2:30 a.m. on the Matilija Dam, with another 100 feet of dotted line left to paint. California. *DamNation Collection*

tools for grassroots activists

Edited by

Nora Gallagher & Lisa Myers

patagonia®

tools for grassroots activists

Best Practices for Success in the Environmental Movement

Edited by
Nora Gallagher & Lisa Myers

Introduction by Yvon Chouinard

contents

Why a Tools Conference? — Yvon Chouinard <pg.XIV>

PG.VI-VII Riders in the 2007 Cabalgata Patagonia Sin Represas (Horseback Ride for a Patagonia Without Dams) protest HidroAysén and its plan to put five massive hydroelectric dams on the Río Baker and Río Pascua, Chile. *Henry Tarmy*
PG.VIII-IX The confluence of the Río Baker and the Río Nef, Aysén, Chile. *Ross Donihue/ Marty Schnure*

Why a Tools Conference?

Yvon Chouinard

Over the years, I've been influenced by many nature writers like Henry David Thoreau, Rachel Carson, and Edward Abbey. I pretty much got to know what the problems were but it was lost on me what I, as one person, could do to fix them.

The first time I came to realize the power of an individual to effect major change was in the early seventies. A group of us went to our local theater to watch a surf movie. At the end, a young surfer asked the audience to attend a city council meeting to speak out against the city's plan to channel and develop the mouth of the Ventura River, one of the best surf points in the area and only five hundred yards from Patagonia's office.

Several of us went to the meeting to protest the possible disruption of our surf break. We knew vaguely that the Ventura River had once been a major spawning creek for steelhead and chinook salmon. In fact, in the 1940s, the river had an annual run of four to five thousand sea-run rainbows. Then two dams were built and the water was diverted, killing the fish run and causing the bars at the mouth of the river to be starved of sand. Except for winter rains, the only water left in the river flowed from the one-stage sewage treatment plant. At the city council meeting, several city-paid experts testified that the river was dead and that channeling would have no effect on the birds and other wildlife at the estuary or on the surf break.

Then Mark Capelli, a young graduate student, gave a slide show of photos he had taken along the river, of the birds that lived in the willows, the muskrats, water snakes, and eels that spawned in the estuary. When he showed the slides of steelhead smolt, everyone stood up and cheered. Yes, several dozen steelhead still came to spawn in our "dead" river.

The development plan was defeated. We gave Mark office space, a mailbox, and small contributions to help fight the battle for the river. As more development

PG. XII   Mark Capelli fishing for southern steelhead in the Ventura River, ca. 1978. Ventura, California. *Photo Courtesy of Mark Capelli* PG. XIII   Aerial view of the mouth of the Ventura River in 2014. Ventura, California. *Rick Wilborn* ABOVE Yvon Chouinard at the Elwha Dam removal ceremony in 2011. Yvon is representing his own hometown action with his T-shirt calling for the removal of the Matilija Dam in Ventura County. Olympic Peninsula, Washington. *Michael Hanson* plans cropped up, the Friends of the Ventura River worked to defeat them and to clean up the water and increase its flow. A second stage was added to the sewage plant and then a third. Wildlife increased and a few more steelhead began to spawn. Mark taught us two important lessons: grassroots efforts could make a difference, and degraded habitat could, with effort, be restored. Inspired by his work, we began to make regular donations to small groups working to save or restore natural habitat, rather than give the money to large, nongovernmental organizations with a big staff and overhead, and corporate connections.

There are many scientists and smart people who work tirelessly to bring us knowledge and facts, but they are too introverted or afraid of losing their jobs to champion their beliefs. Science without action is dead science. I also don't have the courage to be on the front lines, but at least I've learned the power of activism and I want to support it.

We held our first Tools Conference in 1994 at Chico Hot Springs, Montana. We knew we'd hit pay dirt when the local newspaper ran a front-page story about how we "greenies" asked the hotel we were staying in not to change the sheets every day to save water, a revolutionary idea at the time.

While I am often embarrassed to admit to being a businessman—I've been known to call them sleazeballs—I realize that many activists could learn some of the skills that businesspeople possess. When I told that first group of activists that they were businesspeople, there was some snickering in the group. They all thought business was the enemy. I told them that their little NGOs had expenses, did marketing, and had to follow budgets: they had all the problems of business. At that time, many universities had schools of business that had no classes in envi-ronmental responsibility, and the schools of environmental studies had no classes in business. I thought I would bring some activists together with purposeful people who knew about strategic planning, community organizing, technology, and money.

Participants from the 2015 Tools Conference. Fallen Leaf Lake, California. *Amy Kumler*

Now, twenty-one years later, the Tools Conference has really come into its own. Every two years, we bring together 100 activists at Stanford Sierra Camp on Fallen Leaf Lake near South Lake Tahoe and let them feast on what the best trainers available in their fields can give them: grassroots organizing, lobbying, planning strategy and communications, getting the most out of social media, fundraising, using Google tools, and how to work with business. And we don't just bring in good trainers, we bring in the best.

It's easy to be depressed these days, as so much of the wild world has been denigrated or destroyed. But I like to remind myself that things change. You see nothing happening, and then all of a sudden, it changes. It was like that with to-bacco. Remember when people smoked on airplanes? The tobacco industry held sway, the way the oil industry does now. They had teams of PR people and lawyers; even though the medical world knew that smoking caused lung cancer and so did they, they continued to thrive. For fifty years, people worked to connect cigarettes to lung cancer and to ban smoking. The tobacco companies appeared invincible. But the anti-smoking groups kept at it, year after year, slowly and steadily until smoking was banned on airplanes, and then in restaurants and bars, and, finally, CVS stopped selling cigarettes. It was like that with gay marriage, too. Unthinkable and then … done.

The people who won these battles were like those Patagonia supports. Some examples:

Royal Dutch Shell wanted to drill 1,500–10,000 coal-bed methane gas wells in the Sacred Headwaters, where three of Canada's greatest wild salmon and steelhead rivers, the Skeena, Stikine, and Nass, are born. The Skeena Watershed Conservation Coalition—which describes itself as a mix of redneck bravado, First Nations culture, and logger work ethic with a dash of hippie passion—defeated them.

A young woman we supported in her efforts to protect mountains in Appalachia from coal mining went on to organize for the Sierra Club. When they began this phase of the campaign in 2010, the nation was getting 50 percent of its electricity from coal. Today, it's less than 40 percent.

Twenty years ago, dam removal was barely even discussed, but in 2013, com-munities in eighteen states, working in partnership with nonprofit organizations and state and federal agencies, removed fifty-one dams. And in 2014, the people of Chile united to stop what would have been the biggest energy project in the country's history—five huge dams built on two of the wildest rivers in Patagonia.

In these pages, you'll find the best practices and tricks of the trade from those who teach and lead at Patagonia's Tools Conference.

This book, we hope, will reach well beyond those 100 activists who come to Fallen Leaf Lake to everyone who needs the tools to carry the work forward. Thank you and good luck.

CHAPTER 01

The Business of Changing the World

Vincent Stanley

For environmental activism, progress can be hard to spot, let alone measure. If the Hemingway line about bankruptcy—it happens in two ways: slowly, then all of a sudden—haunts us all for the future of our one and only world, we can take heart that "all of a sudden" happens sometimes for awareness as well, and then generates action. Often the action is local. As Yvon said in his introduction, legally smoking cigarettes in public disappeared one community at a time, then everywhere. No one argued for gay marriage, as an abstraction, until nearly every family learned that someone they loved and inside their circle was gay. Everyone becomes more equal, and real, face-to-face. Now we need to see nature, and her needs and rights, less as an abstraction but more as the world in front of us, and a part of us, face-to-face. Then we'll see whether we can change course in time to save the planet—or, to be more modest, to give it a rest and let it take its own time and means to heal.

Why would a clothing company sponsor a "Tools for Activists" conference—or turn the meat of it into a book?

The answer lies in our origins as a climbing-equipment company based in Ventura, California, near the great surf breaks at Rincon. Our founder, Yvon Chouinard, and his original employees were surfers and climbers. For them, the wild began ten feet from the shore, in the power of the waves, or a mile or so from the roadhead on a mountain trail or angler's path. You have to get away from "the hand of man," as Margaret Muric put it, to shed the sense of protection you get from our social systems and relearn the sense of simple, sturdy self-reliance many of us last had as children. It is easier in the wild to feel awe in the presence of a force greater than ourselves, though hard to explain to someone who has never felt the power of the wild why it is so essential to life. Anyone who has felt that power has no quarrel with a deep, lively impulse to preserve it.

PG.XVIII Patagonia Thanksgiving feast with staff and friends high above the Owens Valley on Tuttle Creek, California, ca. 1974. *Gary Regester* PG.1 Arriving in Patagonia, 1988. *Barbara Rowell* ABOVE Ancient history, the Chouinard equipment gang, back in the day. Ventura, California. *Tom Frost*

3

That most of Chouinard's tribe knew and loved some place wild explains the company's modest but steady commitment, beginning in 1985, to donate 1 percent of its sales to grassroots environmental organizations working to save a patch of forest or high desert, or stretch of water or shoreline. We helped groups that the big foundations tended to ignore because they believed them to be too small or too local in scope. We believed the opposite. Because they are local, smaller groups are often more effective. Their people really know and love the spot they're working to defend from the developers and drillers, who more often than not are based outside the community.

We started out small ourselves, with Yvon hammering out pitons or peening carabiner gates alone in his parents' backyard in Burbank, then with his friends in tin sheds in Ventura. We started out unprofessional; we learned on the fly and from each other the skills it takes to run a business, and to play constant catch-up with its growth, all the while never imagining any one of us to be a "businessman." For Yvon, that word was synonymous with "sleazeball."

If, for us, the sleazeball businessman occupied a low point in the spectrum of nobility, at the opposite end of the arc stood the environmental activist, the unstoppable crusader who gave up a good job (or never had one) in order to do the good work we should all be doing—saving the world from sleazeballs doing business. What we at Patagonia had in common with the activists, besides sympathy for their causes, was empathy with their struggle to manage their enterprise. We knew how hard it was, as inexperienced amateurs, to learn how to run our own business.

Those of us who stayed learned to respect good business skills. Even Yvon, as reluctant and ambivalent a businessman as any of us, in the handbook produced from the first Tools Conference praised the word "businesslike" for the qualities it suggests: practical, thorough, purposeful. These are thin-blooded virtues on their own, but appropriate—and necessary—attributes for those doing good who want to be effective.

Anyone familiar with a community church, summer theater, or farmers' market will have an idea of what it takes to run even the smallest environmental organization.

Looking for somewhere to start? Go plant a tree. Only an optimist would do that. *Amy Kumler*

Many of our grantees have an annual income of anywhere from nearly nothing to a million and a half or so dollars. The number of staff can range from one to a half dozen, often part-time, more if you include volunteers; boards of directors can be devoted but distracted; the local community sympathetic (with some elements antipathetic) but preoccupied by daily life and subject to a barrage of conflicting commercial, political, and civic messages.

The executive director, often the organization's founder, has to adapt constantly her original vision to changes in local politics or the economy, run the campaigns, manage the staff, keep up the books and file the taxes, lobby the officials, find new office space when the landlord raises the rent, get the brochure produced pro bono, mobilize the board, and inspire a membership that usually has lots of room to grow. For the environmental activist who may have come into the work (as did some of Patagonia's first employees) as a biologist or river guide, the most critical tools can be the least familiar and hardest to master—small-organization governance, but above all the marketing and storytelling skills that help win hearts and minds for your cause.

From the first Tools Conference, we concentrated on marketing and communication skills, which, as counterintuitive as this sounds, can help ground a small or fledgling organization in both the freedom and discipline it needs to succeed. Marketing is just another word for self-presentation—and works to make as many friends as possible for your organization. Self-presentation has to be, should be, reasonably true (*authentic* is the current buzzword) and specific. If no two snowflakes are identical, nor any two people, why should your organization be described in language that could apply to another? It is different, but how so? And how do you convey that?

The closer the presentation to the self, the more credible (especially over time) and engaging your story is. The more generic and the less forthcoming you are about what you're about, the more you force people to work harder than they should to become your true friend. The reason the best marketing both grounds you in the freedom to act and the discipline you need to be able to make the most intelligent choices: To show who you are, you have to know who you are. To know who you are forces your organization to "live an examined life." And the point of living an examined life is to help you identify where and what to do within the limitations of your resources, where you need to form alliances (or not), and how to communicate to your friends and potential friends.

It's almost impossible for you to hide your organization, especially in the long run, behind a generic screen if you have limited time and money. Your friends and potential friends want to know who you are, what you're doing and why—and what you're asking them to do to help. That is what so much of this book is about.

• • •

Working to save or restore an ecosystem is a fundamentally conservative activity, however radical it can seem politically. "Conservative" in the old American grain of Emerson, Thoreau, our adopted Scotsman John Muir, Rachel Carson, Marjory Stoneman Douglas, and Edward Abbey, all of whom held that nature is our most

important teacher and not a force to be (or that can be) tamed. Saving or restoring an ecosystem is local work that follows the contours of a ridgeline or a watershed, pays attention to plant succession and the composition of wildlife. One constant: Nature is resilient. She rebounds, given a chance to recover. Take down a dam, and the fish return. Move the sheep around more often and carefully, and grassland comes back to life. This is not to urge complacency. Nature has for her lungs a single, thin layer of atmosphere. Poison the soil and it runs into the rivers that reach (or fail to reach) the ocean. The health of our ecosystems, and ultimately the single world, underpins the social and industrial systems by which we make our living. Pull the cloth off the table and the crockery breaks.

This information, this more frequent and pervasive news of systemic natural failure, is too close for comfort for most people yet feels so far away, except—these days—when a hurricane guts America's tenth largest city or odd things crop up in the garden and familiar things won't. It is the task of environmental activists to figure out how to tell people what they're not asking to hear.

We all have to do things we did not expect to have to do at a pace faster than planned.

From the beginning, the Tools Conference has been built around that task. Patagonia pays the way but gets back something that's difficult to describe yet simple. Aldo Leopold said, "A thing is right that tends to preserve the integrity, stability, and beauty of the biotic community." Tools tends to preserve all three, and so does sponsoring Tools. To do the right thing instills in us at Patagonia the confidence to do the next right thing. Even if it's what you might not expect from a business, it is what we expect from *ours*.

I've worked for Patagonia off and on since its start in 1973. I've seen—experienced—the progression and heightening of our sense of both environmental and social responsibility over the years, from a love of nature as something other (the wild places the company's climbers and surfers went off to play in); to something close but hurt (the Ventura River); to the web of life (and relation and obligation)

Benevolent protesters at the 2014 Climate March in New York City, New York. *Tim Davis* that underlies familial, community, and economic life everywhere. Nature is the North Sea, the Hudson, the Pearl River, the Ogallala Aquifer, Glacier Park, the Great Barrier Reef, or little San Francisquito Creek running from the Santa Cruz Mountains to the Bay.

Nature is where we have a retail shop, or textiles dyed, their wastewater released into a river that flows into a sea. Nature is the trees that go into this book.

As yet, very few things we do as a business could be called sustainable. Almost everything we do (including feeding and housing an environmental conference) still takes more from nature than it gives back. But since the early 1990s, when our sense of environmental responsibility first crossed the threshold to include what is done in the supply chain in our name, we have worked steadily to reduce the damage we cause. This includes our switch from conventional to organic cotton, development of recycled polyester, the introduction of high-quality recycled catalog paper, and our messages to customers to dim the glitter of the brand-new bauble and shine light instead on the well-made, useful, but not necessarily new thing. We have learned from our failures, but it is our small successes, our progress, that has created in our business culture a confidence that makes possible the next step, makes that step *ours*. And we know, from what people have told us, that this confidence has been infectious enough to inspire others in business.

That work to change our habits will require every kind of human skill and tool, including the ones we characterize as businesslike. As a Patagonia old-timer, I'm proud of many things our company has done, but nothing we have ever done is better than our sponsorship of Tools. This book, the work of many people over two decades, brings its benefits to a larger audience.

Brock Evans joined the environmental movement as a citizen volunteer in Seattle during the 1960s, when there were no environmental laws whatsoever. Angered by relentless attacks on his beloved Pacific Northwest wilderness, he left a law practice to become the Sierra Club's Northwest representative (Alaska to California) for six years, followed by twenty-five more in Washington, DC, as head lobbyist for the Sierra Club and National Audubon Society. He has won the Sierra Club's highest honor (the John Muir Award), is the author of the award-winning book on eco-tactics Fight and Win, *and has often been a featured speaker at the Tools Conferences.*

Brock Evans

2008 KEYNOTE SPEAKER

Keepers
of the Door

W hen I hear someone say, "It's really hard right now," I think, *Sure, but so what?* It always is. It always has been. I bet I wouldn't get very many hands raised if I asked, "Hey, do you have an easy cause?" Because we didn't sign up for easy, did we? That's what I always keep in mind. But, I am still an optimist. And I want to tell you the three reasons why.

First, it's still a beautiful little planet, isn't it? I just saw the Sierra Nevada mountains flying up from Phoenix this morning, and that great Range of Light is still there. And, I know that somewhere else, wild waves are still crashing down on wild beaches in their ancient rhythms. And, somewhere else, in many deep forests, the wind is sighing through the trees in the late afternoon. There are all sorts of wonderful, lovely places like these everywhere around us in this country—and in many other places as well. It is so beautiful, our lovely Earth, isn't it? Still is. And so I am very happy to be alive in these times. I enjoy them greatly, as I think, and hope, you do, too.

Secondly, I think we live in very special times. We're alive right now, and so for us—we here now—it is given to us to fight for these places. In thirty or forty more years, so many of the places we love will either be protected or they will be gone. We don't know what's going to happen. But we have a chance—right now—because it's all still there. And people like ourselves have not been idle; such places are being protected every day. We have a chance to make a difference. That is a great blessing indeed. There may not be so many such opportunities later on. But they are still before us *now*, in our own time.

Sometimes when I'm feeling really down about something, I remember a metaphor. It always reminds me of who we are and what we are trying to do—and it always makes me feel better. In my mind, I call all of us who are a part of this beautiful environmental movement "Keepers of the Door." What's the door? Well, I see in my mind's eye a door out there. On one side of that door is all of the turbulent present and all of the turbulent past: all the passions and emotions, ups and downs, victories and defeats. On the other side, we don't know. We can have our opinions about what it might be, and I believe it might be and can be a more benign future.

And so our job now, as long as we choose to be a Keeper of the Door, is to shove every acre and every species through that door into the future, as much as we possibly can. Day by day, piece by precious piece, rare animals and plants. For me, it is this knowledge, this understanding, of what our duty and purpose really is that keeps me going—and makes me feel better, too.

The third reason is the most important reason of all why we should be optimists. And that is because we win. *We win a lot!*

Skeptical? Take a look at all the green areas on the map—the really protected places, the national parks, wilderness areas, the state parks, and the wildlife refuges, and places like that. Well over two hundred million acres in this country alone, one-tenth of the entire nation and still counting—every day more special places are being added to our great land protection systems.

You're all doing this right now: new national parks and monuments, wilderness areas, endangered species habitats, protected by law. That's quite a record, I think, for a supposedly materialistic society.

I remember hearing about a statement made by the British ambassador to the United States in 1912. He said, "The national parks are the greatest idea America ever had." When I first heard this I thought, "Wow!" And that was even before we had the Wilderness Act, and the Endangered Species Act, and all the other policies and regulations, too.

So all this makes me very happy, but it's not just those special places that make me feel like an optimist, even though they're beautiful and precious and thank goodness they're still there. But, for me the best part of all is that I know that each one of these places has a beautiful story behind it, a story of people like you and me, ordinary people who, when the time came, stood up and fought for these places. And I know this because I've been involved in so many of the battles and the struggles, passed through them over the many years. So it has come to pass that whenever I fly across the country, I feel like I know every valley and every place. Every place down there has a story, and I know the people behind those stories. They are the ones who made those stories happen. They are stirring tales of amazing people who, when the time came, stepped forward and stood up and fought for these places. And we should all learn the history of these places, because it's a beautiful history. That's why—the only reason why—those places are here today, safe.

In other words, they weren't given to us by the grace of God or any politician. All these special, protected places and habitats are there right now because we took action. We did this ourselves. And we should feel very good, and proud.

PG.8 **Mount Dana at dawn over Mono Lake, California.** *Galen Rowell/Mountain Light*
ABOVE **Todagin Mountain is home to what may be the largest herd of Stone's sheep in the world. The mountain is also home to a deposit of gold and copper, which Imperial Metals plans to extract via an open-pit mine. British Columbia.** *Paul Colangelo*

11

(02)

Campaign Strategy

Brian O'Donnell

Several years ago I was headed for a stroll along the National Mall in Washington, DC. But my walk was soon brought to a halt by a crowd of at least 5,000 people who had gathered there to protest.

The progressive in me felt glad to see people participating in democracy, but the skeptic in me soon took over. Were all these people making any difference whatsoever? My skepticism wasn't aimed at Congress (which deserves plenty) but rather at the leaders of the protest. Did they realize that Congress was *out of session* that week? Nearly every one of the 535 members of Congress they were trying to influence were not in Washington, DC. And where was the media? I looked around and didn't see a TV camera anywhere. It didn't take long before a pamphlet was shoved in my hand. Why were people trying to hand *me* pamphlets? I thought of all the time and money it took to organize the protest. Someone had real organizing skill and drive, and money. They effectively coordinated dozens of buses, secured permits, made signs, and arranged for the travel for thousands of people. It was a huge job, but it wasn't influencing anyone who mattered because the organizers lacked the most important component of a campaign—a strategy to win.

Nature faces huge challenges. We are in the midst of a global struggle to halt the destructive forces of climate change. We are trying to stem the ongoing loss of thousands of acres of forests and open space every day. Our oceans are being polluted and overfished. Habitat loss is imperiling species at an alarming rate, causing the worst extinction crisis since the demise of the dinosaurs. If we want to protect nature, this is no time for ineffective campaigns.

So, how do we ensure that our campaigns are truly making a difference? How do we avoid spending vast amounts of time, energy, and money on efforts that don't win?

PG.12   In October of 2015 the Free the Snake Flotilla paddled from Wawawai Landing to the Lower Granite Dam to protest the four obsolete dams on the lower Snake River, Washington. *Ben Moon*   PG.13   An airborne orca in Puget Sound. A healthy orca population is dependent on a healthy salmon population. Washington. *Hiroya Minakuchi/Minden Pictures/National Geographic Creative*

Focus on Strategy

That sounds simple enough, and it can be very simple indeed, but it is also absolutely mind-boggling how often leaders across disciplines, industries, and at all levels screw up when it comes to developing basic strategy.

Many don't think about strategy until after launching their campaign. For example, in November 2005, the White House published a document called the "National Strategy for Victory in Iraq." The Iraq War was launched in March 2003.

Others seem to never get around to developing a strategy at all. For example, in 2008, POLITICO ran an article in the midst of Senator John McCain's campaign for president questioning why he was spending precious time in states he had no chance of winning, and questioned if he even had a campaign strategy.

Leaders fail to appreciate the importance of developing a strategy, how tactics fit into a strategy, and the difference between the two. With alarming regularity, campaigners don't spend the time to develop a campaign strategy, only to find themselves surprised when their campaigns lose.

Believe it or not, failure to develop a coherent campaign strategy is not limited to the White House and high-level elected officials; even environmental campaigners occasionally mess this up. I know, shocking!

Why do campaigns often struggle with strategy? One of the primary reasons is that people tend to think that strategy development is the realm of Civil War generals, or high-priced marketing gurus. They falsely believe that learning to develop strategy takes years of education at West Point or Harvard Business School.

Additionally, there is a misconception that in order to be successful, strategies must be complex, mysterious, and completely new and innovative. Take a moment to Google "strategy chart" and see what comes up. You may want to put on a raincoat first because you will be deluged by a torrent of crap. Dozens of flowcharts, matrixes, and diagrams attempt to make a relatively simple concept into something on par with mapping the human genome.

Another, perhaps more prevalent, reason why people struggle with strategy is that people simply don't like to answer the hard questions. The questions like: Why are we doing these things? Will this really win our campaign? What is it going to take to influence the key decision maker we need? Often these questions challenge long-held assumptions, expose weaknesses in our campaigns, and force us to face the reality of what it will truly take to *win* the issue, not just *work on* the issue.

Be honest, have you ever really doubted that your campaign had much chance for success but dared not share your fears with campaign allies, colleagues, or volunteers because saying so could confirm that you've wasted lots of money, effort, or time (perhaps even years) on the campaign?

Because we often rush, or worse, skip the strategy part of campaign planning, we frequently end up inventing reasons why or how our campaigns will succeed—reasons that we, the campaign leaders, often don't even fully believe.

A favorite cartoon of mine shows a student and professor in front of a blackboard. On the blackboard is a difficult math equation that the professor asks the student to solve. The student struggles with the problem, and ends up writing, "Then a miracle occurs," in a blank spot in order to "solve" the equation. The professor looks on, befuddled, and says, "I think you should be more explicit here in step two."

Similar scenarios play out regularly in conservation campaigns. Campaigners can articulate where they are now, and where they would like to be, but can in no way say how they are going to get to that desired outcome other than by "working on the campaign," "raising the profile of the issue," and "hoping" that the campaign somehow reaches its goal. Without directly stating it, they are relying on some outside force, or in many cases, a miracle, to win the campaign.

A campaign strategy fills in that blank spot in the equation. It clearly articulates the way forward, and when challenged, can offer a convincing and realistic path to success.

As a campaign leader, being able to develop and articulate a winning campaign strategy is your *most important* job. Nothing else is worth more of your time, your focus, or your energy.

So let's jump right in. We are going to start with the basics and determine if you currently

"I THINK YOU SHOULD BE MORE EXPLICIT HERE IN STEP TWO."

have a strategy or not—and if not, how you can develop one.

What Is a Strategy?

First, let's make sure we all understand what the word *strategy* means. *Webster's Dictionary* defines it as "a careful plan or method for achieving a particular goal, usually over a long period of time."

Sounds simple enough, right?

Now think about your particular campaign:

- Do you have a clear goal?
- Do you have a careful plan that, if followed and well implemented, will *guarantee* that you will achieve your goal?
- If I asked your colleagues, key volunteers, board members, and allies what your strategy is, would they all say the same thing?
- Can you tell me specifically when your campaign is going to win?

If you answered "yes" to all of these questions, congratulations, you are on your way to success. Go ahead and skip to the next chapter of this book.

If you answered "not really," "kind of," "sort of," "maybe," "I'm not sure," "it might," "it's possible," or my favorite response, "I hope so," to any of these questions, then Houston, we have a problem.

Hope is not a strategy. You need to stop what you are doing in your campaign right now and fix this problem before doing anything else.

To fix it, we are going to walk through some of the key steps to developing a campaign strategy and winning your campaign. These may seem very basic or obvious, and in many ways they are, but I would venture that the majority, if not the overwhelming majority, of environmental campaigns underway today have skipped or inadequately completed many of these basic steps.

Develop One Specific, Clear Goal

Make sure your organization is *crystal clear* about the goal your campaign is trying to achieve. If you don't have a *very specific* goal that everyone, and I mean everyone, in your campaign organization understands, you will struggle to develop a strategy for success.

Many campaigns have too many goals (or priorities) all wrapped up in one campaign. This makes developing a strategy significantly harder because there can be distinct strategies needed to achieve different goals. Commingling multiple goals and strategies into one campaign is a recipe for confusion and dysfunction.

Business strategist and author Greg McKeown expands on this in his book *Essentialism*:

> "The word *priority* came into the English language in the 1400s. It was singular. It meant the very first or prior thing. It stayed singular for the next 500 years. Only in the 1900s did we pluralize the term and start talking about *priorities*. Illogically, we reasoned that by changing the word we could bend reality. Somehow we would now be able to have multiple 'first' things."

When developing your strategy, pick one goal and be as specific as possible.

Find Your Target

Too often campaigns aim to influence too many people and spend vast amounts of time and resources trying to target people who can't help the campaign reach its goal. Campaigners often dilute their efforts to the point that they don't have enough resources to truly influence those who matter most.

Usually there are a handful of people, or fewer, who will ultimately determine the fate of your campaign and can secure your goal. They may be US senators, city council members, state agency directors, or corporate leaders. Determine who these people are. Ask, "If this person is on my side, and enthused and active for my cause, will that bring about success?" If the answer is yes, they are your primary targets and will be the focus of your campaign strategy.

Your campaign should focus like a laser on the decision makers who can give you what you want. Unless your campaign has a lot of time and a ton of financial resources, you are not going to be able to target dozens of people. Fortunately, you usually don't have to.

For example, when it comes to land decisions in Congress, we in the environmental community often argue that our public lands belong to all Americans and all Americans should determine their management. While I agree with that sentiment, the reality is that the members of Congress who represent an area are looked to for decisions on that area. Most other members of Congress follow the lead of the local representative on land issues. You can often influence the entire elected body by getting the most local elected official(s) on board. Congress rarely passes public lands conservation legislation without local support.

Keep in mind that the target of your campaign needs to be the person or small group of people who can *truly deliver* success for your campaign. Don't fool yourself that you can win by focusing on people who already agree with you. If they could deliver the goods, you likely wouldn't need a campaign in the first place.

Targeting shouldn't be an exercise that keeps you completely in your comfort zone. If the ultimate decision maker who holds the key to your victory seems at first to be impossibly hard to reach or convince, that's OK. Reality sets in for many campaigners when discussing the appropriate target for a campaign. "We need to convince that senator? Yikes!" But after the initial bout of self-pity, you will start to think creatively about influencing your target. Campaigns have successfully gotten members of Congress who had a zero League of Conservation Voters score to champion conservation causes. As a campaign leader you can't skimp on picking the right target. You may face pressure from allies to focus on easy targets, people who can't deliver your goal, in order to simply show progress. It's your job to spend your limited campaign resources only on targets who can ensure that you will win.

Know the Difference Between Strategy and Tactics

All too often, *strategy* and *tactics* are used interchangeably or one is confused with the other. Hundreds of campaign training manuals have been written about this topic, putting thousands of readers to sleep. Please stay awake for this one, because if you get this right, your campaign will start winning and you will be able to sleep better at night.

Tactics are the everyday actions that a campaign undertakes. Petitions, mailings, rallies, lobbying visits, and press releases are all tactics, not strategies.

Here's a scenario that will help you distinguish between strategy and tactics. You want to get across a river. A strategy for getting across would be to build a bridge, while the tactics would be getting some wood and nails, finding the ideal location to build the bridge, and constructing trusses and beams.

Developing tactics is the easy part of campaign planning. It's the fun part, very often the creative part, and the part that can be most deceiving as to whether you are winning your campaign.

Many campaigns start to engage in planning and undertaking tactics long before ever determining what their campaign strategy is. This can be fatal to the campaign. There is a constant pressure from coalition partners and colleagues to spend campaign planning time developing lists of tactics and getting into the minutiae of them. "Where should we host the press conference? What should the tagline be on our sign? Should we order bumper stickers? How many? Can we get a celebrity to endorse our campaign? Does anybody know Bono?"

Often campaigns have very visible tactics (for example, getting thousands of people to show up at a rally) that can easily be mistaken for strategy. They can roll out high-profile tactic after tactic, generate a ton of press, raise truckloads of money, engage many people—and yet not be one step closer to achieving their goal. At times these campaigns become so wedded to tactics that they continue them even if they aren't tangibly moving the campaign toward its goal. Questioning the tactics can be viewed as heresy by entrenched campaigners. "But we always hold the campaign fly-in rally the second week of September. We've been doing it for the last ten years, people expect us to be holding a rally then!"

How many of your coalitions or organizations have held detailed discussions about the wording of your press release, the location for your campaign kickoff announcement, or the color of the paper to be used for your action alert before you have discussed a winning strategy? Those are tactical discussions, not strategic discussions.

A list of tactics (actions that your campaign plans to undertake) does not amount to a strategy. I've seen many of these lengthy lists of tactics compiled during campaign planning meetings. Often they are titled "Strategic Campaign Plan," when there is nothing strategic about the plan.

A strategy, by contrast, includes a clear goal, and a target. A strategy also articulates the specific venue and method that you will use to achieve victory. A strategy is a plan to get a law enacted, not a bill introduced in Congress. A strategy is a plan to end (win) a campaign, not to start a campaign.

The simplest description of the difference between strategy and tactics I've heard is the following: Tactics is doing *things* right. Strategy is doing the *right* things. You can win a campaign with a good strategy and mediocre tactics, but you will lose every time with mediocre strategy and good tactics.

Bill Clinton's successful campaign strategists, James Carville and Paul Begala, know all about developing effective strategies and why it's more important to focus on strategy than tactics. In their campaign book, *Buck Up, Suck Up ... and Come Back When You Foul Up*, they write:

"So much of the energy of a campaign goes into the small questions, the 'How' questions. Not nearly enough goes into the big, existential questions like 'What are we doing?' and 'Why are we doing it?'

"Those questions seem simple. And they are. But simplicity and importance are not mutually exclusive.

"If you as a leader lose sight of your strategic objective for even a single moment, you will be astonished by how quickly everyone under you begins to focus on the most inane, irrelevant, goofy crap imaginable. They've got to focus on something and if they're not being given a strategic focus from the top, they'll focus on something else. Which will only force you to focus on fixing their mistakes and so on, leading to a death spiral."

Developing Your Strategy

Now that you know the difference between strategy and tactics, it's time to start developing your strategy.

Remember, a strategy has a tangible, specific goal. It identifies a target (person) who can deliver on the goal, it articulates the method and forum by which success will be achieved, and it has a plan that, if implemented properly, will generate the necessary influence, support, and pressure to convince the target to attain the goal.

Don't Rush Developing
Your Strategy

As you work to develop your strategy, there will be all sorts of pressure from fellow campaigners to avoid the hard questions about what it will really take to win. You will have colleagues wanting to skip this step and immediately jump to tactics. Resist this! Stay with it. Keep asking the "why" questions. This is your role as a campaign leader.

It's rare that the best strategic thinking happens within the confines of a planning meeting. Most people get their best ideas in the shower, on hikes, or during one-on-one conversations with colleagues. But campaigns consistently limit their strategy planning to a single planning meeting. Worse still, agendas allocate only an hour for strategy discussions. Once that meeting is over, facilitators push to stay on schedule and move on to discussions of tactics and budgets, even when the strategy discussion is not even close to being fully developed. Efficiency and structured meetings are important, but when you are planning for how to win a campaign, one that may take years and cost tens of thousands of dollars or more, don't box yourself in to some

arbitrary time limit. An unstrategic campaign will cost much more time in the long run. Take as long as is needed to develop a winning strategy. It's OK if it takes many weeks to develop your campaign strategy. Don't give in to those who urgently want to "get going on the campaign" but cannot articulate a plan for long-term success.

Be a Devil's *and* an
Angel's Advocate

You've come up with a strategy. Now it's time for you and your colleagues to challenge it. Try to poke holes in it. Why could it fail? What are its shortcomings? Can we really pull this off? Be the devil's advocate, the skeptic who challenges the strategy to make sure it is truly viable. But, as I know you are well aware, no one really likes a devil's advocate, so your role doesn't end there. You need to also be an angel's advocate—a person who offers a path forward and a solution. For every potential weakness in the strategy that you point out, offer a way to improve it, or an alternative that is stronger. Ask your campaign colleagues to do the same.

Don't move on from this step until you and your colleagues are convinced that you have a solid strategy that will guarantee the success of your campaign. After spending all the time you need on this step, you should welcome the "what are we doing" and "why" questions.

Get the Right Team
on Board

You've put in the time to develop a strategy and worked to the point where you can articulate your strategy. Now your job is to be a missionary for your strategy. Bring your board of directors, your key volunteers, your funders, and potential coalition partners in on the strategy. The fact that you spent the time and truly considered the best path forward will give you confidence. That confidence will get others behind you and your strategy, which is what you need as a campaign leader.

There's a chance that not everyone will agree with your new strategic approach. You may lose some of your original campaign partners who don't want to shift approaches or abandon long-held tactics-oriented campaigns. That's OK. These groups or individuals weren't going to get you to your goal—and they may still come around later, once they see that your approach is making progress. While consensus is ideal, don't let common denominator thinking prevent you from a strategic campaign.

The people you need to fully embrace and understand the strategy are the individuals and groups who will be implementing it. That may mean bringing in new groups and individuals and even severing others from your campaign. Starting fresh with new people and a focused plan can be a very good thing. No one thinks Mick Jagger made a mistake by leaving Little Boy Blue and the Blue Boys to help form The Rolling Stones.

Write Your Campaign Plan

As we just covered, there are a lot of steps to take before writing your campaign plan. By completing the steps I outlined above in advance of writing the plan, you will have given strategy planning the time it needs and you won't be as tempted to immediately jump to tactics.

Make sure you have a *written* campaign plan. As my friend Bob Bingaman from the Sierra Club says, "If it's not written down, it's not a plan."

Every component of your plan should be consistent with your strategy. It helps to start the plan with a brief description of your strategy at the top of your document so that you can keep referring back to this essential element of success.

For example: "Congress will pass a bill designating the 13,000-acre Pineridge Mountain Wilderness Area. The campaign will build overwhelming grassroots support in the local congresswoman's district, focusing on the constituencies most important to her and the state's two US senators: religious conservatives, sportsmen, and businesses."

Now is the time for tactics. List the activities that the campaign is going to undertake. Again, ask questions: Is this tactic consistent with our strategy? Is this tactic going to influence our target? If the answer is "no" to these questions, jettison the tactic, even if it's something you did in the past.

Let the ideas flow, but be prepared to say "no" to twice as many tactics that are proposed as you say "yes" to. Be a guardian of your strategy

and don't include any proposed tactics that are inconsistent with your strategy no matter how easy, fun, or creative they may be.

Make sure you build accountability into your campaign plan. Who specifically is going to undertake the tactics? When will they be completed? How are you going to measure their impact?

Stop and Re-Plan When Things Change or Go Seriously Awry

Occasionally the most well-planned strategies don't play out. Elections can change the political landscape. The economy can tank. Or, your strategy just turned out to be unfeasible or was poorly implemented. As a campaign leader, you have to be able to admit when things aren't going well. It's easy to put a happy face on campaigns that aren't winning, blame the money and power of your opposition, and take solace that you are fighting the good fight. But true leaders fix problems and see failures as an opportunity to learn and improve.

What If You Aren't in Charge of the Campaign?

One of the regular questions I get about strategy comes from campaigners who aren't in charge of their campaigns. They may be local organizers, media, or fundraising people who report to a campaign director or organizational leader. They've often experienced an epiphany that the campaign they are engaged in lacks a coherent strategy, but they don't feel like they are in a position to change it. What to do?

My advice is fairly simple. Start asking questions. Ask the campaign director to explain when you are going to win the campaign. Ask why you are engaged in various activities and what your strategy is to win.

The campaign leaders will take one of three approaches. They will either (1) articulate a clear strategy to you that they hadn't shared previously. This is good news, and you should encourage them to share it more broadly so everyone in the campaign understands it. Or, (2) experience the epiphany that you experienced and use the discussion as a chance to think about the lack of strategy and the need to develop one. This is also good news; you showed leadership and helped improve the campaign. Or, (3) give you a wholly unsatisfactory answer and ask you to stop asking questions.

You want to work on a campaign that welcomes ideas, and has leaders who are comfortable articulating a strategy. If you receive answer number 3, it's time to reconsider your engagement in the campaign. Your time is too important to spend on an unstrategic campaign. Nature needs your talents on campaigns that can win.

If You Only Take Away Two Things from This Chapter

I distinctly remember my Geology 101 professor from my freshman year in college saying, "If you only remember one thing from this class, this should be it." I have long since forgotten what he said next, but I think it had something to do with the rock cycle. With that, I am profoundly optimistic that you will retain the following two simple ideas after reading this chapter.

1   MAKE SURE YOUR CAMPAIGN HAS A GENUINE STRATEGY TO WIN. Your strategy should include a specific goal, a target who can deliver on that goal, and a plan that will generate sufficient support for your target to deliver on your goal.

2   SPEND MORE TIME AND ENERGY GETTING THE STRATEGY RIGHT THAN ON PLANNING TACTICS. Make sure your campaign doesn't jump to tactics before getting the strategy right. My six-year-old daughter asked what I was writing this morning, and I told her I was writing a chapter for a book. She told me I had to end it with "And they live happily ever after." If you get the strategy right for your campaign, that's a fitting ending.

Resources

Begala, Paul, and James Carville. *Buck Up, Suck Up … and Come Back When You Foul Up: 12 Winning Secrets from the War Room*. New York: Simon & Schuster, 2003.

Bobo, K., J. Kendall, S. Max. *Organize for Social Change*. 4th ed. (Midwest Academy Manual). Santa Ana, Calif.: The Forum Press, 2010. http://www.midwestacademy.com/manual/.

McKeown, Greg. *Essentialism – The Disciplined Pursuit of Less*. New York: The Crown Publishing Group, 2014.

Spitfire Strategies. Planning to Win. http://www.spitfirestrategies.com/tools/#tab3.

At the far south end of the Wyoming Range, Commissary Ridge forms the divide between the Smiths Fork and LaBarge Creek, Wyoming. *Susan Marsh*

Sportsmen for the Wyoming Range

This campaign wanted to protect more than a million acres of national forest in the Wyoming Range, a spectacular mountain range in southwestern Wyoming. The area was threatened by large-scale oil and gas drilling that would permanently alter its wild character.

Wyoming hadn't seen a land conservation measure succeed in Congress in decades. Its congressional delegation was among the most conservative in the nation and had consistently opposed federal land conservation legislation. Conservationists recognized that to be successful, they needed to convince the state's congressional delegation of the importance of protecting the Wyoming Range. They also knew that the voices of liberal-leaning environmental groups wouldn't be persuasive to their targets.

Instead, they organized a campaign run by the Sportsmen for the Wyoming Range that garnered support from the state's hunting and fishing organizations—many of them very conservative organizations whose voices would be influential. This coalition of sportsmen's groups advocated effectively with the Wyoming congressional delegation and saw the Wyoming Range Legacy Act passed by Congress in 2009, permanently safeguarding 1.2 million acres of land.

– Brian O'Donnell

A lone male antelope finds forage on the grasslands. Rocky Mountain Front, Montana. *Steven Gnam*

Rocky Mountain Front

Bob Ekey

The Rocky Mountain Front is a striking 150-mile-long swath of country in Montana where the sheer limestone cliffs of the mountains meet the northern prairie, an area so wild it is the only place in the lower forty-eight states where grizzly bears still leave the mountains and roam the plains. Imagine the Colorado Front Range without Denver and Boulder and, instead, ranches and wild country. The Front in Montana was rescued from oil and gas drilling after local residents and conservation advocates launched a campaign to protect this special place. This is how it was done:

Despite a century of conservation along the Front, the threat of oil and gas development still loomed on leases issued decades ago. In 2002, the threat resurfaced when Startech Corp. applied for a permit to drill on federal public lands in the heart of the Front, threatening prime grizzly bear habitat and largely roadless wildlands.

At the time Startech announced its plans, a Texas oilman was in the White House, urging energy development (above all other uses) for public lands.

But local ranchers, hunters, tribal leaders, and elected officials teamed up with conservation and sportsmen's groups to initiate a campaign that developed sound strategies and employed creative tactics. They, we, eventually built a campaign worthy of the landscape. The Coalition to Protect the Rocky Mountain Front

was formed with the theme "Keep the Front the way it is."

One of the keys to the success of the campaign was making sure that the coalition members developed an overall strategy that represented a shared vision. This was not a case of one part of the group deciding the vision and persuading the others to sign on. Instead, everyone was engaged from the beginning and had long-term ownership of the campaign.

The most basic formula for a land protection campaign is what we call "Values-Threat-Solution." The first step is to educate the public about the *values* of the place you're trying to protect. Although you know how great a place is, don't assume that everyone else knows, too. In this case, we knew that to be successful, ours would have to be a statewide campaign, but not everyone in the state understood the incredible wildlife and wildland values found along the Front. So, we launched an earned media campaign with naturalists, wildlife professionals, and others describing that wildlife biologists say the Front is home to some of the best wildlife habitat in the lower forty-eight states.

Next, we outlined the real *threats* of oil and gas development and how that activity industrializes the landscape with a network of roads, pipelines, and compressor stations, displacing wildlife and forever scarring the landscape.

Finally, we described the *solution*: that Montana's Rocky Mountain Front was too wild to drill.

The strategy was to build a bipartisan campaign that would result in a short-term success in stopping the immediate drilling threat, extinguish leases, and eventually achieve permanent protection.

The coalition recognized that with President Bush and a Republican governor in office, as well as a politically mixed congressional delegation, any campaign would have to have bipartisan appeal. Local ranchers, sportsmen, and community leaders would be the face of the campaign. In fact, the local ranchers and sportsmen insisted that we target Republican delegation members.

Once the strategies were developed, tactics were aggressively implemented. This is where coalition members were creative in developing opportunities for political engagement and media coverage.

One of the early strategies was to make the Front the leading environmental issue in Montana's 2004 statewide election. This was accomplished by organizing coalition members and supporters to have a presence at every candidate forum or call-in show to ask about the candidate's position regarding the Front.

The coalition successfully elevated the issue and in October 2004—just weeks before the election—the Bush administration announced it was stopping the drilling application process to make room for other actions that could be taken, including buying out the leases.

At this point, coalition members wanted a campaign that went beyond playing defense against specific threats. We decided to build off the immediate success of stopping the permit to drill and work toward stronger protection. This strategy included buying out existing leases from oil and gas development companies, banning future leasing, and a long-term goal of permanent protection for the Rocky Mountain Front as wilderness or some other permanent protection.

For any buyout of the leases to be successful, we needed Congress to pass a bill.

To make this happen, the coalition's strategy was to target the entire congressional delegation to take action, including Senator Conrad Burns, a Republican whose rhetoric was often anti-public lands. But, the one thing that could trump the senator's point of view was the desire of the local community. In this case, the locals prevailed. They told Burns they wanted to keep the Front the way it was, and that meant stopping the oil and gas development threat.

Burns eventually introduced legislation that would permanently withdraw all the public land in Montana from future oil and gas leasing. While the legislation was pending, Burns lost his re-election bid in 2006. Senator Max Baucus, a Democrat who was in line to become Finance Committee Chair, stepped up and got the legislation passed in late 2006, permanently withdrawing 500,000 acres from any future leasing. Leases started being relinquished or bought out, including the leases for the parcel with the immediate drilling threat—and that stopped oil and gas development along the Rocky Mountain Front. While some leases remain, much of the oil and gas threat was blocked.

After the huge victory of having the oil and gas threat reduced, the coalition went to work on a bill that would designate 67,112 acres of wilderness and 208,000 acres in a conservation management area that limits future development.

The bill was introduced in the Senate in 2011, and despite widespread popularity in Montana, including broad editorial support in the media, it languished in a dysfunctional Congress for three years. But, late in 2014 the Rocky Mountain Front Heritage Act was included in a public lands package that passed in a post-election, lame-duck Congress. Passage of the act meant the first new wilderness designation in Montana in thirty years. What started as a sprint turned into a marathon, but campaign leaders were resolute and experienced. Deep buy-in and engagement by all partners sustained the campaign—and eventually led to success.

A grizzly bear endures the first snow of autumn. Rocky
Mountain Front, Montana. *Steven Gnam*

Annie Leonard is obsessed with stuff: Where does it come from? What is it made of? Where does it go? And how we can find better answers to those questions? Her Internet film, The Story of Stuff, *has been viewed more than 30 million times around the world. She's worked with a number of environmental groups, including Greenpeace, Health Care Without Harm, and the Global Alliance for Incinerator Alternatives.*

Annie Leonard

2011 KEYNOTE SPEAKER

Taking Our Work to the Next Level

PG.28 A Greenpeace activist parachutes off a smokestack at the Gavin Power Plant—one of the largest and dirtiest in the nation, ca. 1984. Cheshire, Ohio. *John Myer/Greenpeace* TOP Greenpeace activists display a banner on the Mobro barge—saddled with 3,186 tons of solid waste—that reads, "Next Time Try Recycling," ca. 1982. Islip, New York. *Dennis Capolongo/Greenpeace* BOTTOM Marine conservationist Charles Moore displays a toothbrush found in the Central North Pacific Ocean off the coast of Hawai'i as part of the Greenpeace Ocean Defenders Campaign. *Greenpeace*

've been working as an environmental activist since I was a teenager, more than a quarter of a century now. During this time I've met super-smart activists and seen effective research, outreach, organizing, and advocacy—all of which has helped stop environmental threats and promoted environmental solutions. It's impressive, and yet it's not enough. Thanks to all this work, things are getting worse at a slower rate, as Donella Meadows, author of *The Limits to Growth*, said. It's time to rethink what we're doing and figure out what we can do better.

I'd like to share three ways that I've learned we environmentalists can work smarter, rather than just harder. I am sure there are many more ways too, and I'd love to hear your ideas as well.

1 WE CAN GET BETTER AT TALKING ABOUT THE ISSUES WE CARE ABOUT.

We environmentalists tend to be a whiney and wonky bunch; we understand the grim science and wish everyone did. But sometimes in our vigor to recruit people, we inadvertently end up pushing them away by coming on too strong and being overly technical and depressing. This isn't news to organizers; almost fifty years ago Saul Alinsky, author of *Rules for Radicals*, taught us to talk to people where they're at, not where you're at. The more we communicate in ways that are accessible, inviting, and relevant, the more diverse people will want to join the movement—making us stronger and smarter overall. So practice: practice talking to your neighbor, your uncle, the grocery store clerk. Find ways to connect the issues you care about to the issues they care about and be sure to offer meaningful ways to get involved.

The best antidote to depression about the state of the planet is taking action!

2 WE CAN THINK BIGGER, AIM HIGHER, AND DREAM MORE COURAGEOUSLY.

In the 1970s, environmentalists were enormously successful, passing more than a dozen major environmental laws and regulations. Then came the 1980s, and a president with such disdain for environmental issues that he blamed pollution on trees. After years of being marginalized in both politics and mainstream culture, many environmentalists have been socialized into submission. We too often hold ourselves back, the result of a culture of caution or a politics of what we think is possible in today's corporate-dominated democracy.

We need to break out of this trend. We need to start demanding the kinds of environmental policies and leadership that the science says are needed—and we know are possible. We need to stop compromising out of fear of appearing unreasonable; the unreasonable ones are those who want to continue extracting fossil fuels when we should be fast-tracking a transition to clean energy!

Dreaming big and bold not only gives us the best chance at a healthy, sustainable future, but it's also the best way to build our movement. Think about social movements in history: leaders didn't rally millions through compromised calls to action. The moment calls on us all to be strong, be bold, and be courageous.

3 WE CAN MOVE BEYOND BEING RESPONSIBLE CONSUMERS TO BEING ACTIVE CITIZENS.

Advocating for environmental solutions from government is painstakingly hard. And changing "business as usual" in most of today's corporations can feel even harder. In response, many environmentalists have taken a de-politicized approach to eco-concerns, focusing on perfecting their day-to-day consumer decisions rather than on making big change. We recycle, avoid buying bottled water, carry our own shopping bags to the store, and use public transit. These are all very good things to do, and we should all do them. They provide value by modeling a more sustainable way to live and aligning our values and actions—which feels good. But we need to remember that recycling and using a refillable bottle is not how we make big, bold, transformational change that is so needed in this country—and is needed by the planet. As activists, we must move beyond focusing on eco-perfect living to changing the broader system so that the best environmental option is the new normal for everyone. We do that by moving beyond our consumer self and re-engaging our citizen self. Yes, consume responsibly but also vote and register others to vote, organize petition and letter drives, write letters to the editor of local papers, and when necessary, march in the streets.

Polls show that a significant portion of the population shares environmental values. Turns out that most people want their babies born without toxic chemicals already in their blood. Most people want the climate to stay within the range in which human life can flourish. Most people want clean air and water. Seventy-four percent of people in the United States support stricter regulations on toxic chemicals in this country. Eighty percent of people support the EPA taking action to reduce carbon emissions. Eighty-five to ninety percent of people think corporations have too much influence in our democracy.

These are really high levels of support—high enough to make serious change. We have higher numbers of support than the suffragettes had fighting for women's right to vote a century ago. We have way higher numbers of support than Martin Luther King Jr. had at the time of the "I Have a Dream" speech. It may not always feel like it, but we really are "most people."

If we can figure out how to communicate in a way that invites people to take part and be bold and courageous in what we aim for, and work together as engaged citizens, we really can build a diverse and powerful movement strong enough to turn things around. Together, we can build a sustainable, healthy, and just future for all.

<u>TOP</u> Greenpeace activist Maxine Tang occupies a yarder in protest against Western Forest Products' plans to clear-cut the Great Bear Rainforest, British Columbia. *Mark Warford/Greenpeace* <u>BOTTOM</u> Greenpeace activists hang a banner at the Bridgeport Harbor Generating Station, Bridgeport, Connecticut. *Greenpeace*

33

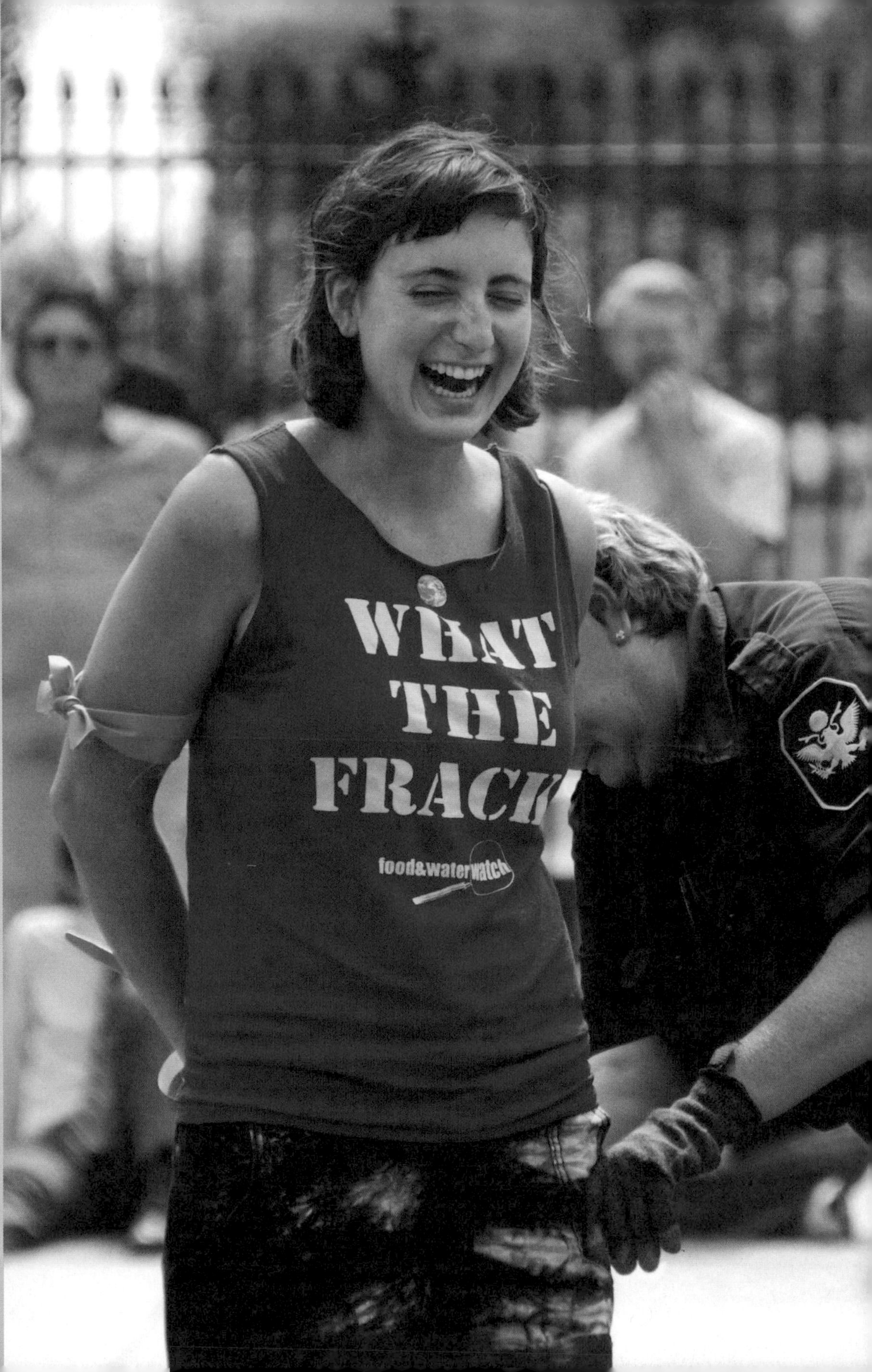
WHAT
THE
FRACK
food&water watch

CHAPTER 03

Marketing

Strick Walker

What is marketing? Some would suggest it's an exercise in shallow, celebrity-slathered, product-driven manipulation and deceit. Perhaps it's the domain of the sleazeball that Vincent Stanley references in "The Business of Changing the World." After all, marketeers always seem to be selling us things we don't need via overblown storytelling. It's a professional landscape littered with directionless liberal arts grads, failed writers, and hack filmmakers. It's the evil but necessary face of capitalism. Right?

Well, I'm a formerly directionless liberal arts graduate and wannabe writer who has grown to love the craft of marketing and its potential to create positive change in the world. Years of manipulation by big companies selling useless widgets have certainly given the endeavor a bad rap. But understanding the fundamentals of marketing—storytelling, self-presentation, or, better yet, meaningful consumer engagement—is a key and often missing ingredient in the difficult and important work of the public sector.

In fact, if we as environmentalists expect to make a real difference, consumer outreach and engagement is an absolutely critical component of our work. At Patagonia, it's what enables us to build petitions around dam removal, raise funds to protect from development the places where we play, and inspire other businesses to help us scale more sustainable materials and embrace more responsible manufacturing practices. We'd better warm up to the idea that meaningful audience outreach is an essential part of the solution. Otherwise, we will continue to publish studies that go unread and preach to our own choirs.

So Let's Talk About Marketing

The way people communicate continues to change rapidly and dramatically. Attention spans are narrowing. The time people have to engage with new issues continues to shorten, and the number of messages we receive in a single day is staggering. In order to get an issue to break through the clutter in a compelling way, it seems we must become communication ninjas. To break through and then actually motivate people to take difficult action—well, that may seem straight-up impossible, particularly on small budgets. But I'm here to tell you that you can do it.

The good news is there are more channels than ever to connect with people. We no longer need to rely on paid media to send our message. But that proliferation of media has created as much challenge as opportunity. So much media—we now live in the bubbles we create.

When it comes to communication, the same old interpersonal rules apply:

- Say what you mean.
- Don't take too long.
- Be yourself.
- Try to relate to people.
- Being like everyone else makes you forgettable.
- Don't interrupt people.

These are lessons we've all learned over time. Yet many companies and organizations ignore them. They attempt to manufacture a false image. They interrupt us. They waste our time. They're confusing and they don't seem to have a real grasp of who they are or what they want us to know. They forget how to be human.

Proper planning and messaging can help you make the most of finite resources and short attention spans. This chapter will help you build a strategic foundation to enable effective customer engagement. The process requires discipline and decision making. But if done properly, it will make your outreach efforts more effective and it will focus everyone on the same goal. Great brand work can actually change the shape of an organization and recalibrate priorities. So working through these eight steps can be a game changer if you're willing to dive in:

1. Positioning
2. Tone of voice and look and feel
3. Brand ID
4. Targeting
5. Key performance indicators (KPIs)
6. Building a plan
7. Creative development
8. Tracking and optimization

Step 1: Positioning

In my view, the key to effective customer engagement (and the hardest trick) is concisely sharing with people who you are, what you do, and why it matters. It's step one when developing a marketing strategy. It's the foundation of all communications. It's an exercise that will ultimately make every dollar and every hour you spend on customer engagement more effective. It is particularly important when dealing with complex subject matter, as many NGOs do. Yet some companies and organizations rush right past it and start posting on Facebook. They are wasting their precious time.

Communicating with people in a meaningful and efficient way requires that you actually know who you are. Getting there typically requires real discipline, tough decision making, and a bit of soul searching. You must distill your reason for being down to a digestible chunk. Sometimes that means leaving things behind that you thought were important. Sometimes it creates disagreement internally. It can feel as if you're dismantling the engine. But I guarantee that when you rebuild it, it will be more powerful than ever—and you'll get way better gas mileage.

This is often referred to as brand positioning work. Brand positioning has always been critical and is becoming even more so. In a multi-medium, sound-bite world, you can't always expect people to read the book. You need to hook them when they hit. Brand positioning is a process of boiling everything down so that you can quickly articulate the following things:

- Who are we?
- What are we trying to accomplish?
- Why and for whom?
- What will be the result if we succeed or fail?

- Why should people care about that?
- What makes us unique?

Use these questions to build an articulation of your brand position. There are books you can buy. There are multiple frameworks to use. I'm sure there are classes you can take. But I suggest that you simply start by answering the questions above and fashioning the answers into one concise paragraph. Get ready—it's not as easy as you think.

Here's a fictional brand positioning statement to illustrate the idea:

> "Eco.org is the only innovative digital platform whose primary goal is to connect small nonprofit groups with a mainstream audience in order to fund the environmental activism needed to address the climate crisis."

How is this sentence actionable? What does it help us do? Well, let's break it down:

"Eco.org is the only innovative digital platform"—this creates internal alignment on the scope and approach of the service. It grounds the offering in the digital space, but suggests that the organization will continue to innovate in that area. This is really clarifying from a product/service development standpoint. The word "only" suggests that they are totally unique in mission and approach.

"whose primary goal is to connect small nonprofit groups with a mainstream audience"—this articulates exactly who the organization has been built to service. They have decided to focus on small nonprofit organizations. Again, this really helps when speaking to why the organization exists, and it enables them to better understand the needs of their audience. They can then design for those specific needs.

"in order to fund the environmental activism needed to address the climate crisis."—this describes what they hope to provide to that target audience. They are very clearly focused on providing financial support for environmental activism. They are not a volunteering resource. They are not designed to educate or lobby. They are not focused on social issues. They exist to drive funds to small enviro groups.

When put together, those components create relevance, separate Eco.org from the pack, and give them the beginnings of a clear development playbook. Brand positioning provides both a lens to look through and a springboard for innovation and ideation. It ensures that you're keeping your eye on the ball, that you're consistent in your efforts, and that your brand communications are efficient.

Step 2: Tone of Voice and Look and Feel

Step two is to identify your voice. How does your organization speak? Are you funny? Serious? Witty? Calm? You also need to think about your visual language. How do the visuals in your work support that tone of voice and round out your identity?

I won't go into great detail on this point, except to say that some articulation of these things will provide needed guidance. It will enable people to know you, recognize you, and feel good about supporting you.

Tone

Tone refers to written language and it should be evident in all copy. This includes your website, press releases, social media posts, print ads—everything. Even the way you answer the phone should be reflective of who you are and your unique tone of voice. Try identifying three to five adjectives that best describe the tone of your organization—then refer to those adjectives when developing communications materials.

Look and Feel

According to your tone of voice, what imagery do you choose? Do you populate your materials with imagery of deforestation and drought? Do you use an illustrator who can provide a more approachable style? Is your tone scientific? What does your graphic design look like? Or is it more human than graphic and, if so, how can you communicate that through visuals? Give yourself a few rules here too. It will pay off.

Step 3: Building a
Brand Identity

Now you have a clear articulation of your position and the tone of your communication to the world. It's time to build a solid brand identity. This is step three.

When marketing types speak about brand identity, they're typically referring to your logo. The logo is the visual stamp for your organization. It needs to communicate quite a bit. Not only does it need to provide the world with quick visual context for your group, it also needs to establish the tone of the organization. To do so, many companies pair a logo with a line of copy. This is what's known as the dreaded *tagline*.

As you develop or review your logo, consider the positioning statement you built in step one. Ultimately the logo, or the logo/tagline combination, should feel like a clear illustration of that statement. Getting the brand identity right will really help. That little lockup will do some pretty heavy lifting for you. If done well, it will intrigue, communicate, and drive interested folks to you for more information.

Step 4: Targeting

Step four is to clearly identify your audience. Who should you connect with and how much of your precious resources and time should you spend on them? Is it one specific audience? Where are they located? How do they consume information (do they read more or spend more time on Twitter)? What do they care about?

Many times, your core audience actually consists of a number of different groups. Audience segmentation is the process of making decisions about how many groups you will target, what makes them different, and how best to engage with them. The trick to effective segmentation is twofold:

1 Be disciplined about how many groups you target. The more narrow the focus, the more effectively you will utilize your resources.
2 Get as insightful as possible within each segment. Try to learn as much as you can about that group. You want your engagement to be as meaningful as possible, so you need to get beyond a quantitative, analytic understanding of your target.

The more deeply you understand your target audience(s), the more effective you will be in designing messages and outreach strategies. Spend time on step four. It will provide you with a road map for building a communication strategy.

A Word About Empathy

Between segmenting your audience and actually developing marketing communications is another fundamental step: establishing real empathy with your target. This is a step that many brands never really accomplish. That lack of intimate connection between brands and customers is why customer insight and innovation design firms are making so much money. Large brands just lose connection with their audience.

I would argue that empathy is even more critical for nonprofit organizations. Customers may still buy a six-pack of Coke, whether or not they feel understood by the Coca-Cola Company. Because it's easy to buy a six-pack and the benefit is clear. But what will motivate people to get involved with your issue? Why should they care? How can your issue be made relevant enough for them to donate time and/or money? To answer these questions, you need to understand what matters most to the target groups you've identified.

There are many ways to establish and maintain empathy with your target audience. Host dinners. Spend time with them. Set up small focus groups. You need to keep learning about them and capturing your findings. Data that comes from empathy can help you design new service offerings, and it can inform outreach strategy, copy, etc. In a world where resources are scarce and investment must be targeted and efficient, emotional connection and understanding is a real benefit.

Step 5:
Establish the Key Performance
Indicators (KPIs)

You've heard the term and it's just vague enough to be dangerous. This is where we attempt to measure our efforts. It's where we talk about Return on Investment (ROI) and optimize our work. It's not very cut-and-dried when you're doing customer engagement work. This is primarily because customer engagement is about relationship building. It takes time. As in real life, if you come on too strong at party number one, you might not get invited to the next party. Really, the fourth party is where you begin building lasting friendships.

In the private sector, sales are the ultimate ROI. But how should we compare short-term bumps in sales to long-term customer loyalty? Isn't it better to have slow and sustained growth? Isn't that more stable? Or are we after significant short-term sales increases? Is that success? Is making the quarter the goal? Each of these goals gives birth to different marketing strategies, but many companies want to have their cake and eat it, too. So they end up chasing both goals.

In the case of the public sector, perhaps the answer is clearer. It's about generating lasting support for issues that often have longer time frames—right? But maybe there are key moments when the troops need to be rallied quickly and results need to be measured in the short term. Understanding what the appropriate KPIs are will help you design your plans. This is step five.

Many believe that awareness is to marketing what location is to real estate. They say awareness of a brand's existence is everything: awareness, awareness, awareness! I disagree. There are two concepts that I believe are more important than awareness:

1 RELEVANCE — why is what you do relevant to my life?
2 DIFFERENTIATION — what makes your organization the one I should support? As Vincent Stanley writes, why would you want to speak in exactly the same way as another organization?

In my view, awareness alone is not a meaningful measurement. For example, I know Chick-fil-A exists. It doesn't mean I'll be going there any time soon. They have failed to create relevance to my life, and they have not differentiated themselves (positively, anyway) from any other chicken joint. To some, however, they have differentiated themselves via their stance on social issues. So perhaps they have their target audience in mind after all.

Now that you've got a clear sense of self via the brand positioning, you know and understand your target audience, it's time to identify your KPIs. What does success look like for you? Feel free to make up your own KPIs. Try to get as detailed as possible. Here are a few examples:

· We want to have fifty people attend the rally.
· We want to raise $20,000 over the next three months.
· We need to generate 50,000 petition signatures by the end of the year.
· We want to build our email file by 30 percent year over year.
· We want 50 percent of our email list to attend at least one event this summer.
· We want 30 percent of previous donors to give again this season.

Spend some time identifying KPIs that are a reach, but are also attainable. Then you can continue to learn from your efforts, ratchet them up, and optimize the initiatives. It is important to have a clear sense of your KPIs before you create a plan. You have to know what you're aiming at.

Step 6: Build a Plan

You've got the strategy. You know your audience. You've nailed your tone of voice. Your brand identity is working hard for you. You have a clear view of what success looks like. Now it's time to take your budget and build a powerful outreach plan.

Subsequent chapters in this book delve more deeply into the public relations and social media realms, so I won't spend much time on those areas here. I will, however, say a few things related to what's known as the "earned and shared" media space:

· As you consider the landscape of potential tactics and touchpoints, these earned media spaces (public relations, social, digital, emails) will be fundamental.
· Each of the channels requires continuous upkeep and attention. They aren't magic bullets. Once you enter into a real-time relationship with someone, that relationship needs to be maintained. If they're following you on one social platform or another—or if they've opted in to your email list—not engaging with

them is the worst thing you can do. I look at earned media in the digital space almost like sweat equity. It's not free—you pay in time and effort instead of media dollars.

- Each of these media will drive people to your website, so it's important to keep that property dialed. They will move from social media, email, or press to your site for more information. Make sure the URLs are correct and the information is there. Then be ready to pick up an ongoing relationship.
- Keep the quality of the content high. If you believe that relevance and differentiation are more important than awareness, then you should care more about the impact of the content than the number of people with apathetic eyeballs on it. Spend your money making great content, and the impressions will follow.

With respect to other touchpoints, traditional media can still be effective if you have the budget. Print is still alive and well—but it's much more fragmented today than ever before. This can be good if you want to reach a very specific audience. It's also good because media prices for these more niche publications have come down significantly—as a consequence of smaller circulation numbers. So consider a reasonable print spend for your larger initiatives if you have the budget.

Real-world customer engagement is always a win. Getting people together to interact face-to-face is never a bad investment. So don't stop investing in events. The beauty these days is that you can promote those events widely both before and after the events via earned media. So the content from the event becomes great brand-building content—and generates earned media on the back end. But I would suggest owning the events, rather than frittering your marketing budget away on sponsorship of events in hopes of logo inclusion on the signage. That's an awareness-building tactic and can be a significant waste of money.

Budgeting Is Not a Four-Letter Word

The money allocation is often the least fun part. But keep in mind that customer engagement

done right is about generating positive interest and support. As stated before, earned media enables you to generate that support with sweat rather than cash. But you still might need to allocate funds for production of assets or fees for external help. Marketing budgets are typically comprised of three types of costs:

PRODUCTION – This is money required to build content or marketing assets. This could include: usage rights for music or photos, event materials and expenses (travel, gas, food, collateral, etc.), and development of film/video content.

MEDIA – These are costs related to promoting existing content. Examples include: reserving media space for print ads/TV spots/digital ads, sponsorship of existing events, boosting content on social media (Facebook, YouTube, etc.), and advertorials.

FEES – These are costs to external partners, potentially including: graphic design support, PR firms, photographers, and site developers.

It used to be that you'd want to spend the majority of your budget on media to really get the word out. But with the advent of the earned media space, you might decide to invest more heavily in producing great content. That would mean you spend more on production and possibly on fees with creative partners. The mix really depends on the plan and the KPIs you've set out to achieve.

I've always found it helpful to go into a planning discussion with a budget in mind. Rather than create a blue-sky plan that can't be funded, going into a planning process with a sense of the budget forces people to be more resourceful. Decide how much you have to spend and let it drive ideation along with the outcomes you hope to achieve.

Step 7: Creative Development

Many nonprofit organizations deal with complex subject matter. But you can really solve for that complexity through creativity and smart communications planning. As you consider development of assets related to the different elements of the communications plan you've built, think about how much your audience can digest. For example, you might hit the main, most provocative point in proactive media, then drive back to the heavier information online. It's often more effective to bring people along slowly rather than dumping all of the complex information on them at once.

Brief Writing – Keep It Brief

All of the work you've done to this point is critical as you approach creative development. You need to know who you are, who you're designing for, what you want them to know, and how all the touchpoints relate to the journey you'll take them on. Whether you're creating a video, a print ad, a social post, or a press release, you should organize your thoughts first.

Here's a set of topics/questions you can use as the basis for creative development. The answers to these questions are often referred to as a creative brief and they can be used as guidance for both internal and external creative resources.

BACKGROUND – What's the backstory? Why are we involved?

COMMUNICATION OBJECTIVE – Why are we developing this communications effort? What are we asking people to do?

CUSTOMER – Who are we talking to? (which of our core targets, demographics, geography, etc.)

INSIGHTS AND OPPORTUNITIES – What is the customer insight that makes this effort particularly relevant or beneficial to them?

CORE IDEA – In a nutshell, this is what we want the audience to take away.

SUPPORT – Why should they believe us?

POSITIONING AND TONE – Are there visual or tonal guidelines we really need to consider for this category and/or audience?

TIMING – What are the key dates to consider?

KEY DELIVERABLES – List creative assets that make up the plan.

BUDGET – A ballpark figure is better than nothing here.

MANDATORIES – Additional must-haves in the work itself.

SUCCESS METRICS – What does success look like? What are the key performance indicators?

Constraint Is Good

Some people would suggest that constraint has a bad influence on real creativity. I would suggest that they've never made a film or designed anything. Constraint is necessary—and it's what you've just created for yourself with the brand positioning statement.

I started my career in the mid '90s on Madison Avenue in New York City at an agency called Young & Rubicam. Here's how an old creative director schooled me with respect to constraint and developing communications:

Think about designing a single-page print ad for a new car. You need to communicate the following things, as they are imperative:

· It's fast.
· It's less expensive than competitors in its class.
· It gets great gas mileage.
· It comes in a special shade of red.
· The stereo is specially designed.
· It's safe.
· If you don't like it, we'll give you your money back.

What would your print ad look like? Can you picture it? What would the headline be? How would you photograph the car? Do you think you could be sure that readers take away everything on the list from that one ad?

OK, now think about what your print ad would look like if you had to communicate just the following: *This car is really, really fast.*

I bet you could design that print ad and I'll bet the customer would get it. I also bet the car would sell.

So much of the strategic work done up front is in service to the creative process. It's not meant to be confining or limiting. Quite the opposite, it's meant to freeing. But in my experience, I can guarantee you one thing: if you don't make decisions early, you will fail.

Challenge yourself to make decisions. Make the core idea as clear and as concise as possible. No more than one sentence. Less if possible. Whether you're a huge packaged goods brand or a tiny nonprofit organization, if you don't take the time to make those decisions up front and provide the necessary constraints, your marketing efforts will be forgettable and ineffective.

I guarantee it, or your money back.

Step 8:
Track and Optimize

Practice makes perfect. The only problem is we're practicing with real money and people's time. Also we're not really shooting for perfect. We're shooting for real. So forget that adage.

However, we can learn a lot as we go. You will continue to learn about your audience. You will understand how best to tell your story, and it will continue to get more concise and more impactful. You will figure out what channels work best for you and how to lead people into the richer content via communications planning. You'll get a better feel for how much money to invest in outreach annually and per initiative. It will become a real tool for your organization. But don't expect it all to click into place at once. Track, learn, speak to people, and adjust. You'll get there.

Conclusion

Embracing the fundamental principles of marketing strategy and communications planning can have a huge impact on your outreach efforts. When done properly, customer engagement can build relationships, rally support for your organization, and get your story out to the world. It doesn't require huge budgets and special effects. It just requires creativity, some storytelling discipline, and a willingness to tell the truth. Sometimes it can feel vulnerable. But that's likely when you're really connecting with people.

There's a quote from *Let My People Go Surfing* that I think about at least once a day. In the chapter on image, Yvon Chouinard says, "Patagonia's image is a human voice. This means that it will offend, and it will inspire." This is freeing to me as a marketer. It means honesty is job number one. It means that the conversations I start with people are real and the relationships I build are based on authenticity. It casts all that sleazeball stuff aside, and lets us in marketing get on with the important work. It encourages us to take risks. To me, marketing is good, clean fun.

So take the time to build your strategy. Let it guide you and help you make decisions. Bring your creativity and your passion. Be human and remember the fundamental rules of interpersonal communication. Then get out there and make it happen. I hope these tools and thoughts are helpful in some way.

Oh, and hire a few liberal arts interns if possible, too. They need the work.

Dolphins ride the bow wave of a boat off the coast of Southern California. *Corey Arnold*

Including Everyone

Environmentalists. Business. Government. So often, we paint the protection of nature as a battle waged between entities. But at the end of the day, the so-called battle plays out among individuals.

Without compromising our reputation as the last and best chance for protecting water in San Diego (or wildlands in the West or endangered species across the globe), building fluid relationships and understanding the goals and frustrations of our so-called opponents becomes a tool in itself. It allows others to come to the table with an open mind.

At a recent gathering, "San Diego and the Ocean," I moderated two groups of speakers, and was very visible to the audience but not involved in any planning. An agitated young man who identified himself as a third-generation longshoreman took me aside and launched into a tirade about how the presenters ignored the ship-building industry and the hundreds of jobs and millions of dollars it generated: "They just talked about tourism."

There were many things I could have said, but, "I understand," had to be the first. The young man's distress, which likely plays out to differing degrees among his family, co-workers, and friends, provides insight into how I might protect the environment and some of the challenges that the San Diego port faces when I request or demand that it take action. So I talked to him. We didn't resolve anything, but I heard him and learned. He (I hope) felt validated and heard what I could share about how the port and environmental community understand and value our longshoremen and women.

Investment management theory says that for sustainable long-term gains, we should invest in a diverse portfolio. To bring our world into alignment—for long-term sustainable environmental gains—bringing a lawsuit or having someone scale an oil rig and hang a banner are important tools, as long as we also recognize that the people working on that oil rig have families, and needs, and values, and we talk to them as such.

– Megan Baehrens

45

TOP   Delia, the trusty Worn Wear truck, designed by the artist Jay Nelson. *Erin Feinblatt*   BOTTOM   The ubiquitous Worn Wear patch, often distributed at Patagonia stores and Worn Wear events. *Donnie Hedden*   RIGHT   The Worn Wear tour poster. *Patagonia Archives*

Worn Wear

Bill Boland

Patagonia products have always carried an Iron Clad Guarantee and with that, the promise to be repaired or replaced as needed. But it wasn't until the Worn Wear program was started that Patagonia's commitment to keeping its products "in play" and out of the landfill gained its own identity.

Patagonia's Worn Wear program started as a blog that allowed our customers to share photos and stories about their favorite Patagonia clothes, http://wornwear.patagonia.com/. From the outset, the program's positioning was clear: an informal and personal conversation between Patagonia and its customers. The blog's simple statement or tag line, The Stories We Wear, captures this nicely. This set the tone for the campaign and helped shape the Worn Wear identity as a conversation among friends, an identity that has remained consistent in all of the communication avenues and continues to this day.

Since its inception in 2013, the Worn Wear program has evolved far beyond the blog. We've also used the campaign to highlight programs we already had in place, such as our repair services and online repair guides. Then we found ways to extend the program, by creating Patagonia's mobile repair truck (her name is Delia), establishing a unique Worn Wear presence on all of our major social media platforms, opening a used Patagonia clothing section in our Portland store, and building on-site repair shops in a few other stores, including one in SoHo.

As the program grew, the need for more marketing materials became evident. By adhering to a consistent look and feel for these pieces, the Worn Wear program gained synergy. Each new flyer, ad, sign, or web page added to the strength of the Worn Wear brand. We made sure to keep the tone consistent, maintaining the conversational feel that was established with the blog. The result is a very recognizable brand identity that resonates with our community and beyond.

One of the keys to the success of the Worn Wear program is that the core message or position remains consistent across different communication channels. It's the variety of platforms or channels that carry the Worn Wear message that allows it to reach different groups within the greater Patagonia customer base. These channels range from face-to-face events in our stores or on the road with Delia to posts on Instagram and the Worn Wear blog.

Establishing the Key Performance Indicators (KPIs) of the Worn Wear program is actually

one of the more straightforward aspects of the campaign. We have hard data: the number of repaired garments; customer participation online, in our stores, and at events; and the amount of used clothing sold. All of these make measuring the impact of the Worn Wear program fairly easy. They also suggest clear, achievable goals and focus for the Worn Wear team.

The relationship customers have with their Patagonia products has always been the foundation of the Worn Wear campaign. With the guidance of KPIs, we are able to develop clear and effective yet flexible strategies and tactics to continue our part in fostering the relationship. Staying engaged with our community—and keeping our customers engaged—is of utmost importance.

The various parts of the program, as illustrated here, come together to form a cohesive, effective campaign driven by a clear, measurable goal—to get more people to keep their stuff longer.

LEFT   A Worn Wear ad printed in the Village Voice on Black Friday, 2014. *Patagonia Archives*   TOP   Individually numbered Worn Wear repair tags used on the tour for tracking product through the repair process. *Matthew Locascio*   BOTTOM   Delia (the truck) in her open-for-business mode, with Dominique Buncio, a Patagonia repair tech, helping a customer assess his repair. *Donnie Hedden*

In 2015, Bill McKibben, the founder of 350.org, won the Right Livelihood Award, sometimes called the "alternative Nobel," for his work on climate change. He also had a new species of woodland gnat named after him by the biologists who found it in a West Coast forest.

Bill McKibben

2013 KEYNOTE SPEAKER

Leaderless

PG.52 On March 2, 2009, some 12,000 young people gathered to show their elected officials that young voters demand real action on climate change. Washington, DC. *Robert Van Waarden / Survival Media Agency* ABOVE In 2009, 350.org events took place across the African continent. Clockwise from upper left: Cape Peninsula, South Africa; Cape Town, South Africa; Niamey, Niger; Cairo, Egypt; Togo; Nigeria; Okavango Delta, Botswana; Addis Ababa, Ethiopia. *Photos Courtesy of 350.org/Anthony Allen/Emily Taylor*

I want to talk about the first big day of action that 350.org organized in 2009. We'd started the year before with seven college students, and no money, no organization, no lists or anything, just this thought that we would go out and try to do the work of building a global movement that hadn't been there before. Which, of course, was a ludicrous idea. There were seven students and seven continents, so each one took one. The guy who took Antarctica also had to take the Internet. So we went to work. And, a year later, on that day we expected, well … we didn't know what to expect on that day.

We got the first sense it might work two days early. We'd asked everybody to do something to dramatize the number 350, what it means, and the sense of peril.

We were sitting around a table in our one-room office with our laptops open, and the satellite phone rang and it was our leader in Ethiopia, who like many of our leaders was a she. And like many of our leaders was seventeen. And she was crying. She said, "The government took away our permit for Saturday, so we're doing our rally today before they can stop us." Which was brave, but that wasn't why she was crying. She said, "We just want to do this the same time as everybody else. We want to be part of the big thing, we don't want to spoil it for everybody, we want to do it the same time as everybody else. And we're so sorry, and we have 15,000 kids right now out in the street in Addis Ababa, chanting."

"It's okay, don't worry about the date," we said.

The pictures were rolling in from every corner of the world; there were 5,200 of these demonstrations. And the thing to understand about that is the fact that there were 5,200 of them does not mean that we were great organizers; it means just the opposite. There's no way that any group of seven people organized 5,200 events. People organized them themselves. It was like a potluck supper. We had set the date, and a general theme, and told everybody, it's up to you to bring the dish. And people were completely capable of it, and creative, and funny, and powerful. There was a big involvement of religious communities for the first time. The leaders of Muslims in South Africa, the leaders of indigenous traditions, the Anglican archbishop of South Africa, our biggest evangelical college in the United States, and a group around the Dead Sea. The Dead Sea is shrinking, so the Jordanians made a big three on their beach, and the Palestinians a five, and the Israelis, the zero.

The point is that this leaderless movement is constructing itself, and that's exactly what we need. The enemy that we face, this incredibly powerful fossil fuel industry that is the richest thing that there's ever been on Earth, the richest enterprise in human history, is protean; it's everywhere, in every corner of every government. And so the kind of movement that rises up to struggle with it, it's going to have to be protean, too; it's going to have to be in every place, in every culture, and in every shade of ideology. That's the kind of movement that is starting to arise. But it's not exactly leaderless. Actually, a better word for it would be *leaderful*.

CHAPTER 04

Organizing

Owen Bailey

On Monday, April 9, 2007, California's powerful State Lands Commission held a public hearing in the city of Oxnard regarding a massive and polluting Liquefied Natural Gas (LNG) terminal proposed off California's coast. The project could not move forward without the agency's approval. BHP Billiton, the world's largest mining corporation, had spent four years and many millions of dollars lobbying all levels of government and demonstrating corporate largess to make their case, while a handful of community leaders and activists led the opposition. The financial and influence disparity between the two sides could hardly be overstated.

The stage was set for a showdown. The hearing room was equipped with 600 chairs—but by mid-afternoon the room was at capacity. Those of us opposing the offshore terminal filled most of the seats and our overflow lined the walls. At the same time, our rally outside was designed for all those we anticipated would never fit in the room. Police estimated the rally alone at 2,000 people.

We concluded the rally while the hearing was still going on so that our crowd could gather in the courtyard as a sea of blue shirts in full view of the commission and everyone inside the hearing room.

More than 2,000 people—realtors and farmworkers, surfers and teachers, kids and grandparents—had all taken a day off from work, missed dinner and helping their kids with their studies to stand up for their community and their environment. After a hearing that lasted more than thirteen hours, the commissioners, having spent the day staring into the faces of this concerned and highly engaged community, voted to deny the project.

How did this happen? Clearly, our David didn't beat this Goliath solely because of an engaged community. To get to the point where we even had a chance at winning enough commissioners' votes, our side needed, among other things, experts to refute the opposition's messaging. We needed to strategically, and over time, educate decision makers and the media, and we needed to have a sound legal strategy. In this case, the successful community coalition had a strong, strategically minded leader in place from the California Coastal Protection Network and expert research and legal support from the Environmental Defense Center. But it is undeniable that seeing such overwhelming community commitment made an impact on the decision makers. A diverse and empowered crowd, united to protect their community and health, made a powerful statement and gave us a significant edge.

PG.56 Protesters during the 2014 Climate March in New York City, New York. *Tim Davis*
PG.57 Seagulls swarm behind a fishing boat in the Arctic's Barents Sea. *Corey Arnold*

59

Mobilizing Support

Unfortunately, not enough of our environmental groups put this much of a focus on mobilizing support. All too often, environmental leaders and organizations act as though all that matters is that we are right—that we have the facts on our side. All too often, while our work represents the values of the communities we represent and work within, we do not spend the time and effort to effectively communicate with and engage these communities to help. Being right is not enough. To win, we must organize.

Wikipedia defines grassroots organizing as "build(ing) community groups from scratch, developing new leadership where none existed and organizing the unorganized." Grassroots organizers work within their communities in an effort to build political power among the disenfranchised. We provide people with opportunities to participate in solutions to the problems facing their families, their neighborhoods, and future generations.

Regardless of the issues we are working on, to win, we must organize. Whether we are trying to win over the city council, convince our local congressperson, move a state agency or any other body, or win at the ballot box, we need to build support. Organizing allows us to demonstrate constituent support to decision makers, generate media attention, and engage new leaders and supporters. Strong attendance at a hearing will also mean that any decisions will be made under the bright light of public scrutiny. Mobilizing people to participate will increase the odds of a thoughtful decision, as leaders will know they are on the record and will be held accountable. In our LNG fight, we had just cast the bright light of several thousand faces and lit the way to a clear victory.

If more campaigns and organizations prioritized in the same way, just think of the changes we could make for our communities and future generations. Unfortunately, I am sure we have all worked on issues where someone has simply announced that since "this is an important issue, people will come" or all we have to do is "get it out there" and people will join us. But the reality is, as we all know, that sending an email—or a lot of emails—will not educate, motivate, and mobilize an army of volunteers and it will certainly not

guide, nurture, and maintain your volunteer corps for the extended period needed to see a project through.

To do that you need someone who will create and then follow an outreach program. You need someone keeping volunteers engaged and on track—providing updates and jobs that need to be done—and you need someone to encourage activists to stretch outside their comfort zones. You need someone to constantly close the loop, letting volunteers know the results and value of their actions, and the results of each tactic attempted. Again, that means you need an organizer.

The Organizer

An organizer's job is evenly split between the inspirational and the mundane. It is her job to bring in new volunteers, to ask and inspire people to action taking on jobs they may have never done before, and also to make sure the campaign is hitting its numbers. He needs to track people's attendance, their actions, and their successes, and monitor what needs to be done—and to do this day after day after day.

The organizer is in a very real sense the source of a campaign's strength; she builds and keeps your volunteer list, and there are few more valuable resources to a campaign. She is either out in the community or identifying and training volunteers to fill this role. He tables at the farmers' market or the street fair with a sign-in sheet, gathering contact information from potential supporters at every community event or meeting. The organizer is behind the scenes encouraging new leaders and providing support for all volunteer actions. The organizer is identifying compelling messengers who can make the campaign's case to specific audiences.

But the organizer isn't simply about doling out and tracking tasks. To successfully build community around an issue, you need to connect with people, to listen to what they are telling you about their concerns, their reasons for joining, and what they need from the campaign. The organizer takes the jargon-rich, and often alienating, technical language that a campaign's experts provide and translates this into messages that volunteers can use and act on. The organizer is listening as much as she is talking in order to make sure she understands what her volunteers need so they can meet the campaign's goals.

Bringing People Together

For our work to stop the LNG project, many of these functions were administered through regularly scheduled group meetings where community members gathered at least monthly—eventually more often as the campaign moved closer to the finish line—to check in on progress, answer questions, update supporters, and assign tasks. These regular meetings were essential for creating community and building accountability to each other.

Over time, our supporter base grew more and more diverse. What began as a clear reflection of the conservation activist community grew to include people we would never have met if it were not for their shared concern about the project we opposed. As partner organizations accessed their networks and we created additional opportunities to reach beyond the communities we were already connected to, our supporter base began to resemble a true cross section of the diverse cities in which we lived. This made it even more critical that everyone meet and learn what issues were of primary importance to each other. These community meetings were the perfect place for new supporters to join and plug in, and for long-time activists to report in and stay informed and connected. Regardless of the size of the group, we would always each take a moment to introduce ourselves and mention what brought us there. Having everyone participate was key to helping move attendees from being an observing audience to becoming an active, cohesive community.

We would then talk briefly about what had happened since we last met, thank those who had taken specific actions for the campaign, and list what needed to be done before we would next assemble. And in front of the group, we would ask people to volunteer to do these tasks—knowing that people are far more likely to follow through on commitments made in front of their peers.

Volunteer Leaders

These meetings are also an opportunity to learn more about your volunteers. In any gathering, ask: Who is here? Why are they involved? What skills and experiences do they have? What do they want to do to help? What are people afraid to do? What are people unwilling to do? Only by actually talking to people do you get a picture of how you can help personally guide them to move up a ladder of activism. For example, we had one volunteer who had never done any campaign work and was afraid to speak in public. Over time, she began by writing a letter to the editor, and built confidence as she took more and more actions. With guidance and help in creating her goals and completing her assignments, she ended up being one of our leaders, testifying at hearings, tabling at festivals, and volunteering to manage a speakers' bureau.

When we began working to defeat the LNG threat, we had immediate goals and long-term strategies. Over the short term, we needed to mobilize people to attend early hearings, so all our activities focused on engaging our base to meet that specific need. The first thing we needed to do was figure out who was in that base.

I was an organizer for the Sierra Club with a built-in network, the organization's membership, for us to start communicating with. If you are working with an established organization, chances are you have a contact list. However, even with this network as a starting point, we also took the steps that a newly established group would. We reached out to other potentially supportive organizations and requested an opportunity to brief them and asked allied groups to share their lists or reach out to their memberships. It was at this time that we began an invaluable partnership with another local organization named CAUSE, which focuses on building grassroots power for environmental justice and other issues, and which ended up being one of our most important and effective alliances throughout the campaign. We also set up tables at community events and fairs and personally reached out to community leaders, influencers, and anyone who could possibly be interested—always asking everyone who they knew who might want to learn more. We always kept very careful track of everyone who expressed any interest.

It is always easier to engage people to help if the clock is ticking loudly. If your hearing is in three weeks, you can ask your strongest supporters and campaign leaders to take on specific roles to help ensure success. This was the situation when we started organizing. We were engaging people to learn more about a project they had never heard of, but which sounded ominous. It is another challenge altogether once that hearing is behind you. The fact is, in many of our conservation efforts, we face long delays. Some projects last for years and years, some simply go dormant for extended periods, and it is always challenging to keep people engaged if the threat is off the front pages for any length of time. Once that happens, you may need to create your own deadlines to keep people working together—you do not want your volunteers to disperse and take on other projects. Your leaders and supporters are among your most valuable resources, and it is far easier to keep people engaged than to let them go, only to try to re-engage them later—or to try to find new volunteers for the next deadline.

Have your volunteers help decide on future projects—whether a rally or media event, a speakers' bureau, a letters to the editor drive, a push to generate handwritten notes to decision makers, a tabling committee, a drive to generate resolutions from local groups, or any number of other options. Empowering your volunteers to take ownership of projects or large pieces of projects will magnify your impact and increase the intensity of the work you are doing together. When volunteers are free to lead the way, their new ideas and energy often allow everyone on the campaign to consider new approaches and solutions to challenges.

Planning the Next Move

In our campaign, shortly after the initial hearings, we entered a period where we knew our issue was likely to be out of the headlines for some time, but we had a hot list of intensely engaged volunteers and activists who we did not want to cool off. So we used our monthly meetings to do some planning: What decision makers or local influencers do we need to educate on our issue, and how do we reach them? To what communities or constituencies do we need to build inroads? And when will there be community events for us to participate in to help us do that?

We decided we needed further visibility, additional media opportunities, and ways to bring in more new volunteers and build our list of general supporters. We met to discuss options and our group decided we would create a public event highlighting some of the community concerns underlying the project. We decided to create a "Hands Across" event, where we would line up and hold hands along a gas pipeline route proposed for the street in front of a major local school. There would be speakers and an opportunity for new leaders to join our campaign. We would invite the media and, as in everything we would do, we would gather contact information from every single person who attended to build our list.

Building Your List

List building is the critical aspect of a community organizing effort. If someone attends your event, that means they have taken time away from their busy life for your cause. If they write a letter, attend a hearing, make a phone call, or even sign your petition at a farmers' market table, they are telling you they share your values, and you need to keep them informed of what is happening and how their participation will make a difference. People generally have very limited time for volunteering, and if someone takes an action for you, that is significant. They should be thanked and then re-engaged.

Our team learned from the early days that supporters and volunteers are everywhere—and the best ambassadors for the cause are other volunteers. Whether you are at church or a pancake breakfast, a PTA meeting or a birthday party or even standing in a checkout line at a grocery store, you always want to have a clipboard or a notebook with you. Don't just give people a flier and hope they call you. If you are speaking to people who express interest, get their contact information and let them know how and when you or someone else will follow up with them. If they simply walk away with your flier but you can't follow up with them, chances are their busy lives will override their good intensions and you may never see them again.

So when people showed up at what we called our Hands Along the Pipeline event, their first stop was the welcome table and the first thing we asked them to do was to sign in. Even if we had worked with them before, we would ask them to sign in and provide their contact information. It sent a good message to everyone and ensured the campaign always had the most up-to-date information and could get back in touch with them.

Constant Forward Movement

Patience and tenacity are what's required when organizing against a well-funded operation that can afford to slow down and wait for your organization to dissipate. We needed to continuously come up with ways for activists to engage and to always make sure that they helped move us closer to our ultimate goal. So month after month we tabled and rallied, we built our lists, helped get supportive resolutions passed, and found other groups to join our coalition. We wrote and collected letters to the editor, engaged young people, and continuously circled back to our volunteers to validate their participation.

It took us three years to get to the home stretch on this "fast tracked" project. We originally expected to have only a matter of months from start to finish on the public process, but the campaign was able to ask enough questions and put enough obstacles in the way to draw the time frame out for several years. While delays can often provide some benefit in this work, giving you additional time to understand the complexities of the project and educate decision makers, it can also present organizing challenges to keeping volunteer activists and supporters motivated for an extended period.

Beyond the basic fact that people are busy and over time your key people can be pulled away for many reasons, as an organizer you are working to knit together a diverse group of people who might not have much in common aside from their concern about your issue. Personality issues are all too common; in our work over more than three years, there were leaders who did not even like each other. The organizer's job is then to keep people focused on what they can do and how their shared opposition to the LNG terminal—or the coal plant or the fracking operation or development project—is more important than their reasons to dislike some other campaign volunteer.

The Final Push

Finally after three years, our critical public hearing was upon us. This was our final push and we needed to pull out all the stops with a massive organizing meeting, phone calls, door knocks, emails, mailings, newsletters, and letters to the editor. We asked our volunteers to commit to bringing friends and relatives. People made pledges for how many people they could bring.

The result was the best-attended hearing in the history of the State Lands Commission to date, a long day, and a victory that led the way to having BHP Billiton close up its offices and move away from Southern California.

Throughout this effort we made sure to stick with our basic underlying philosophy: People help because they are asked. And the most compelling way to ask for something is one-on-one. There is no substitute for one-on-one communication. There is a reason why political campaigns do not just depend on social media, texting, or even email to mobilize voters. The direct conversations you have by phone, at the door, or at a community meeting are the most persuasive and compelling interactions that your neighbors and fellow community members will have throughout your campaign.

Obviously, one person or even a handful of organizers cannot directly communicate with every volunteer or even every leader every time. It takes training and delegation to ensure you have the leaders you need. And of course there is great value in one-to-many communications by email or mail, especially for reminders and follow-up. Many of our causes require mobilizing people across the state or a wide geographical range. The principles of the work are, however, the same: an organizer needs to build a team of leaders who will each organize their own teams of activists and supporters to ensure these one-on-one interactions.

What guided our work was the idea that if we were not creating these interactions, working to organize the community, to find new activists, to make sure there was a steady flow of handwritten notes and letters to the editor, to turn people out to rallies and hearings, then who was? And if nobody was, then we would never be able to convince even those elected officials who might want to do the right thing but needed support. If we couldn't help them stand against the immense pressure that they most assuredly felt from the deep-pocketed special interests pumping big dollars into their community, then we would not earn their support. And if we couldn't win over those who we might expect to be most friendly to our side, how would we ever convince the coveted swing votes on which virtually every campaign relies?

To win, we must organize. If we don't mobilize, work the phones and the farmers' markets, if we don't educate and inspire people to help us, we are alone. Organizing puts the community out in front, leading the way. Organizing builds power to hold decision makers accountable and provides the strength to push back against the big money your opposition invariably brings to bear. And as we learned one Monday in April 2007, a deliberate, passionate, and diverse movement has power and the unique ability to make positive and transformative change for the community and for the future.

Resources

Alinsky, Saul. *Rules for Radicals: A Pragmatic Primer for Realistic Radicals.* New York: Vintage Books, 1971 (reissue 1989).

Bobo, K., J. Kendall, and S. Max. *Organize for Social Change.* 4th ed. (Midwest Academy Manual for Activists.) Santa Ana, Calif.: The Forum Press, 2010.

Brown, Michael J. *Building Powerful Community Organizations: A Personal Guide to Creating Groups That Can Solve Problems and Change the World.* Arlington, Mass: Long Haul Press, 2007.

Ross, Fred. *Axioms for Organizers: Trailblazer for Social Justice.* San Francisco: Neighbor to Neighbor, 1989.

Sierra Club Grassroots Organizing Training Manual. http://clubhouse.sierraclub.org/ training/programs/grassroots-organizing/ Default.aspx.

BEYOND COAL.ORG

A SIERRA CLUB CAMPAIGN

66

Beyond Coal

Mary Anne Hitt

Indianapolis. North Omaha. Memphis. San Antonio. If you're listing hotbeds of US environmental activism, these cities might not be the first that spring to mind. But they are among dozens of communities leading a revolution in how we power America and the world, a movement *Mother Jones* called "a grassroots rebellion [that] is winning the biggest victory yet on climate change."

This is the Beyond Coal campaign, a people-powered, open-source network of more than 100 organizations that have stopped the construction of 184 proposed coal plants, won the retirement of 190 existing coal plants—one-third of the fleet of US coal plants, including those in the cities listed above—and opened the floodgates for record deployment of clean energy such as wind and solar.

As the director of the Beyond Coal campaign at the Sierra Club, I've been down in the trenches, and I've also had a bird's-eye view of this remarkable movement. We've worked with dozens of partner organizations in what Politico called "the most extensive, expensive, and effective campaign in the [Sierra] Club's 123-year history, and maybe the history of the environmental movement."

In 2002, I was working in Appalachia and seeing proposals pop up for new coal-fired power plants. Environmental advocates faced with these proposals around the United States began connecting the dots. The total was staggering. More than 200 coal plants were on the drawing board nationwide. If they were built, it would truly be "game over" for the climate, coal would swallow up future markets for clean energy, and Americans would bear the brunt of another fifty-plus years of air and water pollution.

There was only one option: fight every single proposed power plant in the nation. In hindsight, it seems obvious. So that was what the Beyond Coal movement pledged to do, despite the fact that, given our limited resources and the power of the industry at the time, many advocates and observers thought that taking on such a big goal was crazy.

I had been working to stop coal companies from blowing up mountains in my home region of Appalachia to extract the coal beneath, a practice known as mountaintop removal. In working to fight proposed coal plants in the region that would fuel demand for more mountaintop-removal coal, I met people outside Appalachia affected by coal and learned that everywhere coal was mined, burned, or disposed of, people were getting sick, beautiful places were being destroyed, and democracy was paying the price.

One of the people I met was Bruce Nilles. Bruce was doing this work at the Sierra Club as an attorney based in Illinois, where he had found himself at ground zero in what we would later call the coal rush. He began working with tenacious volunteers (including Verena Owen, now the volunteer leader of the Beyond Coal campaign) to challenge over a dozen new coal plants proposed in Illinois. And they were winning in a true David versus Goliath fashion that inspired others to get in the fight—including me. I joined Bruce on the Sierra Club staff in 2008.

The coal industry seemed invincible at the time, and we had few resources—just a ragtag band of committed advocates and volunteers. Fast-forward to more than a decade since the campaign began in 2002, and this movement has stopped 184 proposed coal plants, with no new plants on the drawing board.

The coal rush is over.

In 2010, the campaign made a major pivot to focus on retiring the most vulnerable of the 500 existing coal plants that were, at that time, providing half of America's electricity. The fact that the nation's aging coal plants were not going to be replaced with a new fleet left operators of the existing plants with a choice: spend money to retrofit them to meet modern health and safety standards, or phase them out.

Our current goal is to win the retirement of half of America's coal plants by 2017 and replace them with clean energy. In 2014, we were well on our way there. When we began this phase of the campaign in 2010, the nation was getting 50 percent of its electricity from coal. In 2015, the amount is less than 40 percent. Of the nation's 500-plus coal plants, 190 were currently announced for retirement, one out of every three US coal plants. That means not only less carbon and smog and mercury pollution, but also less power and influence for the industry that was the biggest obstacle to passing federal climate legislation.

Mobilizing grassroots power has been at the core of our strategy, because fundamentally, these are all local campaigns, each with its own distinctive decision makers, communities, and leverage points—and local grassroots leaders know that landscape best. Owen Bailey's chapter highlights the essential elements to building that power, including enlisting supporters face-to-face, creating organizing opportunities to keep people engaged in a long struggle, identifying the right targets, choosing strategic moments to flex your collective muscle, and demonstrating momentum.

I'll give you just two examples of what that looks like on the ground for the Beyond Coal campaign. Indianapolis was home to an urban coal plant that's a major air and water polluter, the Harding Street plant. Indiana is a conservative, coal-producing state, and when we launched our campaign there, we knew that phasing out the plant would not be easy, despite the serious health and environmental problems it caused in the city. Early in our campaign to retire the plant, I came to town and was greeted by the headline "Beyond Coal's Director Faces Tough Sell in Indiana."

Over the course of two years, we not only readied our legal case targeting air and water pollution problems at the plant, but we organized and organized and organized. We reached out to dozens of community groups, held numerous visibility events, and worked with local reporters. We also met with the utility that owned the plant, Indianapolis Power and Light, to make our goals clear to them and begin a conversation about retiring the plant and replacing it with clean energy.

Two years later, our coalition was fifty organizations and thousands of people strong, and we were poised to pass a resolution in the City-County Council calling for retirement of the plant. The vote was slated for a Monday, and on the Friday before the council meeting, Indianapolis Power and Light announced it would cease burning coal at Harding Street.

Another victory on the West Coast underscores the power of cities to lead the way to a nation powered by clean energy, regardless of gridlock in Washington, DC. On a picture-perfect California morning in March 2013, Los Angeles Mayor Antonio Villaraigosa stood with former Vice President Al Gore, billionaire businessman Tom Steyer, Sierra Club Executive Director Michael Brune, and cheering community leaders and supporters to make a huge announcement: the city of Los Angeles was going coal-free.

After a three-year campaign that engaged 15,000 people, the city was ending its contracts with two coal-fired power plants that provided 40 percent of the electricity to the city of Los Angeles, and replacing much of that coal power with solar power and energy efficiency.

In announcing the news the day before, Mayor Villaraigosa had stated, "The era of coal is over."

When Gore stepped up to the podium, he looked out across the audience and said, "This is a big deal. This is a really big deal."

The Los Angeles event was part of a wave of announcements from coast to coast that cities were moving beyond coal, and that power companies were retiring their old, aging, polluting coal plants. The coal plants that are the nation's number one source of not only the carbon pollution that's throwing the climate into chaos, but also the sulfur pollution that causes tens of thousands of premature deaths, asthma attacks, and heart attacks every year, as well as the mercury pollution that every pregnant woman in America is warned about by her doctor, because exposure in the womb puts babies at risk of lifelong developmental problems like lowered IQ.

Connecting these individual victories to the bigger picture is a key element of our long-term success. Demonstrating momentum in the long climate struggle is an essential element of the Beyond Coal campaign. Repeatedly, we've set an aggressive target for turning the corner on climate change, achieved it, and then stretched for an even bigger goal. When people win campaigns like these coal plant-retirement victories, it connects them to their own power, sometimes for the first time. As it turns out, there's nothing like winning to fire up a movement and inspire them to achieve what seems impossible.

Recent research has shown that people find climate change especially disempowering because the solutions usually proposed seem pathetically small (change your lightbulbs) or impossibly large (reform the US Congress). The Beyond Coal campaign has found at least one empowering middle ground where people can act locally, win victories that matter at the scale of the climate problem, and apply their collective wisdom to aim even higher. It's a strategy that has, so far, transformed the electric sector and slashed US carbon emissions. And we're just getting started.

It's time to stop scaring people with visions of an unavoidable apocalyptic future, and to start inspiring them with the conviction that, together, we actually can turn the corner on climate disruption. After all, we're not just here to fight climate change.

We're here to win that fight.

Protesters from the Moapa Band of Paiutes and the Sierra Club walk from the Reid Gardner Generating Station Plant to the Moapa Southern Paiute Solar project to bring awareness to the need to rapidly transition from coal to clean and renewable energy. Nevada. *Photo Courtesy of the Sierra Club/Gary Thompson/Light Forge Studios*

Counselor to the president, Oberlin College; Minter Fellow at the Cleveland Foundation; founder and chair of the board, Oberlin Project, David Orr is also the author of seven books and several hundred articles on the environment, climate change, politics, and philosophy. He's received eight honorary degrees and other awards, including a 2014 national leadership award from the US Green Building Council.

David Orr

2009 KEYNOTE SPEAKER

The Haircut

W hen I was still a young boy, I was given my first example of leadership. My dad had been raised in Charlotte, North Carolina, during the Jim Crow era and had seen some of the ugly side of racism. He was a Presbyterian minister and for seventeen years, the president of Westminster College in New Wilmington, Pennsylvania. Sometime, probably 1950 or 1951, he decided to integrate the college. Segregation was still in force in Pennsylvania and in most colleges in the region, so it was a tough go. He personally recruited African-American students to Westminster and took an active interest in their college experience in an all-white small town in western Pennsylvania. As part of his commitment, he interviewed students regularly.

One day after school, I stopped by his office. He was talking with one of the African-American students, who said that his experience at the college was fine but that he couldn't get a haircut at the local barbershop.

"That's not a problem, come on with me," my dad replied.

So they walked a block to the barbershop, with me tagging along behind. Walking into the barbershop, Dad said, "Harry, my friend here needs a haircut."

"Dr. Orr, I don't know how to cut that kind of hair," Harry replied.

"Well, Harry, here, I'll show you," my father said.

He sat the student in the barber chair, put the bib around him, and went to work. After a minute or so of some of the worst barbering ever, Harry got the point. "OK, OK, I'll finish up."

It was a small thing to do, but it made a big statement for merchants in that small town: discrimination was not acceptable. I didn't realize it at the time, but that was leadership. And it was done in a way that Harry couldn't refuse. It was everyday leadership where human dignity comes into friction with prejudice.

It's not the sort of leadership in which the guy on the white horse rides into town, makes short work of some bad guy, and rides out again. It's leadership with the people we meet every day as friends and neighbors and have to work through differences of politics, policy, religion, and garden-variety disagreements. We certainly need leadership in state capitals and Washington, but it won't amount to much if we don't have lots of leaders on Main Street, at work, in churches, and in civic organizations.

At either level, the hallmarks of leadership are rock-solid integrity, independent thinking, a refusal to accept injustice and indignities, and courage—all with a smile.

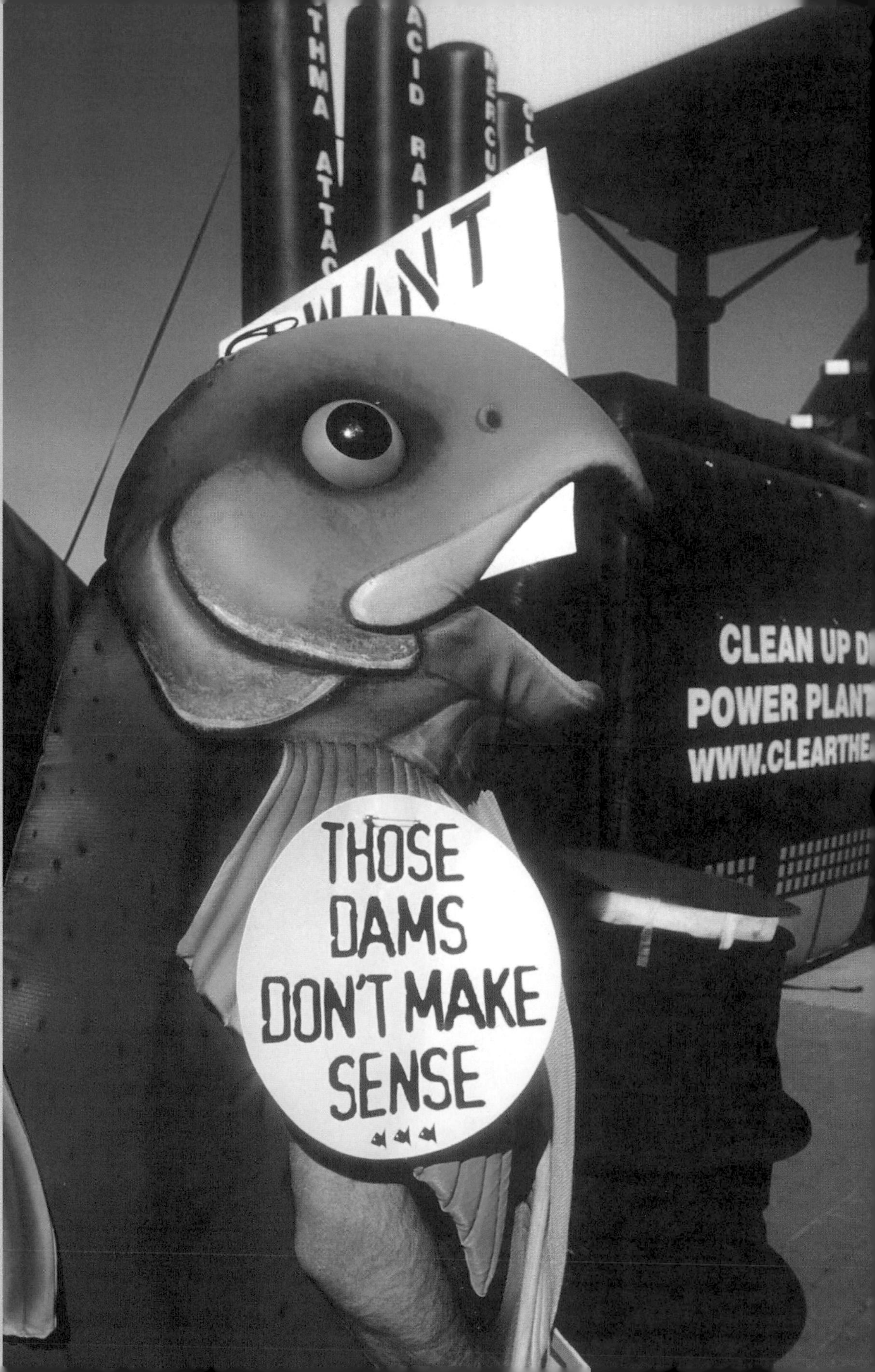
WANT
THOSE DAMS DON'T MAKE SENSE

(05)

Fundraising

Diane Brown

I've never heard little kids say they want to grow up to be a fundraiser. A firefighter or marine biologist maybe, but never a fundraiser.

And really, I'm not offended. I didn't start out with that goal in mind, either. I had worked as a grassroots activist for a lot of different causes, but the common thread running through all of them was that I was passionate about the mission. I wanted to make change happen, but it was hard to feel very effective when we kept losing staff because we couldn't provide livable wages, and we continually struggled to find the money for critical campaigns.

I was putting in long hours to create a sustainable environment and economy, but was working in an unsustainable organization.

To change that, to create a healthy, sustainable organization that could accomplish great things, I broke down and learned how to raise money.

And what I found out is that fundraising really is not rocket science. We all know something about it, and pretty much anybody can learn how to do it.

Maybe you've been frustrated by a lack of resources, too. If you think your organization could accomplish more with a bit more money, then read on for some practical tips on how to bring it in without selling your soul.

PG.74 A rare upright-walking salmon attends a protest to promote the use of clean power. Seattle, Washington. *Colin Meagher* PG.75 Sockeye salmon approach their spawning grounds. Shortly after laying their eggs the salmon will die and decompose or be eaten, and contribute to the upstream ecosystem. Adams River, British Columbia. *Paul Colangelo*

Let's Start with the Basics

Just where does money come from for nonprofit organizations? Many people submit grant applications, but only about one in ten are funded. Grants from foundations seem like the Holy Grail but, in fact, they account for only about 14 percent of the $300 billion donated every year. Corporations account for another 5 percent and mostly give in-kind gifts plus some grants, but rarely to environmental advocacy organizations. So what's the source of the remaining 81 percent of the donations?

Eight percent come from bequests, gifts that are left to your organization in someone's will when they die. The remaining 73 percent—nearly three-quarters of all donations every year—comes from individuals. Know any of those? You may not have personal connections with any business CEOs or foundation board members, but you *do* know individuals (hundreds of them, by the counts on your social media address books).

The good news here is that *most of your money will probably not come from wealthy people*. It will instead come from people of relatively modest means who share your values and dreams. Seventy percent of Americans donate every year. Ninety-one percent of these folks make under $100,000. Starting to look more like the people you know?

Since most grassroots environmental groups have a very small budget to spend on fundraising and limited staff and volunteer time, you'll want to focus on your most likely prospects.

Draw a Bull's-Eye Target

Into the center of the bull's-eye, write your best supporters (specific individuals, businesses, foundations, schools, other organizations, media outlets, volunteers, staff, board members, former board members, allies, demographic groups such as baby boomers, politicians, whoever you can think of who has given a cash or in-kind gift). This is your primary audience. Then, write the names of people you know or have done business with on the rings outside the center. The farther they are from the center, the less likely they are to be a donor.

Now you have a pretty clear map of where to focus your limited resources: in the center and

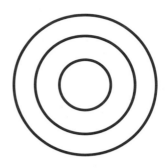

the first ring, because these are your best bets. In the long run, you would aim to upgrade folks in the outer rings closer to the center, but most of your money will come from people who share the values of the people in the center.

So, you need to know more about those values: What motivates your most loyal donors? Brainstorm a list of "Why Someone Would Give to Us." Try to come up with about twenty reasons ranging from the specific (had a great time at the creek cleanup) to the general (believes in the mission, wants their grandkids to live in a beautiful, safe world).

Everybody's list will look different, but most folks miss the most important reason that people give: Because they were asked. It seems so obvious, but think about how many times you've made a donation without being asked versus when you were actually invited to do so—whether by a Girl Scout selling Thin Mints in front of the grocery store, in a membership renewal letter, on a website, or at a rally.

Now, brainstorm another list, this time of all the Grinch reasons: "Why Someone Would Not Give to Us." This list will include things like: didn't get a thank you, thinks we get a lot of government grants, already gave at the office, got us confused with that other group whose bookkeeper embezzled money, and of course, because he or she wasn't asked.

So why make this list? Because you don't want to send any staff, board member, or volunteer out into the world without having a reasonable response to each one of these potential objections. Most are easily corrected misinformation, but some really need careful thought about how to frame an answer. Think about how you would craft a response to each objection, with one exception: If the person really does not believe in the mission or cause. My advice is to be polite to these folks, but do not spend your precious time or resources on them; they are not going to become donors.

Now, bring this "Why Give/Why Not/Snappy Responses" list and the bull's-eye target exercise back to your staff and board members. I'm always amazed at the great input this generates, since people in your group touch different parts of your community, and it gets everyone involved in creating fundraising strategy. Convert all these responses into a simple FAQ handout with bullet point answers to each of the "Why Nots," and you've got a simple, uber-practical tool.

One day, one of my board members told me about this fellow who had just built a luxurious vacation home in a nearby, gated community. He wondered where to put him on the bull's-eye target map. So, I asked a few questions: Did anyone know this fellow or his family? Has he done anything that would indicate he cares about the environment? Has he made a donation to any group they know of?

Why the questions? Because we need to make an educated guess about which people to approach and which are too far in the outer rings of the bull's-eye right now. You should be able to answer affirmatively to at least three, and preferably four, of the following questions in order to qualify someone as a high-priority major donor prospect, one really worth actively pursuing:

> ## Why would someone Give to Us?
> ### (List all the reasons)
>
> 1
> 2
> 3
> 4
> 5
> 6
> 7
> 8
> 9 …

- Do they have discretionary money?
- Do they give any of it away?
- Do they care about your issue?
- Are they connected to you or your organization?

How do you find out if they're philanthropic and give any money away? Use a search engine to see if the press reported on a donation; also search the donor recognition section of websites or newsletters to see if they are listed.

How do you know if they care about your issue? Is there evidence they have given or volunteered for the same or a related issue? People who want to save the whales usually want to save the dolphins as well.

How do you find out if they're connected to you? Ask your staff, volunteers, board members, friends, allies, and stakeholders if they know the person, and try LinkedIn and social media. This is the easiest qualifier to remedy, and actually is a strength we have over big national and international environmental organizations. Many of us work in rural areas with limited wealth. But we know our communities, our neighbors, and the unique cultural and social values and traditions that knit us together. We meet friends who share our values at the farmers' market, in the bleachers at our kids' soccer games, and at work. This gives us many opportunities to talk one-to-one, answer their questions, and invite them to volunteer with us next Saturday—opportunities that Greenpeace or NRDC can only dream of.

Most People Want to Give Locally

They want to see the results of their investment in their own backyard, and have a connection to people they know and trust. While the big national and international organizations certainly do important work, we know that people care most deeply about the places where they live and play. Given the opportunity (that's your job), they want to protect the quality of life for their family and their community, and they want to protect their values. The little guys don't get big breaks like this very often, so get out there and talk to people about what you're doing locally to protect the people and places they love.

You don't want to ask strangers for money, you want to ask friends. It's also important to remember that when you're fundraising, you're not asking for money for yourself, you're offering people an opportunity to support your campaign and the cause. They may or may not choose to make a donation to your organization, but that's not the same as rejecting you personally.

Your Board Members Are a Terrific Asset

The two most challenging questions I have been asked while meeting with a prospective major donor are if 100 percent of the board members participate in fundraising activities and if 100 percent of the board members make a personal donation. More and more people are asking whether one's board is putting skin in the game, and it's sparked some deep conversations. Those organizations whose boards can claim bragging rights to 100 percent giving and 100 percent participation have put themselves in an enviable position in relation to their fundraising competition.

Board members are especially important ambassadors for your organization. Because people in the community know them, they are trusted. And because they govern the organization, people view them as knowledgeable leaders. Telling your organization's story and listening to other folks' stories is the most critical thing that board members can do to strengthen relationships with potential supporters. Whether they ask for a major gift or set up the chairs at a special event, fundraising needs to be a part of your board members' job description.

But remember: No one is born knowing how to fundraise. These folks are "Super Volunteers" and deserve training and support. Teach everyone how to be a great ambassador, feed them new success stories, build their confidence by practicing how to respond to quirky questions, and create a list of all the ways board members might help with fundraising in the coming year.

Then sit down with each member individually and work with them to map out their own personal fundraising action plan. Let them pick which of the fundraising activities they can do. Encourage them to choose tasks that play to their own strengths, but also to take on at least one new thing, even if it's a bit outside their comfort zone. Write down their fundraising action plan including activities, due dates, and whom they can go to for information or help. Schedule time to give them the training and ongoing support they will need to be successful, as well as dates to check in on their progress.

And of course, it's much easier to ask for a donation if you've already made one yourself. ("Please join me" is much more powerful than "I'd like *you* to please give.") Include a discussion of what donation pledge your board member would like to make this year, perhaps spreading out the payments if that is the most convenient method. One rule of thumb a lot of organizations use is to ask their board members to consider all the charitable donations they plan to make this year, and make their largest gift to the group where they are a board member.

While everyone can make some financial contribution, even if it's $5 a year, it's often hard for board members, volunteers, or staff to ask others for money. They may say that fundraising feels like begging, and thus, they don't want to do it.

Asking for money is an emotional subject, laden with taboos and issues of class, but one that people can and should be given a safe space to talk about. People usually give money to beggars because they feel sorry for them, and expect nothing more than a thank you in return. But "feeling sorry for the organization" probably didn't show up on your "Why Give" list.

Please allow me to offer you a different way to look at asking for money.

Give People the Opportunity to Support Your Work

When you fundraise, what you're really doing is giving people an opportunity to accomplish things they can't do by themselves.

If your community understands and appreciates what you're doing, then they will want to support your work. It's an equal exchange—you do good work in the community, and they support you with a donation. That's not begging.

They may be making different choices in their lives about how they spend their time or where they want to work. If you are campaigning for the change that they want done but can't do by themselves, then you should feel good about giving them the opportunity to make their world a better place. Your job is to listen to what they see as an environmental problem and then talk to them about what your organization is doing to help solve that problem. If you are producing the change they want to see in the world, then they will invest their charitable dollars with you because they know they will get a good return.

We are all alarmed by the environmental problems we face. But since compassion fatigue sets in if we only talk about the threats, it's very important to also talk about results. Gather, polish, and share your success stories, and you will give the gift of hope to your donors. Of course you need to acknowledge the problems, but environmental groups are having the most success when they move on to talk about the results of their hard work. We need to know we *can* create change, and we owe it to our supporters to share the stories of our victories—both large and small.

Below Are Three Exercises to Try

- FEEL GOOD EXERCISE: Take one minute to write down or tell a friend a ten-second success story.
- FEEL EVEN BETTER EXERCISE: Start your next meeting by giving everyone a chance to tell their own ten-second success stories.
- MAKE IT A FUNDRAISING TOOL EXERCISE: Schedule three minutes at the beginning of each board meeting to share those amazing stories with your board members, who can then share them with their family, friends, and colleagues. No more waiting for the local press to cover your issue; you are in control of your message and can spread the word about your great work to the people who share your values (also known as your current and potential donors and volunteers).

Once I was working with an executive director who had a great memory; she knew the organization's history with every major donor and hit every deadline for mailing fundraising letters and executing flawless events. Everyone was in awe of this person (and a little jealous of her unique brain cells) until she unexpectedly resigned to take a terrific job in another state. She left, and took the organization's mental fund development plan with her. In the chaos that followed, we vowed to invest the small amount of time it takes to create a *written* fund development plan.

Write a Diversified Fundraising Plan for Your Group

Every organization's plan will be different, but the process can be fairly simple if you figure out the answers to some basic questions and then select a few smart strategies that match your available resources.

- How much money do we need to raise?
- How much money do we have available to invest in fundraising?
- How much time do we have to spend on raising money?
- Who has some time to do it?
- What skills or experience do we have?
- What fundraising activities have we done in the past?
- What did each activity cost, both in cash and labor?
- How much money did each fundraising activity bring in?
- What was the net profit for each activity?

Unless you are one of those rare environmental groups that has a hefty fundraising budget and a gaggle of development staff, you'll have to be really strategic about which fundraising tactics you choose. Think about that last special event … which exhausted a lot of people, brought in less money than projected, and frankly, didn't feel all that special. Clearly, some fundraising strategies will have a much better return on your investment of time and money than others.

To help widen your horizons, here is a short description of the most common fundraising activities, generally ranked from best bets at the top to longer shots at the bottom. For more info, I've listed some books and links at the end of this chapter.

Face-to-Face

The single most effective way to raise money is to ask someone you know, face-to-face, for a specific amount of money to support the work of your organization. Expected batting average: half will say no, half will say yes, half of your yeses will give less than you hoped for. It's a numbers game: ask enough people and you *will* get the money you need.

Telephone

Call someone you know who shares your values, and ask for a donation. Great for membership renewals, recruiting volunteers, upgrading folks to join your monthly givers club, and increasing the response rate by up to 50 percent following a letter appeal.

Write a Personal Letter

Write a personal letter to someone you know, asking for a donation. Less effective: Address it "Dear Friend" and send bulk direct mail to every name on your outdated mailing list. More effective: Tailor different letters to different segments of your up-to-date mailing list, followed by email reminders. Definitely send a holiday letter right after Thanksgiving, and then two other times during the year. Lose the jargon, have a great, one-sentence opening hook, and tell a story describing the problem (from the donor's perspective), what your organization is doing to solve their problem, and offer them an opportunity to help. Be sure to include a P.S. at the end of the letter—one or two lines max that refer back to the beginning problem or create a sense of urgency.

Charge a Fee for Your Services

What are you good at? What do people want or need? Tap your talented staff, board, or volunteers to offer naturalist-guided hikes, unique classes, removal of blackberry thickets, eco-tours, expert testimony, research, photography, summer camp or afterschool educational programs, on-site planning for residential rainwater catchment, restoration contracts with government agencies, Geographic Information System services, water quality analysis, special event or newsletter production, and so on, and charge for it.

Submit a Grant Proposal

Remember, 81 percent of all donations come from individuals, not foundations or corporations, so that's where you'll want to focus your efforts. That said, grant proposal writing should probably be part of your diversified funding strategy.

Fee-For-Service Ideas
(List yours)

1

2

3

4

5

6

7

8

9

10 ...

Even with a terrific program and a crackerjack proposal writer, the competition is stiff and multiyear grants are rare. To increase your chances of success, do a funding search twice a year and apply only if you fit the criteria, especially their geographic focus. Look for free access to The Foundation Directory Online at your local college, public library, nonprofit resource center, or for a fee at https://fconline.foundationcenter.org. You can find information about available federal grants online at www.grants.gov, but your chances of being hit by a meteor are greater. Search the newsletters and websites of organizations doing work similar to yours for lists of their grantors and then research them to see if you might qualify.

If you find a good foundation prospect, scrupulously review their website, application guidelines, type and amount of grants awarded, whether they accept unsolicited proposals, and lists of award amounts to their recent grantees. Then, follow the application instructions perfectly. Tailor each proposal to the goals of the funder and do not shotgun the same proposal to multiple funders.

If you're new to proposal writing or a relatively new organization, establish your credibility by collaborating with an ally that has a track record with the foundation you're courting. Even though it takes more of your time, funders love collaborative proposals.

Host a Fundraising Special Event

The pros are: Everybody knows how to throw a party. And it's fun. The cons are: It's a huge time suck. There is a big "opportunity cost"; time spent on this is time that's not available to execute some other, more productive fundraising activity. And it's one of the most inefficient ways to raise money—overhead is often 50 percent or more.

Events are great for raising awareness, inspiring people to action, getting press coverage, and building camaraderie. These can all be valid campaign tactics but should not necessarily be classified as fundraising. Be clear if you're doing an event as a "friend" raiser with no net income expectations, and build that into your campaign program budget. Just don't call it a fundraising activity.

If you *are* going to do a special event, be sure to maximize your investment. Have your sponsorships cover all your expenses. Use raffles and live and silent auctions to offer additional opportunities to donors beyond the ticket price. Train your staff and board members how to use this as a chance to cultivate relationships with current and potential major donors. Set up multiple information booths or tables with campaign success PowerPoint presentations or video displays. Enlist roaming ambassadors (endangered species costumes optional) to engage attendees and encourage membership sign ups, renewals, and upgrades; update email lists; and to recruit volunteers for specific upcoming tasks.

Make It Easy to Give Online

Online giving is covered in Beth Kanter's chapter, "Networking."

Remind Your Membership of Legacy Giving

Planned giving is when people leave you a bequest in their will, make you a beneficiary of their insurance policy, or save a bunch on their taxes by donating to you shares of their appreciated stock. There are a lot of other complicated vehicles like unitrusts and charitable remainder trusts, but since 90 percent of planned gifts are simple will bequests, just gently but consistently remind your supporters in your newsletter and on your website that they can leave an important

legacy for future generations by naming you in their will. Invest a little time in this, and the payoff could be huge.

Have Your Members Give at the Office

Both United Way and EarthShare make it easy to deduct an automatic donation from each of a donor's paychecks. Find out about the timing of your local campaign and then alert your supporters about the donor designation option for United Way. (You don't have to be a United Way member or grantee to receive gifts this way.) Get registered with the Combined Federal Campaign for federal workers at http://www.opm.gov/combined-federal-campaign/ and find the website for your state workers, too.

Other Options

There are many other easy and often-neglected ways for environmental groups to raise money, including in-kind donations of goods or services, designated gifts from community foundations, scrip and merchant loyalty card programs, employer matching gift programs, memorial or tribute programs, and more.

Remember, Fundraising in a Grassroots Organization Is a Team Sport

A community organizer may meet a prospective donor at a meeting, your bookkeeper may be in a training session and hear about a grant opportunity, a board member can invite a colleague to go on a hike with the executive director, a volunteer can ask a friend who runs a small business to be special event sponsor, and so on.

Fundraising Isn't Rocket Science—Almost Anyone Can Learn This Stuff

The most important qualification is that the person is passionate about your mission. There are so many different roles; everyone can find a comfortable task, as well as a new challenge if they're up for it. Everybody deserves some training and support. You don't have to be a bubbly extrovert. In fact, the best fundraisers often turn out to be thoughtful introverts who are great listeners ... because what is the favorite topic of any prospective donors? Themselves.

Give people a chance to tell their story, show how what your organization is doing helps *them* reach their life or philanthropic goals, and you've just served them the secret sauce.

Resources

Armstrong, James. *Planning Special Events*. San Francisco: Jossey-Bass, 2001.

Foundation Center Proposal Writing Short Course. http://foundationcenter.org/getstarted/tutorials/shortcourse/.

Fredericks, Laura. *The Ask: How to Ask for Support for Your Nonprofit Cause, Creative Project, or Business Venture*. San Francisco: Jossey-Bass, 2010.

Hodiak, Diane L., and Michael J. Henley. *Fundraising and Marketing in the One-Person Shop: Achieving Success With Limited Resources*. 2d ed. Berlin, Mass.: Development Resource Center, 1997.

Klein, Kim. Fundraising for Social Change and Fifty-Three Ways for Board Members to Raise $1000. http://f4dc.org/wp-content/uploads/2013/03/53-ways-to-raise-one-thousand-dollars.pdf.

Planned Giving. http://www.plannedgiving.com/index.php/resources-free-downloads.

Robinson, Andy, and Kim Klein. *Selling Social Change (Without Selling Out): Earned Income Strategies for Nonprofits*. San Francisco: Jossey-Bass, 2002.

Robinson, Ellis M. *The Nonprofit Membership Toolkit*. San Francisco: Jossey-Bass, 2003.

Warwick, Mal. *How To Write Successful Fundraising Appeals*. San Francisco: Jossey-Bass, 2003.

A stand of black spruce silhouetted by the sun. Quebec. *Valerie Courtois/International Boreal Conservation Campaign*

What the Tools Conference Taught Me

When asked how we planned to get in shape for a 2,000-mile Appalachian Trail hike after graduating college, my buddy and trail mate Andrew Goldberg would reply, "We figure the first two hundred ought to do it."

Hiking the AT was the first time in my life that I felt like I was exactly where I should be, with no second-guessing. But it seemed that everywhere I went, the forests were being cut down around me. I had found something I loved, and someone was wrecking it. So, I did what I always do. I jumped in.

It began with starting a grassroots forest protection group with a few other people. We had many successes, but it was rough going. At night I worked as a chef to make money, and during the day I wrote legal briefs and newsletters, battling the Forest Service, timber companies, and local officials. I lay in bed awake at the end of long days, feeling alone, overwhelmed, and not knowing where to go for guidance.

As if in answer, I got a call one day from some folks at Patagonia, inviting me to their first "Tools for Grassroots" conference, and I happily accepted. Here were the instructions, right on time. I learned about strategic planning, fundraising, marketing, and building campaigns based on local pride. Most importantly, I learned that I didn't have to figure it all out by myself.

I have since gone on to play integral roles in protecting the remaining 60 million acres of intact roadless areas on the US National Forest System, and protecting an area in Quebec more than twice the size of all the US National Parks combined.

I'm coming up on fifty years old now. I was half that when I attended the first conference, and I can truly say it has made all the difference. I learned to become a part of the community in which I lived, representing their concerns for a better planet.

– Mat Jacobson

85

Adult chinook salmon and juvenile steelhead trout in a tributary of the Smith River. The Smith River is a highly protected watershed, with Federal Wild and Scenic status, yet is still threatened by open-pit nickel mining. Local groups, including the Smith River Alliance, are working to highlight the importance of the Smith River as a "salmon stronghold" in order to halt the proposed mining activities. The Oregon/California border. *Thomas Dunklin*

California Salmon and Steelhead

Karen Gardner

Salmonids (salmon and steelhead trout) are pretty incredible fish. They're born in freshwater rivers and streams, swim out to the ocean, then turn around and swim back, against the current, to reproduce.

Of the 2,000–5,000 eggs in a salmon's nest, all but a few are destined to die before adulthood. This may sound depressing, but it actually means that these fish are an incredibly important food source for many other species. Oceanic nutrients, brought by salmon, have been traced in hundreds of California organisms, from redwood trees, to bald eagles, to black bears.

For thousands of years, people of all backgrounds have also depended on salmon. From Native Americans to European settlers, to commercial fishermen, the salmon economy has supported entire cultures and communities.

Unfortunately, humans have done many things to reduce salmonid populations to historic lows: dams, diversions, pollution, development, habitat destruction, and overfishing. But a whole field of people is working to restore our rivers and protect these amazing fish.

In 1986 at a restoration forum in Fort Bragg, California, a number of salmon lovers decided they needed a new way to share information, collaborate, and educate others. And from that forum, the Salmonid Restoration Federation (SRF) was born.

Today, SRF works with restoration professionals, landowners, government agencies, and the general public to support restoration efforts across California. Through an annual conference and a number of workshops, we educate people about restoration. We also advocate for restoration and restoration funding at the local, regional, and state levels.

In order to do this work, of course, we need to raise money. And with a staff of three, it falls on our board members to do a lot in the way of fundraising.

Sometimes, when I think of a "fundraising board," I imagine people older and wealthier than I am, who solicit large gifts from their friends, who I also imagine to be old and wealthy. This isn't exactly what we do at SRF.

You're more likely to find many of our board members at the bar, talking about the reintroduction of beavers or the latest water bond with other salmon lovers. We are part of an active and enthusiastic community of people who work tirelessly to restore wild salmon, and developing relationships with people who are connected to our mission builds a sense of shared purpose. This has proven, inadvertently, to be a successful fundraising tactic for us because it has helped us connect with individuals and decision makers who are passionate about our cause.

It also doesn't hurt that specific expectations about giving and fundraising are part of our board member job descriptions—like soliciting items for our annual silent auction and staffing tables at outreach events. And we are proud to consistently achieve our goal of 100 percent board giving.

As far as our development plan, we mostly pursue three main income sources: workshop and conference fees, individual donations, and grants from community foundations and state agencies.

We're lucky that a lot of our mission-related work lends itself to charging a fee for service. By charging attendance fees, our annual Salmonid Restoration Conference is both an educational program and a fundraising event. We hold this conference in a different California region each year, covering the biology, ecology, and policy issues facing salmonids. It all happens through a combination of presentations, tours, workshops, and surprisingly fun networking events.

As a membership-based organization, we receive a lot of individual contributions—mostly in smaller amounts. When we look closely at who donates to SRF, we see that our best supporters tend to be middle-class people who work for restoration groups, live in Northern California, and are passionate about salmonid and watershed ecology. These are the people we try to reach through our direct mail, events, and other donor outreach efforts.

We also get some grant funding, receiving more than 90 percent of the grants we apply for. One year we wrote a particularly ambitious state grant to address historical watershed degradation: a 500-square-mile area on the Eel River in Northern California. We didn't get the grant, but one day at a community event organized by local fishermen, we asked the agency representative why we were turned down. This initiated a dialog about how to strategize and prioritize restoration efforts in the area. Working with other stakeholders, we began to design a program based on where we believed changes in human behavior would most impact water conservation and salmon recovery. We now have 100 percent support for this program from the entities that rejected our initial grant request.

There is a lot of great advice in this book and elsewhere about the importance of one-on-one relationships with individual donors. We believe that this advice applies to other funders too, including government funders. At SRF, we steward our government contacts like many groups steward major donors. We develop relationships, trying to get a spot at the table before there is anything on the table. We keep in touch with them, tell them success stories, ask their advice. And yes, sometimes we go out for a beer with them.

A wild male coho salmon swims among a school of both wild and hatchery steelhead trout. Coho salmon are a state and federally listed species, but are threatened by vague sport-fishing regulations that allow for the take of hatchery steelhead. Those regulations allow for the incidental catch of listed species as "by-catch." Groups, including the Mad River Alliance, are petitioning the California Fish and Game Commission to make sport-fishing regulations that are both meaningful and enforceable. Mad River, California. *Thomas Dunklin*

Wade Davis grew up Canadian and worked as a park ranger and logger before discovering botany and anthropology at Harvard, which led him to the Amazon and the Andes. After six years as a plant explorer he went to Haiti to study zombies, an assignment that led to his first book, The Serpent and the Rainbow. *He became a writer—*One River, The Wayfinders, Into the Silence, *among other works—a photographer, and a filmmaker, serving for fourteen years as an Explorer-in-Residence at the National Geographic Society. He is currently professor of anthropology and the BC leadership chair in Cultures and Ecosystems at Risk at the University of British Columbia.*

Wade Davis

2015 KEYNOTE SPEAKER

Saving the Sacred Headwaters

I would like to reflect on the significance of language, and the power and potential of names to redefine landscapes, shift history, and galvanize social and environmental movements.

Consider the settlement of the American West. Beyond the 100th meridian, a line of longitude that bisects the Dakotas and Nebraska, running through Kansas and Texas, there is no place in a thousand miles, from the Mexican frontier to the Canadian border, that receives more than twenty inches of rain a year. The entire region, an area the size of Western Europe, was once known as the Great American Desert. But deserts are places of scarcity, minimalist landscapes that, however beautiful, are perceived as being innately hostile, austere, and infertile. Austerity is a notion foreign to the American ethos.

Thus as the frontier moved west, the nomenclature of place shifted and the desert was transformed in language if not in fact, becoming the Great Basin, the Colorado and Columbia Plateaus, the Snake River Plain, the Blue Mountains, and the Bitterroot Range. But the stark reality remained. The Great Salt Lake, the Black Rock and the Painted, the Great Sandy and Death Valley, the Mojave, and the Sonora are all deserts, as dry as many parts of the Sahara. The great cities and scattered towns, the ranches and grim farmsteads, the roadside strip malls, motels, and filling stations, the broken-down drive-ins and every blue highway pawnshop and plywood souvenir trading post between Taos and Yuma could not exist without the massive manipulation of water.

Nomenclature in a sense became destiny, and those who controlled the choice of language determined perception, with profound consequences for the great rivers of the American West: the Colorado, Columbia, and Río Grande.

Language can also lead to the protection of wild lands, if only by providing an organizing principle, a beacon of hope around which environmental advocates and ordinary citizens can rally in defense of nature. Growing up in British Columbia, I flew over the midcoast on any number of occasions and always marveled at the continuous expanse of islands covered by rich, temperate rainforests, with few signs of the industrial logging that had devastated Vancouver Island and much of the Alaskan panhandle farther to the north. What I did not see, however, was the Great Bear Rainforest.

But twenty years later a young biologist, Ian McAllister, did see it, envisioning in his mind a place no one else had imagined. He made it real by drawing lines on a map, inventing the name, and defying anyone to challenge the designation. Who, after all, could deny that the largest single expanse of temperate rainforest in the world, home to the Kermode bear, among the most singular of creatures, had not been appropriately delineated and named? McAllister later invoked native lore to transform the Kermode into the Spirit Bear, further sparking the imagination of the public. What ultimately came of his dream was the protection of the largest tract of continuous temperate rainforest on Earth.

In the late 1970s I worked as a park ranger and logger on the Queen Charlotte Islands, the traditional homeland of the Haida. At the time multinational timber companies dominated the economy and determined the mood of the people, everywhere save perhaps in the recesses of memory and traditions maintained by some of the Haida. Among them was a good friend, Gary Edenshaw. One night he and Thom Henley, another friend, pulled out a map of the islands and with a pencil etched a line across the belt of the archipelago and vowed to stop industrial logging south of that mark. Forty years later what they drew is the actual boundary of Gwaii Haanas, a national park co-managed with the Haida Nation. Edenshaw changed his name to Guujaaw just about the time Canadians began referring to the islands as Haida Gwaii. Who the hell, as Guujaaw said, was Queen Charlotte anyway?

In 1976 Guujaaw worked with legendary Haida artist Bill Reid to carve the first totem pole erected in Skidegate in Haida Gwaii since the British colonial authorities banned the potlatch in 1884. Today the potlatch is back, and the multinationals are gone. Haida communities have forests of new poles, and the shores are once again crowded with seafaring canoes carved from cedar. A spirit of renewal and cultural revitalization permeates the islands in a manner that was unimaginable a short generation go.

For more than a decade the focus of my concern has been Klabona, a valley today known to the Tahltan and all the First Nations of British Columbia as the Sacred Headwaters, the point of origins of the three great salmon rivers, the Stikine, the Skeena, and the Nass. A modest fishing lodge I've owned on Ealue Lake since 1987 is the closest private holding to this astonishing valley, a place where in a long day, perhaps two, you can walk through open meadows, following the tracks of grizzly, caribou, and wolf, and drink from the very sources of the rivers that inspired so many of the great cultures that cradled the civilization of the Pacific Northwest: the Gitxsan and Wet'suwet'en, the Carrier and Sekani, the Tsimshian, Nisga'a, Haisla, Tlingit, Tahltan, and indeed the Haida.

For generations the Tahltan have acknowledged Klabona as the best hunting grounds in a region often referred to as the Serengeti of Canada. It is their commissary, kitchen, schoolyard, church, cemetery, and country club all rolled into one. For a nomadic hunting people, no place was more sacred than another; every stream and draw, mountain and glen, and all the creatures of the wild were considered sacrosanct. Ask an elder to describe his or her favorite spot, and invariably they will recall the land where they shot the most moose or caribou. Blood on ice or grass is not a sign of death but an affirmation of life itself.

In 2004, Shell Canada secured an eight-year lease to extract methane gas from shallow coal deposits spread across a tenure of close to a million acres covering the very heart of Klabona. Had this project gone ahead, it would have implied a network of several thousand wells, linked by some 2,200 miles of roads and pipelines, laid upon the entire landscape of the Sacred Headwaters.

It had to be stopped.

Jim Bourquin, a non-native activist married to the daughter of Loveman Nole, a highly respected Tahltan elder, used the word *sacred* whenever he spoke of Klabona. It was the only term that made sense to him, given what he had learned over three decades from his father-in-law, who had hunted and trapped in Klabona all of his life. In an article about the Stikine written for the *National Geographic Magazine* in 2003, I had meanwhile drawn attention to the remarkable proximity of the headwaters of Stikine, Skeena, and the Nass, all born in a rugged knot of mountains soaring over the meadows of Klabona.

Somehow this all came together one night at our lodge by the campfire as Guujaaw, visiting from Haida Gwaii, and Oscar Dennis, my closest Tahltan friend, were arguing about the origins of Raven. To the Haida, Raven emerged from a clamshell at the dawn of time to steal the light of the sun. For the Tahltan, Raven came out of a rock face that soars over the confluence of the Tahltan River and the Stikine. As Dennis pointed out to Guujaaw, the outline of his wings remained clearly visible to this day. Only a fool or a Haida, he added, could believe that such a mythological being would deem to be born out of a seashell.

As the discussion grew somewhat heated, I interjected a comment about Shell's plans for the headwaters, and before you knew it both my friends were referring to the valley in question not as Klabona but as the Sacred Headwaters. The term just slipped into consciousness and took form. It might well have died by the fire that night. But somehow it reached back to the community of Iskut and was embraced by the women. Banners went up, as did a blockade across the one dirt track into the interior where Shell had its tenure.

For weeks and months, in all kinds of weather, men and women, even elders in wheelchairs, stood up to the company and would not let its people and equipment pass. They did so at tremendous sacrifice, both personal and financial. Some lost jobs. Elders who had never broken the law were arrested and taken away to jail. The word *sacrifice* in English is derived from the Latin meaning "to make sacred." It was the courage and fortitude of the men and women on the blockade that ultimately gave meaning, power, and authenticity to a phrase that might have been dismissed as a contrived invention.

In July 2006, the people of Iskut issued an invitation to all First Nations through whose lands flowed the Stikine, Skeena, and Nass to join them at the Sacred Headwaters to celebrate the rivers of origins and the political stand of the Tahltan people. On August 4, 2006, chiefs and representatives of nine First Nations, along with hundreds of supporters, both native and non-native, gathered in a great circle in the very meadows where in a sense the entire movement had begun.

One by one, through a timeless day, the elders of each nation walked forward to place water from their own rivers into a cedar bent box that had been crafted for the occasion. Rita Louie, the diminutive wife of the chief of Iskut, spoke late in the day. She and three sisters of the chief had been arrested on the blockade, an act of civil disobedience that had transformed her life. The sun glowed on her face and her eyes caressed all the distant horizons.

"My name is Rita Louie," she began. "The beauty of this land, we live off. We get our food, our fish, our medicines, our berries. If they take that away, what are we going to have? We'll be standing with nothing. What's going to happen to us? You see that, all those mountains? Our minds are in every mountain. Our memories are in every valley. Our children are in every river and stream that flows here. That's where we belong."

Lillian Moyer, having been the first to be arrested at the blockade, was one of the last to speak at the gathering. Dressed in army fatigue pants, her shoulders covered by an elegant button blanket, she reached out her arms as if in prayer. Sunlight sparkled on her silver bracelets.

"The elders are keepers of the land," she said. "When we stand with them, we stand with the ancestors. I did not get arrested for the fun of it. I did it to protect the land. We have the power to stop whatever we want to stop."

She then turned to address the entire gathering. "We need your help to protect this land. It is not just for the native people. It is for all people. Not just for us. And that is the way it should be. It is all connected. We are all connected."

Within the next months, even as the resistance grew, the media increasingly picked up the story of this quixotic fight, the ultimate David versus Goliath scenario: a small group of native and non-native men and women, not a single professional environmentalist among them, brought together by their love of the country, standing up to the largest corporation in the world.

In the end, the Tahltan prevailed and in December of 2012, Shell to its immense credit announced that it was permanently abandoning its tenure in the Sacred Headwaters. To be sure, there remain other threats to Klabona, all part of a tsunami of industrial development sweeping over the Canadian north. But as long as government and industry have no choice but to refer to the valley as the Sacred Headwaters, how can we possibly lose?

PG.90 The upper Little Klappan River meanders through a meadow in the Skeena Mountains, British Columbia. *Carr Clifton* ABOVE Kermode bears head to their local rivers in the fall to feast on spawning salmon. There are only a few hundred of these rare white "spirit bears" in the world. Great Bear Rainforest, British Columbia. *Ian McAllister*

95

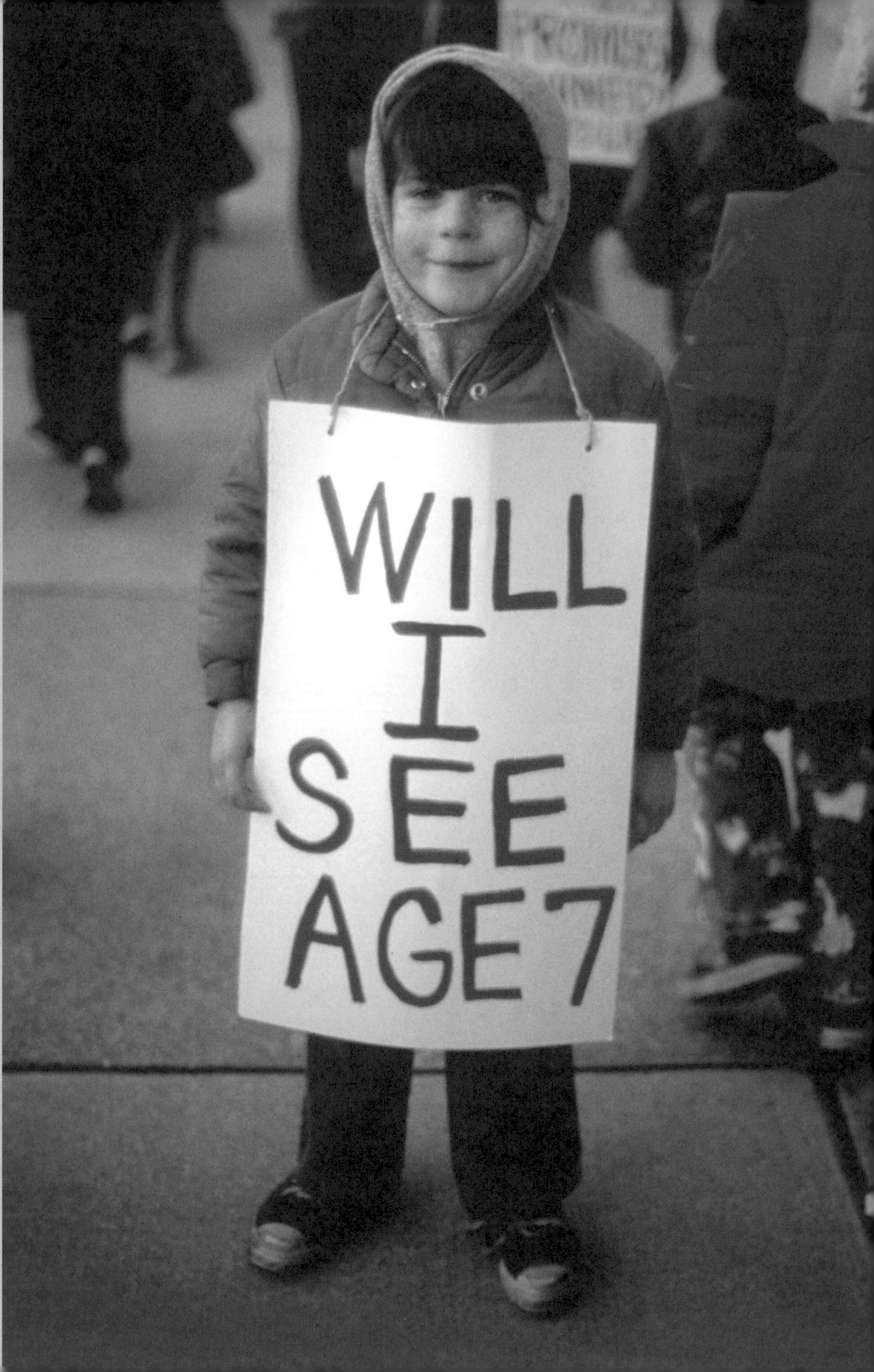
WILL
I
SEE
AGE 7

CHAPTER 06

Communications

Kristen Grimm

I was in Mexico for work: local activists and I wanted to persuade Mexican officials to establish a marine protected area in the Gulf of California. This wasn't going to be easy. Someone suggested we take the officials out by boat to see the area.

"What will they see?" I asked.

"Lots and lots of water," someone offered. I looked skeptical.

Someone else added, "There are vaquita." Once I learned that those are porpoises, I was very excited. (I believe if you can connect your issue to a dolphin or whale, success is all but inevitable.)

"They are very shy," someone else cautioned, "they rarely show themselves." We pondered our dilemma.

"We can get an animal trainer to train them to approach the boat," said the most optimistic among us. Right then I knew we were way off-track.

We had made a classic mistake. We weren't focused on what we wanted to achieve. Instead, we were down the rabbit hole of misguided tactics, mired in process. We were about to hire an animal trainer, for Pete's sake. We needed to pull back, focus on our goal, and get more strategic.

Ambitions become bold social change with good, effective communication. But good, effective communication is difficult. We've all suffered through overly long PowerPoint presentations full of bullets and type that's too small to read. Numbing statistics in "parts per million" bore rather than excite the way the term "dangerous levels" does. Jargon and sterile words and phrases lull us into complacency, while evocative words stimulate and enliven issues—and us. To engage people in your causes, to create the world you want to live in, to move from ambition to change, you need to motivate, persuade, and activate people with the power of communication.

I've been doing this a long time. Twenty-three years, to be exact. I've run some amazing communication campaigns. And I have done some things that make me cringe when I think of them now. Along the way, I have learned six important lessons that help produce more communication successes than regrets.

Lesson 1: Practice Purposeful Communication

Be crystal clear about your purpose, what you want to change. Remove a dam. Get bikers, hikers, and runners to share a trail. Vote with a favorite outdoor place in mind.

In Pittsburgh, folks want cleaner air. As school buses wait for students to get out of the last class of the day, they idle and pollute. The clean air folks want to ban idling. This is their purpose. Their purpose is not to get people to visit a website, tweet that buses shouldn't idle, or pass out bumper stickers that say honk if you want to stop idling buses. Those are all tactics. Tactics help achieve a purpose—they are tools. But communication efforts should focus on the actual purpose of an effort.

Back in Mexico, our purpose wasn't to get public officials out on a boat. It was to convince them to establish a marine protected area. If the tactic of a boat ride helps achieve our purpose, great. If it fails to get them excited about the marine protected area, it is a distraction and a poor use of time and resources.

A purpose is concrete change. Don't say your purpose is to "raise awareness." Many issues have high awareness with nothing to show for it. People are "aware" they shouldn't text while driving; they know it is dangerous. But cars still swerve all over the road because drivers are focused on emoticons rather than driving. They haven't changed their behavior despite being aware of the dangers. The people who want to ban texting haven't persuaded elected leaders and the public to solve the problem. They haven't rallied their friends and families to the cause. You want more than awareness, you want action. The communication you employ should help you get that.

Lesson 2: Know Who You Need to Engage

Ask people around you to tell you about themselves. They'll say they are parents, teachers, omnivores, or the world's greatest gamer. Nobody says they are the general public, so targeting this group isn't effective. Determine who has a vested interest in your cause, who is most likely to get involved to make change. Lavish attention on those groups so that they identify with your cause and engage with you and your efforts.

If you want people to favor utilities that offer renewable energy options, you can focus on anyone who gets a power bill—a large group. But keep in mind, different segments of this group have different motivations for favoring renewables. Some want to save money. Let's call them "thrifty energy peeps." Some love Mother Earth. Let's call them "greenies." Some don't want their partner to nag them. Let's call them "passive aggressive" (but not to their face). Each segment requires tailored incentives to get them to choose renewables. When you know exactly what makes your target audience tick, it is easier to motivate them to make a change.

Don't list institutions as your audiences. If your goal is to persuade the White House or JPMorgan Chase to do something, good luck. Have you been to the White House or the New York headquarters of JPMorgan Chase? These are large, imposing buildings, nearly as imposing as the institutions enshrined in them. Buildings are not persuadable; people inside buildings are. So don't just list institutions when deciding who to engage; list the people inside.

When Georgia Organics wanted to get more schools to offer local, organic foods in school cafeterias, it could have listed "schools" as the target audience. But what do schools care about? Who do they listen to? Schools are just large institutional buildings. Instead, Georgia Organics focused on the nutrition directors at each school—real people with backgrounds and interests. They could look online to find out the name of Jackson County's nutrition director. What college did she go to? Does she have kids? How long has she been in the position? This information is invaluable when you are trying to engage with people.

Identify real people as your target audiences. Then you can dig into what they care about and who they listen to—all the rich detail that is necessary to provoke change.

Lesson 3: Plan for Successful Engagement

You've identified what you want to change, a.k.a. your purpose. You've identified your audience. Now you need to inspire action. You may think,

This is the easy part: an email blast marked 'urgent' and voilà. Stop and think about that for a second. Consider all the emails you get from people and organizations you don't know very well with "urgent" in the subject line. When was the last time you even opened one of them, let alone did what it asked you to do? Too often, groups approach communication with their target audiences as a transaction rather than an engagement.

Sometimes, engagement is simple to think about. You put organizers on the street to ask passers-by for money to help support climate change legislation or protect gay rights or fight for human rights. The passers-by go through a quick mental checklist: *Do I have time to stop? Do I care about the issue? Is the group making the request credible?*

For other efforts, your audience may have a much more complicated decision to make. They may not agree with the facts you present because someone else they listen to and respect has a different opinion or a different set of facts. Or maybe the facts you emphasize don't track with their top concerns. For example, you want to remove a dam to restore valuable biodiversity and foster natural development of the watershed. But they are worried about the impact dam removal will have on area jobs. If you want to engage with these folks, you'll need to address economic impacts.

Remember, your audiences are real people who have real concerns that affect their everyday lives and their families. You can reach them and get them involved in your cause when you take the following steps:

Make It Personal

Explain how your cause personally affects them. For example, make a direct personal connection by showing how pollution compromises their drinking water. Create a personal experience. The Surfrider Foundation does this on International Surfing Day. They ask people to not only protect the ocean but also enjoy the ocean and then share their experiences through posts on Instagram with #myspecialplace. Offer audiences a personal reward. Those bumper stickers that say "My kid's an honor student at Rock Lake Middle School" are rewards. Proud parents get to

brag. Some rewards might be more tangible, but pride and self-esteem are two good incentives that can attract people to your cause.

Trigger Emotions That Empower

Too often, we try to motivate with guilt, fear, and shame. There are a few problems with this approach. First, most people don't need more guilt in their lives. Also, fear and shame are disempowering emotions that make people less likely to act. Use emotions that empower like hope, pride, admiration, envy, and anger. These will engender action. Americans saw admiration work when we met the "Dreamers." These are high school students who are undocumented in the United States. They are top students but they cannot go to college because of their immigration status. They protested. They pushed to get the Dream Act in place to offer them a path to citizenship and to college and into a productive place in American society. They took enormous risks coming out since they could be deported. We admired their courage and their conviction, which generated immense support for their cause from broad swaths of society. Those lists of the best places to live, or the healthiest communities, or the most socially responsible companies? Those create envy. People want to be number one. The Robert Wood Johnson Foundation has leveraged this emotion with their County Health Rankings, which list the healthiest counties in the United States. Johnson County, Kansas, won the top slot in that state in 2014; now other counties will gun for the title next year.

Show How People They Know Are Already Involved in Your Cause

People like to belong. Their political views, religion, lifestyle, or any other personal badge defines them and who they are. If others from their groups already support your cause, that will create a link to draw them in. However, if they believe what you are asking them to do violates the codes and norms of their chosen groups, it will be very difficult for them to engage. Help them navigate a way to get involved without betraying their convictions. We've seen this work with gay marriage and evangelicals. Some people with strong religious leanings have found it difficult to reconcile what is in the Bible and their desire to support friends and family who wanted to marry the person they loved. As religious leaders shared their own journey of reconciliation and how they found peace with supporting gay marriage, it allowed others in their congregations to begin similar journeys.

Leverage Something They Already Care About

You care about collective bargaining, they don't. Maybe they don't even understand it. However, they do want the workplace to be fair for women. Find a starting point of intersecting interests. If you start with something they don't care about or don't agree with or don't understand, it will be hard to gain traction. The starting point shouldn't be an unacceptable compromise for either of you; it should instead offer common ground.

Use Questions to Get Them Thinking

When you start with a statement, your audiences instantly decide if they agree or not. Your cards are already on the table. If they disagree, it's game over. Say you start with "Dams are outdated and no longer needed in this region." If they believe dams are an important energy source for their region or supply water for development and household needs, they will write you off as out of touch with their reality and needs. You've lost the connection. Instead, a question such as "Now that we get our energy and water from other sources, should we take a look at the need for the dam?" gets them thinking. Reasonable people will likely agree that it is a good idea to at least consider whether or not the dam is necessary. There is no downside to that. Questions can put a cause in a different light—providing new perspective. People may not agree that the cap-and-trade program is a good idea. But ask them if it's OK for US companies to produce unlimited pollution. No one wants more pollution and certainly not unlimited pollution. Now you have them thinking that we might need to do more to curb carbon pollution. You've got a foot in the door.

Don't Rely on Data, Use Stories to Explain Your Issue

When you spout data, audiences may question its source or its accuracy. An array of numbers, facts, and figures may not compel. However, stories elicit an entirely different response. Experts say that good stories lower people's defenses—especially if they believe the story is true. Stories can provide context for data. Stories help people identify with a cause. Many people now know the story of Malala, a teenager from Pakistan who spoke out about the importance of girls' education and was shot for her views. There was no shortage of data about the barriers to education that girls face in parts of Pakistan. But it was Malala's story that brought those statistics to life, that helped people all over the world identify with those injustices. Now when political leaders and members of international organizations talk about the need to promote and safeguard education for girls, they say there are thousands of Malalas all over the world—and people understand exactly what that means.

Lesson 4: Choose Words That Create Pictures

Words matter. Words can educate and motivate, but they can also alienate and confuse. The most passionate advocate of a cause can end up sounding like an automaton when trying to communicate with others. It's easy to slip into jargon and acronyms when discussing how allowable sale quantity in a forest plan undermines the aquatic conservation strategy designed to protect benthic invertebrates and terrestrial species in buffer zones. Instead, talk about wild places where families camp and create lifetime memories, where a child can catch her first fish or a couple can spot the only bear they'll ever see. Use words that paint a picture.

When crafting language to connect with your audiences, remember the following tips:

Every Word You Choose Is Valuable Real Estate

Make sure each word packs a lot of meaning. "Unfair" lending doesn't mean the same as "predatory" lending, nor is it as compelling a descriptor.

Big, Vague Words Do Little to Capture Imaginations

Does your audience understand what you mean by *sustainable*, *resilient*, or any other great-sounding but vague word or phrase? If you aren't sure, add context to explain what you mean—or choose a better word that conveys more meaning.

Good Messaging Persuades and Motivates

If your language is factual and grounded in data, but doesn't actually inspire your audience to do something, you may miss the mark.

Words Aren't the Only Way to Communicate

The popularity of social media posts, videos, and Snapchat give you a variety of ways to use visuals to get across important points. National Geographic recently painted an express lane on a sidewalk in Washington, DC, for pedestrians whose eyes aren't glued to their cell phones. This visual message made a point and, observers said, motivated "texters" to walk in the slower lane designated for them.

Lesson 5: Pursue Activities That Give You the Highest Return on Your Investment

Now that you know the purpose of your communication, who you want to engage and how, and what words and visuals to use to get your points across, it's time to get active. You have many options. You can do it the old-fashioned way and go door to door. Or you can go big and cultivate millions of Twitter followers. You can use earned media to get your story out via the local paper and on the evening news or spread the word through social media. There are community meetings, conferences, visits with policy makers, and (my personal favorite) a well-planned "run-in" with an important leader at his or her favorite market. You can do point-of-purchase messaging in stores, put messages on reusable bags, or use paid advertising. You can stage street art, skywrite, or plan a flash mob.

As you consider all the opportunities to reach and engage with your audience, you have to decide which activities produce the highest return on investment. People who run campaign messages on the radio during drive time and then ask people to text a word to learn more aren't thinking things through (at least I hope they aren't!). However, groups that set up information tables at local playing fields and offer messages about the overuse of chemicals on the grass and related health problems in children are smart. Parents are hanging around and have time to listen—and they feel passionately about their kids' health. These groups are engaging people on an issue that is relevant and right in front of them.

Here are some ways to stay focused on high-value activities and avoid being distracted by shiny tactics that may have limited impact:

Timing Is Everything

People aren't open to engagement 24/7. When do your audiences already have your cause in their minds and are they open to having a conversation then? Are there times that create natural windows? People think about taxes on April 15, water quality for safe swimming in early June, and back to school in late August. Is there a natural time period to bring up your issue when it is easy to get people's attention? Believe me, Facebook knows exactly when people are online and will tell you. Use information like that to help guide the timing of your communication efforts.

Sometimes More Is Less

An example is having lots of fans on Facebook, but few donors to a good cause. You may be better off with activities that cultivate a few more new donors than constantly posting on Facebook to keep your fans up to date. Make sure you aren't only preaching to the choir, especially if those fans aren't helping your issue gain momentum.

Figure Out Which Tactics Will Go Furthest with Your Audience

Picture the people who represent your audience. Then think about what happens from the moment they wake up. They check email if they are busy working moms. They listen to the morning news on NPR if they are card-carrying liberals. They plug in their earphones and walk to work if they are smart growth-loving millennials. They

They peruse certain websites even while at work. They talk to friends and family. They go out to dinner or stop at the local market on the way home. When you see how they live, you'll see many ways to reach them and talk with them about your issue. Choose activities that offer you the best opportunity, and ones you are really good at. (Word to the wise: skywriting is always a mistake.)

Lesson 6: Make Sure Your Communication Is Working

Is all of your smart thinking leading to successful engagement? If not, don't talk louder; change how you are saying your message. To determine whether you are making headway with your audiences, you need to know what progress looks like. What's a good result? What do you want audiences to do once you've communicated with them?

Successful groups map a ladder of engagement that shows their audience's journey. It might start with a website visit, then a donation, then a public proclamation, then active engagement, then outreach to recruit others to the cause. If you know what you want your audiences to do—if you have tangible goals—you can track to see if your communications plan is helping you make headway. If you don't measure, you will likely rationalize that there is value in your communications because you like it and have pride of ownership. You need objectivity. This is where the rubber meets the road. You need to prove that your communications strategy buried a policy maker in requests from constituents to protect the habitat of the sage grouse so that it stayed off the endangered species list.

Be honest about the impact of your communications. If your efforts aren't paying off, review and revise your approach and your strategy. It may be that the activities you picked don't connect with your audiences. Maybe your messaging sounds more like a lecture and doesn't motivate your audience to engage. Don't stay on a failed path. It only wastes the power of communication. Be open to experimentation and honor the results. And once you know your plan is effective, stay the course.

I have worked with amazing people around the globe who are on a mission to make the world better. Some are focused on changing local ordinances so people can raise chickens in their neighborhood, and others are trying to stop human trafficking across the entire planet. No matter their ambitions, when these folks stop and think about how to align communication efforts to what they want to achieve, they get results. You will, too.

Resources

"Digital S.M.A.R.T.S. Guide." (A tool to help nonprofits strengthen their digital strategy, including chapters on Twitter ads, Snapchat, building better blogs, creating engaging visuals and using live-streaming to reach your audiences.) Spitfire Strategies. http://www.spitfirestrategies.com/tools/#tab5.

"Free Range Thinking." (Monthly newsletter that features communication advice, particularly focused on storytelling.) The Goodman Center. http://www.thegoodman center.com/resources/newsletters/.

Kitroeff, Natalie. "Why That Video Went Viral." May 19, 2014. *New York Times* (Science section, online edition). http://www.nytimes .com/2014/05/20/science/why-that-video-went -viral.html.

Mobilisation Lab. (Good repository of smart campaigning methods.) http://www.mobilisa tionlab.org.

"Smart Chart 3.0." (A communication planning tool that helps you set goals, identify priority audiences, craft compelling messages, and pursue high-value communication activities.) Spitfire Strategies. http://www.smart chart.org, http://www.spitfirestrategies.com.

"The Ripple Effect: How to Use the Media for Social Change." Ripple Strategies. http:// www.ripplestrategies.com/use-media-social -change-report/.

Zak, Paul. "Why Your Brain Loves Good Story-telling." *Harvard Business Review.* Oct. 28, 2104. http://blogs.hbr.org/2014/10/why-your -brain-loves-good-storytelling/?cm_ven=Spop -Email&cm_ite=DailyAlert-102914+(1)&cm_lm =mitch@twistimage.com.

Mountain biking in Fort Ord, California. *Bob Wick, Bureau of Land Management*

Fort Ord Recreational Trails

Citizens in Monterey County, California, wanted to protect the important plant and wildlife habitat and recreational opportunities at Fort Ord, an army base closed in 1994. They developed a strategy to convince President Obama to use his authority under the Antiquities Act to declare the area a national monument. The president had made it clear that he didn't want to create significant controversy when designating new national monuments. The campaign understood that, in order for a national monument strategy to succeed, they didn't need a large national campaign, but rather overwhelming local support. Fort Ord conservationists focused on garnering resolutions in support of the national monument from all of the local municipalities and the county government. They knew that the local municipalities and county could not directly get a national monument declared, but if the campaign compiled an exhaustive list of supporters and delivered it to their key targets (the chair of the White House Council on Environmental Quality and the Secretary of the Interior), they could win. Because of their strategic approach, the local campaign leaders, most of whom had never been involved in any prior campaign, were able to secure a private meeting with President Obama. They made their pitch and demonstrated the overwhelming local support. They returned to Washington, DC, a few months later to stand behind the president as he signed a proclamation designating the Fort Ord National Monument and protecting forty-four rare, threatened, or endangered species, eighty-six miles of recreational trails, and one of the few remaining large expanses of coastal grasslands and live oak woodlands in the world.

– Brian O'Donnell

Boats burn off surface oil, creating huge black columns of smoke, not far from the Deepwater Horizon spill site in the Gulf of Mexico. *Joel Sartore*

The Gulf of Mexico

Kristen Grimm

Long before the worst oil disaster in US history spilled more than 200 million gallons of oil into the Gulf of Mexico, local and national groups had been working to secure funding for environmental restoration across the Gulf and Mississippi River Delta—a region that had already suffered years of degradation from human use and natural disasters like Hurricane Katrina.

When the Deepwater Horizon oil spill erupted in 2010, the Gulf, its coasts, and its wildlife were devastated, and so were the businesses, fishermen, and communities that depend on a healthy Gulf. But conservation and workforce development groups nationally and in the region suspected the spill could also represent a unique opportunity to decisively change the outlook for Gulf restoration. The companies responsible for the spill would likely pay billions of dollars in fines under the Clean Water Act. The catch? Without a change in the law, that money—up to $21 billion—would go into the general fund at the US Treasury, not to the places hardest hit by the disaster.

To have the law changed, leading national groups—including the Environmental Defense Fund, National Audubon Society, National Wildlife Federation, The Nature Conservancy, Ocean Conservancy, and Oxfam America—needed to convince elected leaders to move a bill through Congress. They created a coalition called the Gulf Renewal Project (GRP) to get it done.

From the very beginning, the groups had a clear sense of who they ultimately needed to convince first—the senators from Louisiana, Texas, Florida, Mississippi, and Alabama. Notice they didn't just say, "the US Congress." The US Congress is a nameless, faceless institution. They needed to have a clear sense of exactly who they were trying to engage and they zeroed in on senators from the Gulf Coast states. Political views in the Gulf states run to the conservative side of the spectrum, so a conventional environmental message wasn't going to carry the day.

With that in mind, the coalition built its communication strategy around an understanding of what their policy-maker audiences cared about: restoring a strong economy and creating jobs in the wake of a recession. The GRP was also eager to move away from using old language that frames environmental protection and economic prosperity as mutually exclusive, or antagonistic to one another.

In short, the campaigners quickly decided that all of their activities would support a simple and consistent truth: "Environmental Restoration *is* Economic Recovery."

The first step in bringing this argument to life? The groups set out to show the Gulf senators that embracing the legislation would be popular at home. The coalition conducted a poll across the Gulf states to demonstrate that voters saw a strong connection between environmental restoration and a strong economy. The poll found that nearly three out of four voters in Gulf states said they'd be more likely to vote for federal legislators if they supported funding to restore the Gulf, and voters believed there was a strong connection between the well-being of the Gulf and their state economies. The groups got the results into the media by having local business leaders across the region share their conviction that restoration would benefit their businesses. The elected leaders heard loud and clear from oyster fishermen, hotel operators, and fishing charter captains about the specific ways a healthy Gulf would help their bottom lines.

From there, the groups built momentum by continuing to create new opportunities to push out the joint economic and conservation argument. In ads, letters, and online communications, the coalition highlighted how conservationists, business and industry leaders, sportsmen, and strong majorities of voters across the political spectrum supported efforts to use oil spill fines to repair environmental damage caused by the spill. They used their coalition to deliver a steady drumbeat so senators couldn't escape hearing the message.

Persuaded by the strong case, and emboldened by the clear evidence of political support in their states, a group of Gulf senators introduced the RESTORE Act (Resources and Ecosystems Sustainability, Tourist Opportunity, and Revived Economies of the Gulf States) in the summer of 2011, which proposed to dedicate 80 percent of the fines from the companies responsible for the spill to restoring areas affected by the disaster.

The coalition stayed the course, creating white papers demonstrating the economic benefits of environmental restoration—including studies on the benefits to the national supply chain. They also continued a steady stream of media work, sign-on letters, and other activities to push business and industry leaders to help carry the message.

In July 2012, after more than two years of work by advocates and legislators, Congress passed the RESTORE Act with strong bipartisan support. To date, it is the largest bill supporting conservation spending in US history.

Ultimately, the simple, strategic message, backed up by smart strategy delivered consistently through multiple channels and reinforced by a diverse and committed coalition, won the day.

A protest cemetery dedicated to all the things that were lost due to the Deepwater Horizon oil spill. Grand Isle, Louisiana. *Joel Sartore*

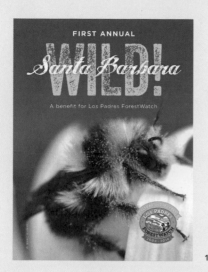

1

2

3

4

Creating Print Materials

Jim Little

Print pieces can say a lot about your group. At their best, they will inspire your audience, communicate your issue as an important one, and represent you as focused and effective. But when poorly executed, they can have the opposite effect.

I've seen some really nice pieces during my years reviewing print materials at the Tools Conference. Their objective was clear and their mission statement concise. The writing was economical and the tone, conversational. Their photos were inspired, and the design was clean, making effective use of typography, headlines, subheads, and captions to tell their stories.

However, these were the few.

But don't despair. While producing an effective print piece does take time, some expertise, and money—things a lot of small groups often lack—it is doable, even on a small budget. We hope these quick tips can help you get there.

Getting Started

Sit down with others in your group to examine your objectives and draft a creative brief that attempts to answer the following questions:

What's Your Mission Statement?

More than likely, you already have one. But is it concise—preferably one sentence—and descriptive? Does it give a good indication of who you are and what you do? It should, and you should use it to reinforce your organization's identity.

What Is the Goal for Your Piece?

Why do you want to produce this? What do you want people to know about you and your work, and what do you want them to do? Are you trying to educate, raise money, build membership, incite action, provide news?

What Is the Lifespan of This Tool?

How long do you see yourself using it before you produce another piece?

Who Is the Target Audience?

Are you speaking to your members, people who may know nothing about you, the media, possible donors, the scientific community, or someone else? The answer will help you tailor your message and tone.

How Will You Use This Piece?

Will you mail it, table with it, hand it out?

What Is Your Hierarchy of Messages?

Make a list of the things you want to say in order of their importance. You may have to sacrifice one for another you deem more important, so it's good to be clear about how they stack up.

Is This Your Only Piece?

Does this one have to do it all, or do you have others (or a website) you can also use to tell other parts of your story and achieve your objectives?

1 Benefit invitation. *Courtesy of Los Padres Forestwatch* 2 T-shirt. *Courtesy of the Native Fish Society* 3 T-shirt. *Courtesy of the designer, Geoffrey Holstad* 4 Newsletter, designed by Colleen Corcoran, cartography by Mehmet Berker, edited by Alissa Walker. *Courtesy of Los Angeles Walks*

What Is Your Budget?

Though always a limitation, even if it's scant, don't let it thwart you.

What Format Is Appropriate (and Affordable)?

Postcard, tri-fold, multipage booklet? Do you have access to good (and hopefully free) photos and artwork? What kind of paper are you going to use? How many copies do you need? It's good to try to determine these things in advance.

Now look around. Many printed pieces do a good job of presenting information; others do not. Find a few that you like. Look at their layouts and their writing and their use of headlines, subheads, and photos. What makes them effective? Where are they lacking? Imitation is the sincerest form of flattery. Flatter away.

Some Editing Principles

Below are a few "tricks of the trade" that can help you create strong content that connects with your readers.

Keep It Simple and Conversational

Communicate clearly. While you may live in a world of planners, scientists, and bureaucrats, try to stay away from the often mind-numbing lexicon and passive sentence constructions of enviro speak. Don't make your audience work too hard. Keep things moving. Say what you mean.

Present a Quick Read

Use photos, photo captions, headlines, and subheads to help tell your stories in short form. Not everyone is a reader; some people are skimmers. And some just like to look at the pictures.

Keep It Positive

Try to frame your issue and your work in a positive light. Speak of challenges and opportunities, not problems. Describe your successes—the

acres preserved, roads removed, volunteers trained, growing membership.

Keep It Active

We "preserve wilderness," not "engage in wilderness preservation." Likewise, we remove roads, build trails, monitor water quality. Use active language to keep readers interested and help maintain a positive, conversational tone.

Your Challenges

Keep these issues in mind to avoid potential stumbling blocks.

Don't Try to Tell It All

With the abundance of information you have about your issue, there's a temptation to try to present it all at once. Resist this! Consider your objective for your piece. Say only what you need to in order to achieve that objective. Provide enough detail, but don't try to tell a story that's too large and complicated for just one piece.

Don't Write by Committee

Assign one person to write and one to edit the piece, unless you have several good writers and want different voices. If you want to include a message from your executive director or a board member who's not much of a writer, write it for them. Before you begin, make sure everyone agrees on the goals and the message. This will save a lot of rewriting later on.

Use Your Connections and Creativity

Funds for design and printing services are often in short supply. Use your connections and creativity to enlist the support of photographers, graphic artists, writers, editors, and printers to get your piece produced more cheaply—or, better yet, for free. Ask for help. People want to help. Ask for free printing. Acknowledge those who help by mentioning them in your piece.

Good luck!

5 T-shirt. *Courtesy of the designer, Geoffrey Holstad* 6 Newsletter. *Courtesy of the Native Fish Society* 7 Logo. *Courtesy of the League to Save Lake Tahoe – Keep Tahoe Blue* 8 Neighborhood Planning Manual, designed by Colleen Corcoran and Tiffanie Tran. *Courtesy of the Los Angeles County Bicycle Coalition/T.R.U.S.T. South LA/the Los Angeles Department of Transportation.* 9 Poster, designed by Rosten Woo, Tiffanie Tran, and Colleen Corcoran, content developed and edited by Rosten Woo and the Los Angeles Black Worker Center. *Courtesy of the Los Angeles Black Worker Center*

5

6

7

9

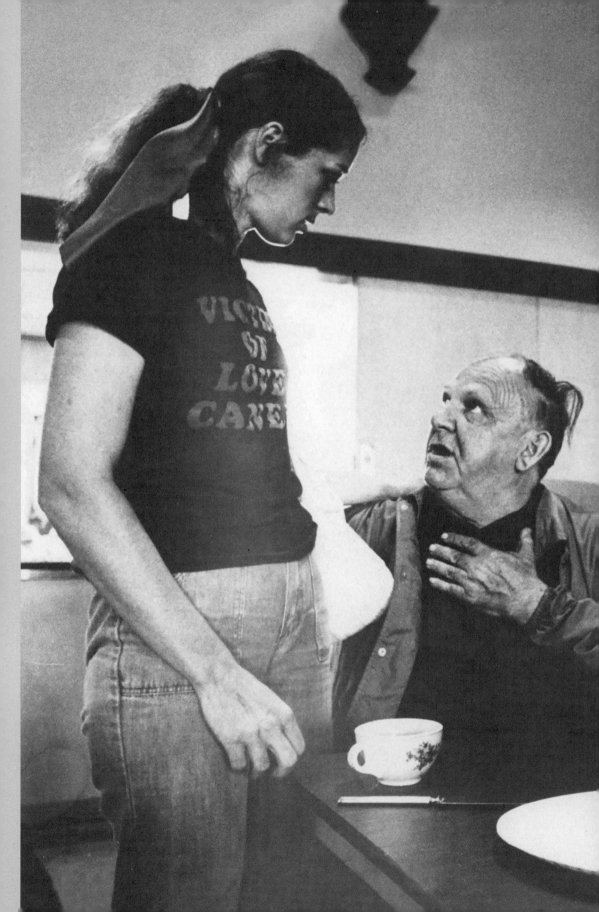

Between 1978 and the early 1980s, the efforts of Lois Gibbs as leader of the Love Canal community in New York led to the evacuation of residents who did not know that their neighborhood and elementary school had been built near a toxic industrial chemical waste dump. Under her leadership, the Love Canal crisis got the attention of President Jimmy Carter and other officials. They obtained evacuations for 833 Love Canal families affected by leaking toxic chemicals in their neighborhood. Afterward she founded the Center for Health, Environment & Justice to help other communities faced with environmental chemical threats.

Lois Gibbs

1997 KEYNOTE SPEAKER

When We Change the Climate, We Change the World

As the Center for Health, Environment & Justice begins its thirty-fourth year of creating change and empowering leaders, it makes sense to reflect on how lasting change happens. One valuable lesson is that long-term change, a cultural shift in society, begins at and grows from local communities to the national level. Peter Montague, who wrote about lasting change in *Rachael's News* years ago, provided a moment of clarity for me.

Peter talked about changing the "climate of opinion." He wrote that today, slavery is not only illegal; it is unthinkable. The "climate of opinion" would not allow a serious proposal to bring back slavery or allow a public debate over a proposal to prohibit women from voting. Once a "climate of opinion" victory has been achieved, it is difficult to reverse.

When I began my struggle at Love Canal in Niagara Falls, New York, I set out to protect my children from the leaking 20,000 tons of toxic wastes buried in the center of our neighborhood. I believed that government would protect me if there was a problem that required its intervention. I believed that science would be pure and never used politically against innocent families. Yes, I was as naïve as a newborn child. I did not set out to change anything beyond my family's situation.

But I did.

What I've learned over the past three-plus decades is that every struggle, every victory counts. Science and laws are tools in our efforts to win change. At Love Canal, it was shocking to hear that the state health department agreed that 56 percent of our children were born with birth defects. But it was more shocking to learn that the health authorities believed that this rate was due to a random clustering of people with genetic defects—not the 20,000 tons of chemicals leaking into our homes, air, and neighborhood. And the burden of proof, beyond a shadow of a doubt, was thrust upon our shoulders.

With this new understanding of how science was used against us in the political arena, our community worked to win over public opinion to obtain justice. Mothers with sick children were credible messengers as they pointed to the governor as being responsible for the cover-up. Moreover, state health authorities looked foolish with their "cluster of genetically damaged people" statement. Essentially, we changed public opinion about how our health department was behaving. It was not protecting public health at Love Canal; rather, it was protecting corporate profits and government resources from being used to resolve the problem and protect innocent people.

Although ours was a local struggle, the story went national and then international. Suddenly, women and men stood up worldwide to say that they, too, had been harmed by environmental chemicals. You couldn't open a newspaper anywhere that was not covering a story about "another Love Canal." People nationwide were educated and felt strongly that innocent individuals harmed by pollution should absolutely be helped. A movement was born of ordinary people, many of low wealth and of color, standing together to demand protection.

The climate of public opinion shifted dramatically. The Superfund law was passed in 1980 that provides federal funds to address other Love Canal–like situations in the future. The right-to-know law was passed in 1986 to give both workers and the community the right to information about chemicals used, stored, or disposed of in their community. A federal health agency was established under the Centers for Disease Control to assess environmental chemical risks. And equally important, not one new commercial hazardous waste landfill has been built since 1984. Although it is still legal to build such facilities, it's no longer acceptable to the American people.

Why is all of this important? Because people must understand that every victory, no matter how small, will add voices and power to change the climate of public opinion, and making certain actions unacceptable. Local victories in which citizens tackle a problem will improve the local environment, give people real experience in making democracy work, create connections between strangers, and seed the idea that the community should be planning ahead to take control of its own destiny.

After a series of local fights has highlighted a problem, government policy becomes ripe for change. Local fights are the basic engine for identifying problems, inventing solutions, and eventually changing government and corporate policies. Local fights "trickle up" to higher levels, where they generate new policies. Policy victories are important but rarely permanent and must be repeatedly defended. The victory of a change driven by the climate of opinion is much more difficult to reverse than a policy victory. The climate of opinion determines what kind of behavior is unthinkable. Climate of opinion changes are so incremental that often we're unaware of them.

New York's governor recently took a huge leap and banned fracking in the state, "... until a health study can prove it is safe." However, don't be fooled by his statement. It was strong public opinion that truly created the motivation for Governor Cuomo to leap as far as he did and ban fracking.

So here's the question for all of us: How can we create the climate of public opinion that demands the prevention of harm; protects our forests, mountains, and rivers; and stops contributing to climate change?

<u>TOP</u> Within forty-eight hours, several hundred families organized the Love Canal Homeowners Association, ca. 1980. Love Canal, New York. *Photo Courtesy of the University Archives, University at Buffalo, the State University of New York* <u>BOTTOM</u> Remediation work at Love Canal, ca. 1980. New York. *Photo Courtesy of the University Archives, University at Buffalo, the State University of New York*

119

Roses are RED, and I'm feeling BLUE
climate change is scary
At least I've got YOU!

(07)

Networking

Beth Kanter

In this chapter, I'm going to give you two views: the balcony and the dance floor. From the balcony, you'll see the big picture, trends, and how all the parts fit together—and how online networks and social media have dramatically changed the way nonprofits connect with their audiences. You'll learn that it isn't about the tools, it's about the connections and relationships that the tools facilitate.

When rocking the dance floor, we'll focus on best practices. Our time and resources are limited, so we need to be efficient. The tips I'll share are practical and tactical, and will help you incorporate social media into your campaign plan and see real results.

The power of networks is about people, not just organizations, as this story demonstrates. I have a very special connection with Cambodia: it's where my adopted children were born. I've traveled there often over the years. On my most recent trip in 2012, I experienced the dramatic change in the level of Internet technology in Cambodia. I was able to get fast Wi-Fi on my smartphone almost everywhere we traveled. I was able to share photos, tweets, Facebook updates, and Instagram photos in real time.

Having Internet access on our drive from Phnom Penh to Siem Reap came in handy. My Cambodian friend Mongkol, a blogger met online through my blog, wrote us a note in the Khmer language to give to the driver. It said, "Please drive slowly and safely. We are not in a hurry to get to Siem Reap. We want to live a long life." But our taxi driver was talking on his cell phone during the drive on unpaved roads through rural Cambodia—and from the backseat (without a seat belt in the car), I posted on Facebook that I wished I had a sign in Khmer that said, "Don't talk on your mobile phone while your are driving." Three minutes later, Mongkol wrote exactly that, photographed it, and posted it on my Facebook wall. I was able to tap the driver's shoulder and show him the note, and he stopped talking on his cell phone. Obviously, we got back safely.

Networks Are Impacting Our Personal, Work, and Civic Lives

What this story illustrates is the power of the technology to connect you with people who share your interests and passions—and you can instantly work together in real time to communicate, solve problems, and take action. It also illustrates three digital revolutions that have disrupted the way nonprofits do their work; three trends behind the rise of the network-centric approach to social change. And, according to recent studies from the Pew Internet and America Life Project, these three things impact our personal, professional, and civic lives.

1. Eighty-two percent of Americans have access to broadband Internet: Internet access is more pervasive and fast in parts of the world, like the United States (and Cambodia, as I discovered). It's no longer a slow, frustrating experience to get online, and more and more of us rely on using it for both our work and personal lives.

2. Eighty-nine percent of Americans have a smartphone that is connected to the Internet. We are no longer tethered to a desktop to communicate or inspire people to take action. We can get on the Internet and use social media anytime, anywhere.

3. Seventy-two percent of Americans use at least one social network. And according to the Pew studies, that network is Facebook. Social media and social networks are no longer just for early adopters or kids; they have become like air to us, allowing us to keep in touch with family, for work, to discover news, and, of course, for social change.

No single nonprofit or individual can do it alone. Collaboration, coordination, and working in networks are becoming the new normal, as leaders across sectors take a network-centric approach to moving the needle on today's most pressing problems.

What does this look like? Grassroots mobilization has experienced a steep climb in speed and power in the last couple of years, as witnessed by the Twitter-enabled Arab Spring, the KONY 2012 campaign that put a long-invisible crisis in Africa on the public radar, and many other political, cultural, and social justice examples.

In 2014, we saw how people turned to their online networks to raise money and awareness for ALS through the Ice Bucket Challenge. Millions participated, resulting in over $100 million in donations to advance research.

And then there are collaborative efforts on sites like Wikipedia that continue to grow and redefine how we access expertise. The power of networks is apparent in field-level collaborative projects such as RE-AMP, a network of environmental organizations that have aligned their policy and advocacy efforts to reduce coal plant production.

The backdrop to all of it is this: Your nonprofit is operating in an age of networks and connectivity, and is part of something larger. It is no longer good enough to simply be an isolated entity on Facebook; you have to be a networked nonprofit.

The Networked Nonprofit

Networked nonprofits are simple, agile, and transparent organizations that are expert at using social media tools to make the world a better place. Everyone in a networked nonprofit is empowered to use social media and to leverage their professional networks and passion in service of the organization's mission.

Embracing a networked way of working for some nonprofits means changing the way they work. And we all know that change can be difficult—and slow. That's why I advocate small, incremental steps—as seen in the framework (and example) that follows.

Becoming a Networked Nonprofit and Using Social Media

"If you can't fly then run, if you can't run then walk, if you can't walk then crawl, but whatever you do you have to keep moving forward."

– Martin Luther King Jr.

Where should you begin?

The Crawl Stage

Crawlers are not using social media or measurement consistently; they also lack a robust communications strategy and either resist or aren't sure how to adopt a networked way of thinking (what this is specifically will become clear as we progress through the stages).

The Walk Stage

These nonprofits use several social media channels consistently, but aren't being strategic about it. They implement low-risk projects that collect stories, learning, and metrics to help leadership better understand the value, benefits, and costs, but they're not interacting with users, or they only share content and messaging produced by their own organization.

Creating a social media strategy that focuses on gaining expertise in one or two social media tools and generating tangible results is key. And integrating social media responsibilities into existing staff jobs (among identifying other low-cost ways to build capacity internally) is essential.

The Run Stage

These nonprofits have an integrated strategy, they're identifying key metrics that drive everything they do, and they understand conversion: moving supporters/donors from hearing about your organization to actively engaging, volunteering, or donating to your organization. Measurement is their religion and data is their God and they adjust their content strategy when needed, based on measurement. Social media is not "owned" by one person or department in these organizations (though they do have a community manager actively building relationships online); it's pervasive and part of the culture.

The Fly Stage

These organizations have nailed everything mentioned above—and then some. They have mastered the networked mind-set and are the Jedi to The Run Stage's padawan: Flyers embrace failure and success alike, and learn from both. They are part of a vibrant network of people and organizations all focused on social change. And they use sophisticated measurement techniques, tools, and processes.

The Story of One Nonprofit's Transformation

Several years ago, the Community Foundation of Santa Cruz County did not have a presence on social media and there was a lot of resistance to changing that, particularly to the idea of all staff members using the tools to connect. They had a communications strategy, but it did not incorporate new media. After looking at the crawl-to-fly spectrum, they joked that they were not even crawling; they hadn't even been born yet!

Knowing that they had to start somewhere, they took the first step of articulating their objectives and the target audience for social media. After a strategy session with staff members, they had identified several audiences (local nonprofits, donors, and community members) and clear objectives: to provide information, educate, and inform. Their staff was small, with limited resources, so they decided to focus on one social channel to start: Facebook.

Scanning local nonprofit Facebook pages in their county and adding the information to a spreadsheet, they discovered that 80 percent of local nonprofits were on Facebook and had an average of 200 fans. Local nonprofits were a key audience they wanted to reach and were missing out, so they took the following steps:

- Developed an editorial calendar of content they would post on Facebook based on what they knew this audience wanted to read.
- Reviewed similar nonprofit social media policies and created their own, detailing do's and don'ts along with a Facebook tip sheet.
- Developed a robust engagement and content strategy, which was integrated with other digital channels.
- Shared the new media strategy with staff members and specifically trained everyone to encourage participation.
- Used measurement to figure out what specific content was inspiring more engagement and more views on Facebook.

They discovered a few things once they got started:

- Photos or updates about the inner workings of the organization got a lot more engagement, especially those posts with a little personality.
- Sharing content from nonprofits in their network got a lot more views.
- When their executive director responded to a post and engaged in conversation in the comments section, both the number of comments and reach soared.

The group has gone on to incorporate additional channels, including a blog, LinkedIn, Twitter, and Instagram—and everyone on staff is active on those networks, serving as champions for the organization's work. The impact of this work is noticeable: More people in the community are aware of their work, and sponsored events are better attended.

Starting small works. Where is your organization now? What do you need to get to the next stage? Remember, it takes incremental steps—and you need to start somewhere. If you are crawling like the Community Foundation of Santa Cruz was a few years ago, I'm cheering you on! Let's dive in to how you can become a networked nonprofit.

Networked Mind-Set Requires Leadership

As we just saw, becoming a networked nonprofit requires cultivating a networked mind-set. This includes:

- Leadership through active social media participation as a personal brand (that is, as the individual versus just the organization's brand) to support organizational goals.
- Listening and cultivating organizational and professional networks to achieve the impact.
- Sharing control of decision-making.
- Communicating through a network model, rather than a broadcast model.
- Open, transparent, decentralized decision-making, and allowing for collective action.

- Allowing—and encouraging—all employees to be champions for the organizations by using their personal social media accounts to share information or engage with their network about the organization's programs and work.

Social Media: It's Part of Everyone's Job in a Nonprofit

The idea that social media is part of everyone's job gets either groans or cheers from people who work in the trenches of nonprofits. Should all staff members represent the organization on social media? Won't that cause confusion? What if someone makes a mistake? What if they end up wasting their time, an important organizational resource? But, the question that nonprofits should ask instead is this: How can we leverage the passion and expertise of our staff members' personal brands on social media to support our organization's work? An example:

Upwell is an activist organization that collaborates with like-minded organizations to coordinate new media campaigns to support ocean conservation. Everyone on its small staff uses their personal brands as well as the organizational brand to support the cause.

Rachel Dearborn is the communications staff and a shark lover who stumbled upon an amazing tumblr blog called "F**K yeah Sharks" that had over 1 million subscribers who actively commented on its posts. The blog owners were going to shut it down due to time constraints, but Rachel convinced them to donate it to her nonprofit. The nonprofit was a bit uncomfortable owning a blog with swear words in the URL, so Rachel took it on as her own and devotes a small amount of work time to updating it. Win-win. Upwell benefits from the many potential new advocates the blog attracts every day, and Rachel is able to pursue her passion in service of the organization's mission.

Having a presence on Twitter, Facebook, or other social media channels can boost the organizational strategy, but CEOs are often very busy. They need to understand that social media can be used to enhance the work they are already doing—not add an item to an already overextended list of to do's.

Trust Is Cheaper Than Control: Social Media Policy

Now, other nonprofits might not have the problem of top-down command and control leadership that does not trust its employees. But what it takes is a willing attitude and a clear social media policy that describes what staff can and cannot do to be advocates on social media for the organization's work.

Structurally, a social media policy has two sections:

1   GUIDELINES — A one- or two-page summary of how your organization can be more effective at using social media. It should lay out parameters around organizational and personal use and how to use the tools effectively.
2   MANUAL — The manual consists of your social media plan, including best practices on using social media with specific examples. Many organizations use this as part of their training.

Your social media policy should be developed in tandem with your new strategy (see next section). There are many examples out there, so there is no reason to start from scratch. And it's helpful to look at what other organizations are doing and pick out the elements relevant to your organization and goals.

Now that we've covered the more difficult aspects of becoming a networked nonprofit, let's look at the organizational strategy.

Creating a Simple New Media Strategy for Your Organization

Many of the hundreds, if not thousands, of nonprofits I encounter every year when I teach workshops realize that what they need is a new media strategy. But they haven't quite defined the desired results, nor have they clearly defined the audience for their use of social media.

You need a new media strategy to:

- Be more strategic in selecting and using social media to reach and measure results.
- Save time—help prioritize limited resources and staff members' time.

- Reach the right audience on the right social media platform. For example, if you want to reach teens, you'd better be using Snapchat, not Facebook.

What are the elements of a strategy? Many nonprofits (wisely) start out with the "POST" framework.

P is People. Understand your audience and how to target it. Take Save the Children, for example. Their audiences include grassroots donors and supporters as well as influencers such as journalists and policy makers. To reach the latter audience, their CEO, Carolyn Miles, has a leadership profile on Twitter where she shares updates directed at this target group. The brand uses Twitter to share calls to donate and news about the organization's programs.

O is Objectives. What is your goal? You need to define your objective(s) before thinking about which technology to use (and certainly before you consider measurement). Objectives should be specific, measurable, attainable, relevant, and timely. The outcomes you can expect from your new media strategy generally fall into these categories: reach, action, engagement, or donations.

S is Strategy. I like to think about strategy as the specific and effective ways of integrating social media. This includes listening, engagement, content, social proofing, reaching out to and cultivating influencers, and identifying champions. It is also about how you integrate leadership—how you empower your executive director and staff to leverage their personal brands in service of the overall goals. It's also about measuring your results to both prove impact and improve what you're doing.

T is Technology. Now you can decide what makes sense regarding different technologies. Should you develop a community, a blog—a wiki, perhaps? There are so many different channels, and it is at this point that you begin to prioritize where you will spend your time.

Below are just a few of the most popular social networking sites:

FACEBOOK: Largest social networking with over 1 billion members

TWITTER: Micro blogging site where people share updates in 140 or fewer characters

INSTAGRAM: Social networking site where people share photos and videos

PINTEREST: Social networking site where people share visual "bulletin boards" on different topics

LINKEDIN: Business-oriented social networking site

SNAPCHAT: Picture-sharing site popular with teens to share photos that are subsequently deleted after 24 hours

PERISCOPE: Live video streaming site connected to Twitter that allows users to live stream video snippets of their lives in real time

Listening

Listening well is the basis of your engagement and content strategy. Listening is discovering. It's hearing what your supporters, volunteers, and potential donors are talking about, understanding what their concerns are and addressing them.

Perhaps the best example of this is from the American Red Cross. This organization monitors social media channels and analyzes what people are saying, and in some cases members of the communications staff will listen and respond in real time. When they hear people complimenting the Red Cross, for example, on Twitter, they may tweet back with a thank you—this helps them build relationships with their supporters.

They also hear complaints. First they try to determine whether the complaints are valid. For example, there was a complaint from a number of supporters that they were being reminded too often to give blood. The staff members forwarded the information to different affiliates, and it turned out there was a glitch in the database software.

They also track whether or not a person complaining is an influencer. When this happens, they address it right away because the situation could escalate into a PR disaster. They're using listening as a giant focus group to help understand how to improve what they're doing. Social media engagement is a great way to address concerns, identify opportunities, and gauge a campaign's effectiveness as it's happening.

Listening to and analyzing online conversations via a variety of monitoring tools (like Radian6 and Tweetdeck) can help you scan available social platforms for mentions of your organization. It can also let you summarize the mentions into positive, negative, or neutral comments that can provide insights in real time about what people are saying.

Listening isn't confined to measuring campaigns and listening to supporters; it's also about listening to your niche, understanding your space (as an expert), and finding content that will help those listening to you advance conversations and move the needle forward. And the first step toward becoming a masterful content curator is cultivating great sources.

What Is Content?

Content is short-form text like tweets or Facebook status updates and long-form text like blog posts, images, photos, or videos. Your content strategy needs to include content curation (content you find on social media channels and build upon), content creation (original content), and a strategy for effectively distributing both. The key to doing this well is all in the mind-set. You need to think of every piece of content (curated or created) as a piece of a larger whole, and you must repurpose, recycle, and reuse every bit of it.

Content Curation

Content curation is about discovering great stuff amid the noise, annotating it, organizing it, and adding your wisdom or perspective and sharing a collection of curated links in a context or time that adds value.

Curation is accomplished using two tools: news discovery, to help you find relevant content in your niche area, and curation tools, to organize and share it.

News discovery tools select and aggregate content based on keyword searches—you'll find a great, curated list of discovery tools from Robin Good in the Resource links at the end of the chapter.

How do you identify great content? Well (this will sound simple, but many skip this step to their own peril), you have to *read* it. First, develop a list of trusted sources, those that share the kind of information you seek, and then organize them with a newsreader (Feedly is a great option for this). Then turn a critical eye to the content and train yourself to "spot the awesome." Awesome is different for each person and purpose, but something that inspires you to stop and reframe your thinking about a topic is certainly it.

When you spot the awesome, spend time looking for more content and context to add to it—making the original resource more valuable by adding additional references, quotes, reviews, citations, or stories that complement the existing view. And then create your own awesome.

So at this point, you've planned, strategized, curated, and created something awesome—and now you need to focus on engagement.

How to Inspire People to Engage with Your Brand and Content

Engagement is connecting with your target audience in a way that either encourages them to take action in some way or encourages them to think of you when they're ready to! Engagement can be as simple as posting a question or conversation starter on your organization's Facebook page as well as responding to people in the comments section.

Some practical tips: Engage around questions that are relevant, fun, nostalgic, or evoke emotions. Hit your audience where their passion lies.

Keep a running list of high-engagement conversation starters and use them regularly. This list should be with you when you are planning your content and engagement for your social media channels. For example, the San Francisco Gay Men's Chorus uses conversation starters regularly related to concerts. They encourage the audience to take "social media breaks" and post photos during intermission. And they post questions like:

- What's your best restaurant recommendation for a quick dinner before our concert?

- What's your favorite piece on our upcoming concert program and why?
- Post a photo of yourself in the lobby during intermission and have an opportunity to win two tickets to our next concert.
- What was your favorite moment of tonight's concert?

Don't have any conversations starters? Conduct interviews with your audiences or simply observe them to find out what they are interested in. For example, a food bank noticed that during actual tours of its food warehouse, people asked a lot of questions about the types of foods that were donated. The food bank decided to test engaging people on Facebook with a weekly "Warehouse Wednesday" post that included a photograph and question about a recently donated food item. These posts were very popular.

Social media is an almost-ideal medium to show donor, volunteer, staff, and audience appreciation. If you can tag the person you're thanking, you immediately increase the engagement of the post. Because people like to put their philanthropy on display, you can almost count on the fact that they will re-share your post.

Texas Humane Heroes shows a lot of love to those who adopt their animals. These posts get an insane amount of engagement. *Be sure to always get your supporters' permission before publicly recognizing them.* While you're asking, be sure to get their Twitter handle or have someone in the organization befriend them so that you can tag them later.

TIP: Add social media channels as communication preferences on your personal information forms.

Make it "buzzworthy" by crafting good headlines. Be sure these headlines aren't linkbait (meaning they promise one thing and then don't pay off in the piece), as Facebook now penalizes content for that—and other platforms are bound to follow suit—and it will backfire on you in the end.

Now that your audience has engaged with your brand, how can you use that to support your fundraising efforts? Using social media for fundraising is a natural progression, but there are some best practices to keep in mind.

Fundraising

You need to set a realistic goal based on benchmarking. If you don't yet have other efforts to benchmark against, this will be your starting point. Research the amounts that others have raised in your niche to use this time around, but don't be too hard on yourself if you fall short—they aren't you.

Don't set minimum gift levels too low. Just as you don't want to set the overall goal too low, don't set the minimum gift level too low either. Based on my past experience with fund-raising campaigns, many people give at the minimum level. Don't worry; if they can't afford to give the minimum, they will still give another amount.

TIP: Come up with creative names for each donor level.

Social proofing helps generate donations. Social proof is peer pressure in a positive way—when people find out others are doing something, they will want to do that something too. Social proofing, or tagging your call to donate, is something that can be replicated.

Build social capital in your network by reaching out personally to ask for (and then acknowledge) donations in a public and unique way.

TIP: I've found that a large percentage of donations come from groups and individuals with whom I have strong ties. The most effective solicitation was one-on-one personal asks

(to donate or help spread the word). When people in your network see that others are donating, they will as well. Giving is contagious.

Offer numerous ways for people to participate. Moving participants from awareness to actively supporting your cause, and then having them take that extra step to influence others to participate as well, no longer follows a linear path. You need to respond with different calls to action offering a spectrum of involvement options from light to heavy.

"Heavy" asks include making a donation, sharing a personal story, or providing advice or materials to support your campaign. Lighter involvement is popular as well though and shouldn't be discounted. These folks are your brand ambassadors and help amplify your message and provide that all-important social proof mentioned above.

TIP: Knowing your audience, and whom to ask for what, is essential and increases the likelihood of success.

Summary

I've shared the big picture about underlying trends and why working as a networked nonprofit is important. I've shared some stories and principles about making that transformation to a more open, agile, and responsive nonprofit and how to do it in an incremental and strategic way. I've also shared tips and tactics to help you get started to integrate social media in your organization's new media strategy. Now it's up to you! I look forward to hearing your success stories.

Resources

Resources

CWRF framework. http://www.ssireview.org/blog/entry/becoming_a_ networked_nonprofit.

Four Magic Steps to Curating Awesome Content. http://www.mobilisationlab.org/mobilisation-tools/four-magic-steps-to-creating-shareable-purpose-driven-social-media-content/.

Kanter, Beth. Beth's Blog. http://www.bethkanter.org.

Social Media Posting Guide. http://topnonprofits.com/posting-guide/.

SSIR: The Permanent Disruption of Social Media. http://www.ssireview.org/articles/entry/the_permanent_disruption_of_social_media.

Top Nonprofits on Social Media. http://topnonprofits.com/lists/top-nonprofits-on-social-media/.

ACLU-New Jersey director Udi Ofer invited his constituents to engage on social media by posting this photo along with the tagline, "Ask me anything." You can too—follow him on Twitter @UdiACLU. *Accra Shepp*

Getting Your ED to Tweet

The executive director for the ACLU-NJ, Udi Ofer, set up a Twitter account, @UdiACLU, and started using Instagram and YouTube to answer questions about marriage equality, DOMA, police misconduct, and other issues on the organization's docket.

Ofer was a Twitter novice, but he was open to meeting with his communications staff for a half-hour tutorial on Twitter and how to tweet from his mobile phone, including a "How To Tweet" cheat sheet that not only included the simple mechanics, but also sample tweets from other ACLU leaders around the country (a subtle form of peer pressure).

By using Twitter, Ofer isn't sharing the news of what he ate for breakfast. Instead, he provides quotes on his organization's most important cases and issues to reporters, in addition to their traditional press release or emailed statement. He is also publicly debating civil liberties issues with reporters, activists, lawyers, and followers. And his occasional personal tweets help make him seem approachable and human.

Udi Ofer is just one example of nonprofit CEOs and leaders who use Twitter and other social media platforms as their personal brand to support the organization's new media strategy. You can find many other examples at http://list.ly/list/l0a-ultimate-list-of-lists-of-nonprofit-social-ceos).

Tips for Getting Your Nonprofit Executive Director on Social Media

1   Get their attention. If you have to camp outside their door, do it. Let them know that this is important and have stats ready to share that show why.

2   Show how social media amplifies the work they are already doing. It only requires asking some simple but powerful questions to engage an audience, as the story of Udi Ofer illustrates. Share that story with your CEO.

3   Give them a "Tweetorial." Show them how to use Twitter on their mobile phone and the basic commands. Knowing who to follow and how to "feed" followers the best content isn't intuitive. Help them map it out.

4   Show examples from peers. Share how other nonprofit CEOs are using Twitter (or whichever platform you're trying to pitch) and be ready to show how easy it is to use.

5   Be ready to show them the impact of their efforts. Using a tool like Twiangulate, you can easily see the overlap of followers and reach for the CEO and the organization's branded account.

– Beth Kanter

132

Grist founder Chip Giller turned environmentalism on its head. *John Clark*

Grist

Katharine Wroth

When Grist took to Twitter for the first time, you could practically hear the uncertainty spilling from our keyboards: "being gristy," our first tweet read—with a winking emoticon for added effect.

That was August 2007. Twitter was a year old, Facebook had reached the advanced age of three, and it was becoming clear that they would transform the online landscape. No one was entirely sure how, but Grist knew these tools could bolster our mission. With a reputation for publishing green news that resonates with the next generation—we've been called *The Daily Show* of the environment"—it made sense for us to meet those users where they were increasingly spending their time.

Because communications is our core focus, it didn't take long for us to grow more confident with these new tools. As we tended our Grist accounts, a responsibility that fell initially to our small marketing team, we also encouraged our writers to develop their own social media presences. In some cases, it took time for staff members to warm up to this idea. Senior writer David Roberts, a leading voice on the site, made his debut in 2009, his tone characteristically wry: "I guess I'm twittering now. Because blog posts aren't poorly thought through and instantly regrettable enough." Before too long, Dave had churned out 100,000 tweets and earned 38,000 followers.

As our social media presence grew, we evolved from simply promoting our latest content to hosting an interactive, ongoing discussion with our readers—one that needed tending. In early 2011, Grist hired a social media coordinator. We immediately saw the benefits of putting resources toward this role. Within three months, traffic referrals from Twitter and Facebook had doubled, and our unique users—for us, a key indicator of progress—had grown 40 percent. Today, our following on Twitter and Facebook is more than 400,000, and social media is responsible for 35-40 percent of traffic to our site.

But social media is far more than a traffic generator. As we pursue our mission of empowering a new generation to make change, we think of our followers as evangelists—people who can activate their own networks to support the aims of the environmental movement. We engage people in many ways, whether we're discussing the economics of bicycling, sharing images from the storm-ravaged streets of New York after Hurricane Sandy, or soliciting recipes for eating local in winter. Seventy percent of our readers tell us they've made change based on Grist content.

Experimentation has also been a key part of our social media work. We held a Twitter power-er-hour fundraiser, seeking twenty donations in sixty minutes and partnering with influential non-green allies to help spread the word.

This social fundraiser spurred twenty-six gifts (with twenty-one of them from new donors), and our efforts were reported in *The Chronicle of Philanthropy*. We've also played with new tools like Thunderclap, which enables simultaneous distribution of a single tweet; we inspired more than 650 Grist fans to send the same tweet about climate change, reaching an estimated 476,882 people. And we've had plenty of fun, like a contest to come up with the best #hipsterfarmer band name—Radicchiohead won.

Why does social media matter to Grist? Because 68 percent of millennials get their news from it. Because nearly 2 billion people around the world use it to talk, share, scheme, commiserate, and communicate. Because it's an important part of our strategic effort to move people from being casual readers to becoming informed, active citizens—in fact, it's a first step on that ladder of engagement.

RADICCHIOHEAD

The winner of Grist's online contest to come up with the best
#hipsterfarmer band name. *Image Courtesy of Grist*

Inspire with Film

Melinda Booth

The South Yuba River Citizens League, affectionately referred to as SYRCL, is a nonprofit river conservation organization located in Nevada City, California, in the foothills of the Sierra Nevada. SYRCL started the Wild & Scenic Film Festival in 2003 as a fundraiser. The event was named after the sixteen-year-long, and ultimately successful, fight to secure wild and scenic status for thirty-nine miles of the South Yuba River, forever protecting it from the threat of dams. The event grew from two nights and a dozen films to a four-day event consisting of eight venues concurrently screening more than 100 environmental and adventure films while also promoting art, music, activist workshops, and special guests, and generating overwhelming community involvement and support.

We quickly realized we had a successful model and felt we had an obligation to share it with other environmental organizations. Thus in 2005, Wild & Scenic On Tour was born. The festival is currently hosted in more than 150 communities around the globe—it's out there using film to inspire activism. The Wild & Scenic Film Festival On Tour is a turn-key "event-in-a-box" developed by an environmental nonprofit for other environmental nonprofits in an effort to raise funds, increase membership, inspire activism, and reach new audiences. Oh, and have fun, too!

Each Wild & Scenic On Tour event serves as a call to action for a different cause. We partner with a local organization to host the event, and that organization presents the event as its own. The host chooses a lineup of films from the sixty-plus options, so the event delivers a specific message tailored to a local audience. The event belongs to the organization—we don't travel with the show. Instead, we provide a toolkit (sixty-eight pages of tips, tricks, time lines, and other resources) for producing and leveraging the festival. The host is walked through planning each step of the way, and we are on-call via email and phone for consultation and troubleshooting. We promote the "teach a woman to fish" model for event success. It worked for us and it can work for you.

Events as a Tool

Events: Fun or daunting? Fundraisers or friend-raisers? Focus on current supporters or engage a new audience? In reality, a successful event will be all of these things. With some guidance, focus, and help along the way, a well-planned event will be more fun than daunting, raise both funds and friends, engage your existing audience and attract new folks—as well as promote your organization's mission, campaign, or issue.

For Kentucky Waterways Alliance, the Wild & Scenic Film Festival On Tour has become their single largest annual membership generator, as well as their signature event that supporters look forward to every year. It's also a way they can engage volunteers in a fun and meaningful way—once people volunteer, they are more likely to join, donate, stay involved, and promote that organization to their friends and family.

Stills from two of the films screening at the 2016 Wild & Scenic Film Fest: *Unbranded*, which draws attention to the 50,000 wild horses and burros currently living in government captivity, and *Speechless: The Polar Realm*, a beautiful visual odyssey through the Earth's polar regions. *Cory Richards and Richard Sidey*

Producing the event is a commitment. On average, our partners allocate two to three staff to work on their event and wrangle a few board members to help, too. Before you embark on this journey, make sure you have a team in place to make it happen—producing a successful event is not a one-person job. It's also time-consuming; ensure you have the bandwidth to make the event happen without burning out. Don't be too discouraged if you're not seeing immediate results—the "friend-raiser" part of the event can take time to manifest into memberships, a donations, or volunteers. But our experience is that it *will* happen.

As is the case with any tool, an event is one piece of an overall strategy for your larger goal, not a magic bullet. But combined with other fundraising and outreach tools, events are a worthwhile investment.

One of our festival's long-time attendees has told us that her husband has a love/hate relationship with Wild & Scenic On Tour. This woman attends every year and from the information garnered from the films she views, she makes a conscious change in her life. Inspired to action, she aims to address a problem she found particularly moving. In 2011, she stopped using plastic shopping bags. In 2012, she traded in her SUV for a hybrid sedan. In 2013, she vowed to buy only organic produce. In 2014, she committed to installing solar panels on her home.

So why the love/hate relationship from her husband? As we all know, change is hard, and her action and dedication to these changes affected both him and their household. Each January, he gets nervous about what big change is coming. But, ultimately, if you ask him, he feels good about her leadership to live in a more sustainable way. She loves it and is giddy with anticipation about what new action she can implement each year that will contribute to larger change. These are results inspired by Wild & Scenic films.

Why Film Works

The ancient tradition of storytelling encompasses every facet of human endeavor and lies at the heart of human experience; it is beauty, community, mystery. We connect with people through the telling of stories. While many traditions have languished in the twenty-first century, digital storytelling is on the rise. Film is one of the most engaging and powerful platforms from which to tell a story.

Film is also a medium that is accessible to a diverse audience—it interests most people and allows you to reach "beyond the choir" in an unintimidating way. A fun event featuring inspirational films can break down perceived barriers between "enviros" and "non-enviros," making reaching new audiences easier than ever.

A long-time partner on California's Central Coast, the Ventana Wilderness Alliance, tells us that Wild & Scenic On Tour has allowed them to do just that. They consider it an essential tool for spreading their message to audiences they wouldn't otherwise reach.

And, we believe this event does more than just reach that new audience; it engages and inspires them. When the theater lights come back up, your audience will want to go out and make things better.

We invite you to join us in the effort to increase the groundswell for the environmental grassroots movement as a whole, and experience using film to inspire activism in your community.

How to Host

Visit www.wildandscenicontour.org for more information.

Stills from two more films screening at the 2016 Wild & Scenic Film Fest: *Co2ld Waters*, a film about fly fishing and climate change, and *A Quest for Meaning*, which documents two childhood friends who travel the world to meet some of the greatest thinkers of our time. *Photos Courtesy of Jeremy Roberts/Conservation Media and Kamea Meah Films*

At different times, a Haight-Ashbury hippie, logger, millwright, commercial fisherman, salmon guide, shit disturber, river rat and boat junky, and putative conservationist. Member of the Loyal Order of Masters of Mischief. Committed to wild salmon, wild places of the heart, home waters, big old trees, and fighting bad shit.

Bruce Hill

KEYNOTE SPEAKER

Let Your Hands Go

PG.140 A wolf and raven fish side by side for pink salmon in the Great Bear Rainforest, British Columbia. *Ian McAllister* ABOVE People of the Heiltsuk First Nation protest the Northern Gateway oil pipeline and super tanker proposal for the Great Bear Rainforest, Bella Bella, British Columbia. *Ian McAllister*

I live in northern British Columbia, an iconic landscape of wild salmon, big old trees in coastal rainforests, and indigenous people who just won't stand down for big oil. Right now this region is ground zero for proposed industrial development on a scale that staggers the imagination: close to a half trillion dollars of development is proposed for the region. We are facing over a dozen massive Liquefied Natural Gas projects, several proposed oil refineries, tar sands pipelines that would cross 800 rivers and see 250 supertankers a year through the Great Bear Rainforest. And then there are some of the largest proposed mines on earth, some as big as the Pebble mine beast—mines on the headwaters of great salmon rivers that require 700-foot-high dams to hold back billions of tons of toxic waste for ten thousand years.

How do you deal with that kind of insanity?

Northern enviros jokingly refer to it as a "target-rich environment."

Behind all the madness are five of the six wealthiest corporations in the world: Sinopec, CNOOC, BP, Exxon, and Shell. The "little" players like Petronas, Mitsubishi, Rio Tinto, and Enbridge are all here too. Enbridge, Canada's largest pipeline company, is spending more than $100 million trying to convince the people of the region—the usual mix of folks up here who like their mountains wild, their rivers full of salmon, and their small towns livable—that pipelines and oil tankers are perfectly safe. So hope, and keeping hope alive, is an issue for us.

Now for the good news. We aren't run over yet, and the world hasn't ended. And we keep winning. Saving some of those special places and critters, even if it's for the next time around, actually seems doable. Hope is important. Winning one once in a while is important.

But you have to "let your hands go."

It's a boxing term. My Uncle Phil, a Golden Gloves champion with 160 wins, taught me to box and told me this: in boxing, when you throw a punch, you become susceptible to the counterpunch, and some boxers never get past that fear of committing. Of getting hit, of failing. They can't let their hands go. So they seldom win, regardless of their talent, power, or speed. Taking risks is important. You can't win if you are too afraid of losing.

I can't count the number of enviro conference calls I have been on, or meetings in myriad hotel rooms, over the past twenty-five years, where innovative ideas, seemingly crazy ideas, wild ideas, are proposed. And then the resistance comes: "But that's too hard" or "That might not work." It makes me crazy. The fear of failure is real in the environmental nongovernment organization (ENGO) world at times, and it's crippling—a beast that will bring failure if you let it. If the work of conservation and making change happen were easy, it would have been done already. It's hard, it takes time, and some days you have to wade through the despair and doubt to get to the good places.

I was driving along the Skeena River one day, when we were fighting Royal Dutch Shell's plans to drill thousands of gas wells on the headwaters of the Skeena, Stikine, and Nass Rivers. My cell phone went off, I pulled over, and it was the vice president of Shell in Canada. He wanted to know what it would take to get us to back off the fight. We talked for maybe a half hour, and he eventually warned me that Shell had billions of dollars in resources, and never lost. So I told him my story, and what my uncle had taught me. I told him I loved fighting big outfits like Shell, because no matter where I punched, I was gonna hit solid meat. As it turned out, mighty Shell Oil couldn't stand the publicity of Native grandmothers getting cuffed and being carted off to jail. They realized that they couldn't get away with that crap in BC. They bailed, left, called it quits, and we won.

Several years prior to that victory I had been talking to the head of the First Nations tribal council in the area, and he told me, "No one beats Shell; we have to cut the best deal we can." But his own elders didn't listen, they didn't give up, they stood in the road and held out their hands and demanded to be cuffed—some of them in wheelchairs. They were scared, some of them were crying, but I never heard them mention the idea that they might lose. And did they ever let their hands go. It wasn't a million-dollar campaign by the big ENGOs, it was a ragtag coalition of citizens—First Nation elders, kids, and families, and local conservationists who ranged from old back-to-the-land hippies to hard-core loggers and ranchers. Maybe we just didn't know better, or maybe we just didn't give a damn anyway, but we let our hands go, and we kept hitting solid meat.

I have been lucky to have been a part of some very successful conservation campaigns over the past twenty-five years, and even more fortunate to have worked with the leading First Nation conservationists in North America and some of the leading conservationists in the world. We reformed major fisheries, protected coastal watersheds, stopped the expansion of salmon farms on our coast, helped protect grizzly bears, and killed some dangerous industrial projects in places that needed to be left alone. In every single instance, we were told it couldn't be done, that we were powerless against big oil, big government, and big timber. If we had listened to the naysayers, there would be fish farms all over the north coast of BC, 5,000 gas wells in the Spatsizi, and a pipeline from the Tar Sands to the north coast of BC, and the Kitlope would be just another logged-out rainforest valley. I have a coffee cup from a crazy hooligan enviro cowgirl up the Skeena. It says, "I Kicked Shell's Ass, What Makes You Think I Won't Kick Yours." Shannon McPhail lets her hands go.

It's been a while since we've had many easy conservation victories, and we are not unique in northern BC, or enviro magicians with a lock on some secret weapon. Maybe we just don't know any better. But I know this: Every single person on this rock is now facing the same challenges and the need to keep hope alive. Everyone has a river, or canyon, or beach that needs protecting. So let those hands go, have some fun with it, and know your gonna hit some solid meat from time to time.

And don't let the bastards get you down.

A grizzly bear fishes for salmon. Great Bear Rainforest, British Columbia. *Ian McAllister*

(08)

Lobbying

Tim Mahoney

When I meet activists coming to Washington, DC, for the first time, they often tell me they feel intimidated by lobbying. They may believe it is beyond their capability, the province of high-powered lawyers spreading money and schmoozing senators at swanky restaurants behind closed doors. There is some of that, but most lobbying is just honest people using shoe leather, email, and the phone. And there is nothing involved in lobbying that you can't do. Frankly, it's hard to imagine you haven't done it already.

The strength of any grassroots campaign is grassroots organizing and support. It's what gives a campaign power. But almost every single campaign will at some point need to lobby a decision maker or maybe a whole bunch of them, whether a county or forest supervisor, a member of Congress, or a delegate to the United Nations. Lobbying is the interface with decision makers. Meeting with them can provide real information that can inform strategy.

Lobbying can help show campaign leaders a path forward, past obstacles and on course to succeed. If local grassroots are the engine, lobbying is the steering wheel.

PG.146 Patagonia ambassador Caroline Gleich, lobbying on behalf of the snowsports industry, urges Congress to support strong climate policy. Washington, DC. *Photo Courtesy of Protect Our Winters* PG.147 Patagonia ambassador Caroline Gleich at her day job, with Liz Daley, Glen Morden, and Carston Oliver, slogging through two feet of fresh powder above La Parva, Chile. *Adam Clark*

How to Get
Your Cat Fed

Let's say you live alone with an unappealing cat: homely, sheds, cries, sometimes claws the furniture and sometimes misses the box. And now let's say you plan to go away for a few days and need someone to come to your place once or twice a day to feed your cat, and maybe even clean the litter box. Big favors to ask. So you walk next door and visit your neighbor.

What would you say? How about, "You know, I've never thought you were a very good neighbor. I thought the neighbor who lived here before you was much better. But I want you to come over and feed my cat for a few days. And if you don't help me this one time, I will be furious with you."

Sound like a winning approach? Amazingly, that is the attitude of a few activists who come to Washington. They've never supported their member of Congress, don't think much of her, and still seem to think their representative or senator is under some obligation to do what they want.

Back to your cat. If you had planned ahead, you might have done a favor for your neighbor beforehand. That would have been smart. But the first thing you might say is to thank her for something she did for you in the recent past. "Oh thank you so much for bringing my paper in from the curb last week. You are so thoughtful. And your flowers look beautiful." Then tell her what you need: "I hate to bother you, but I have a huge favor to ask." It doesn't do you any good to underplay how unpleasant your cat is; if your neighbor doesn't already know, she will soon. So be honest, and emphasize how important the favor is. And say you'll be happy to return the favor in the future.

It's the same with lobbying. Whether you want a county supervisor to vote against a zoning change or you want a US senator to introduce a wilderness bill, you need to make what we call an "ask." You are asking someone to take action—which potentially could involve the decision maker taking some political risk—on behalf of you and your campaign. So, acknowledge that what you're asking of your representative may be politically difficult, stress the importance of the favor, reiterate your commitment to returning

the kindness in the future, follow up with profuse thanks, and make good on your promises. Otherwise, it may be the last time your neighbor feeds your homely cat—or the last time your representative goes to bat for you politically.

You may not agree with your member of Congress about much. In today's era of strong partisanship and rigid positions, you may not be able to work with your member despite your best efforts. But it may surprise you how often a member of Congress, when approached by appealing leaders with a thoughtful, inclusive approach and good local support, will respond positively. You may even become friends with the member or his staff despite your differences. I have. Individuals can make a big difference.

When I was a child—in the middle of the last century—we still had door-to-door salesmen. And except for the Avon lady, they were all men. They went house to house selling Fuller brushes, magazine subscriptions, or vacuum cleaners. Of course they would have a good spiel. But they had something else: a good ear. Suppose the brush salesman started telling you about the wonders of their new set of brushes. "You won't believe the value. It's durable, it's firm, it takes cat hair off clothing."

"I have a cat," you say. Now, do you think the salesman would just continue to run through his list of brush attributes? Or would the salesman ask about your cat? You guessed it. "Does your cat shed? Is cat hair a problem on your furniture? Let me show you what my brush can do!"

When activists come to Washington for the first time, they are often anxious about remembering every talking point, every fact, memorizing every arcane statistic about their issue. Sometimes, their meetings with staff consist of little else than a monologue as they anxiously list every point they can about why their cause is right. But when the member or staffer makes a point or asks a question, they better not rush by it in their zeal to say everything they have to say. Because the member is telling you what she cares about. And what *she* cares about, you care about. So listen and respond. And don't worry about all of your arcane talking points.

A good lobby meeting is like a conversation. People speak, listen, respond, and engage. Depending on the response you receive, you will want to emphasize what is important to the decision maker, not what is important to you. After all, you are trying to find a way to get them to yes in their own mind, for their own reasons.

Suppose the decision maker does not respond. Some just listen and let you blather on, then thank you and let you go. You might learn nothing about them or how they feel about your issue. Congressman Mo Udall, the great environmental leader and legislator of the '60s, '70s, and '80s, had a habit of nodding his head when people spoke and saying "yup." I remember one activist coming back from a meeting with Mo and saying he was with us and would do whatever it was we wanted. What did he say? He said yes to every point, was the reply.

Not exactly. For Mo, "yup, yup" was just his way of telling the speaker, "Message received, please continue." But we needed to know what he thought about our message. He was the decision maker.

So how do you do that? Stop talking about your brushes, and start asking questions. "Have you heard about this issue? Have any of your constituents contacted you about it? How can we best make our case?" And then listen, really listen, to what they have to say.

If the member of Congress says she thinks it would help you to have a favorable editorial in the local paper, she is not only giving you a campaign tip, she is telling you what is important to her. If she asks what an influential local landowner thinks, she is telling you that his opinion counts with her. And if the answer is so terse as to not provide any information, it could simply mean that she is withholding judgment until she learns more or hears more views. But it could be worse than that. Sometimes a decision maker doesn't want to tell you she does not favor your view. In fact, members of Congress often rely on staff to convey bad news. None of us like to disappoint people.

However, don't assume it is bad news if someone hasn't said so. Keep plugging. Try a different tack or perhaps send a different person from your campaign. One person may work better than another.

Remember: getting your cat fed is your ultimate goal. You're lobbying because you can't feed the cat yourself; laws have to come from somewhere, and you need a legislative champion to introduce a bill and lead it to passage. To find that champion, you need a cohesive strategy.

That strategic plan will be very different depending on whether your campaign is trying to do something positive, like passing your own wilderness proposal for your favorite canyon, or negative, like stopping some other champion's plan to build a dam in that canyon.

Tolstoy on Strategy

The Russian novelist Leo Tolstoy wrote, "All happy families are alike; each unhappy family is unhappy in its own way."

And I say, "All defensive campaigns are alike; every proactive campaign is different in its own way." Once we understand that, we can work out effective strategy, effective messaging, and an effective lobby plan.

Defensive campaigns are campaigns to stop something bad from happening. You are trying to get a legislator to vote "no," or, by delaying a decision or perhaps a quiet word to leadership, prevent the issue from coming to a vote at all.

Your messaging invariably is dire as you work to enlist a strong core of committed opponents to whatever it is you're trying to stop. You will necessarily be in a reactive mode, because in a defensive campaign you have less control over timing—which tends to be controlled more by proponents than opponents. But time is just as important to you as it is to proponents, perhaps more so, because the longer you can drag out a process of approval, the greater your chances of prevailing. So your tactics involve finding ways to delay or stop the process, whether it's stymying a bill in Congress or persuading an agency to switch direction and execute a new plan. You must find ways to get extra time for public input; fact finding; and more processes, consultations, and amendments. This time will not only slow your adversaries' momentum; it will also give you the chance to intensify your messaging and recruit more people to your side.

Successful defensive lobbying campaigns seldom result in a vote. Instead, as your side gains traction, the proponents may find their effort stalling because their champions are having trouble gaining additional supporters. And in a legislative body, since they need at least a majority and very likely a large majority, your side can often win with an intense and growing minority. In an elected body, there are most often three camps: those in favor, those opposed, and those who would really rather not be on the record one way or the other. (It's an old joke on Capitol Hill that a lawmaker says "Some of my friends are for this bill, and some of my friends are against it, and I'm for my friends.") If you can build a campaign of opposition based on intensely concerned constituents and increased media scrutiny, some elected officials in the "yes" camp may become queasy as their support begins to soften and waver. Once that happens, proponents will often delay moving forward because they know that avoiding taking a position is something members do well. If enough members want to sidestep a vote, the bill will ultimately die. Your side has won, at least for now.

But how is each proactive campaign different in its own way? First, this is a campaign to make something new happen, something good that will require proponents to find our way through the process with as little controversy as possible and gain the broadest coalition of supporters. So the messaging is positive; it stresses all the good things that will flow from accomplishing the goal. It is reassuring, not alarming, welcoming those who may be unsure to join us as we create this (wonderful) legacy. And we want them to join us!

Then, of course, we will have to navigate our political course with all of its twists, turns, and eddies, and to succeed we have to complete every step of the process, even as our adversaries try to force extra steps. That is the burden of proponents.

As you can imagine, our adversaries will be spreading dire warnings about this new thing we want to create as they try to mobilize their base and recruit doubters.

Each proactive campaign faces different political terrain and each strategy must be chosen to adapt to that terrain. Is your local decision maker in favor, neutral, unknowing, or likely to be opposed to your proposal? What about the other decision makers you and your champion will face? Are there powerful opponents ready to oppose and construct an alarming defensive

campaign against you? And if so, are there ways to evade them, co-opt them, or perhaps co-opt *some* of them (divide and conquer)? Perhaps gaining allies means modifying your proposal to meet their requirements, and that means you and your leaders will face a difficult choice. Are you willing to accept less in order to increase the likelihood of success? Or perhaps include someone else's goals as well as your own? How willing are you to change course midstream—perhaps more than once—if you find that your initial strategy isn't working?

In my career, I've had the good fortune to work with a couple of very powerful champions who will accept and fight for our most hoped-for proposals and use their own political clout to combine with ours to overwhelm some powerful opponents. In public lands campaigns, our side invariably would prefer to see that strategy undertaken, because then we didn't have to give up any or many of our cherished goals.

We have not always been so lucky. We've worked in fairly conservative areas where a stand-alone wilderness bill would muster little support. There, working with open-minded ranchers, local officials, and even timber operators, we've had to negotiate more complex compromises that meet not only our needs but also those of others. In these cases, we might have negotiated directly with other stakeholders before we took it to the decision makers. We have tried to reach out to other groups and gather the broadest support we can. That may mean we modified our proposal: we moved a boundary of an area proposed for protection to accommodate an alternative use, for example. But it could also mean including a priority valued by another group, one that is only tangentially related to our priority. These are hard choices, but they are not impossible if you approach them with a true reading of the politics and options available.

Working together, even with an opponent, you can achieve the support that neither group could achieve by itself.

So now that we've covered the basics of lobbying and defensive and offensive strategy, let's refocus on technique. You want to be a good lobbyist. After all, you love your cat, and his welfare is important to you.

Lobbyists
Don't Lie

Despite our public image, lobbyists don't lie. Perhaps we put the best slant on our case. Perhaps we don't always tell everything we know about a subject. But we don't lie. We don't deliberately mislead. Lobbyists succeed by building relationships with decision makers, and they come to trust our judgments. If one were to mislead a member of Congress, that would end the relationship. The best relationships I have on the Hill are ones where I can be very frank about a situation, particularly the political downside for the member of Congress. In part, because of the trust we've developed, the member is more likely to take my side. He would figure out the downside sooner or later—better to get it from me than from my adversary. (Just as your neighbor will figure things out about your cat sooner rather than later; better to tell him up front about the claws.)

You don't have to explicitly lie to break your trust; giving a false impression can be just as harmful. Or simply not doing your homework well enough. I once witnessed a public hearing in Alaska over what would become the Alaska National Interest Lands Conservation Act (ANILCA). In the southeast panhandle, conservationists were advocating for protection of forty-five different places, large and small. More than one hundred people testified during three days in the southeast, and witnesses had only a couple of minutes to make their testimony. One witness hurried through his testimony about one area then asked to spend a moment to speak of a second, the Sweetwater-Honker Divide. The chairman, John Seiberling of Ohio, was a devoted conservationist with an encyclopedic memory. When the panel of witnesses had finished, he asked the witness to elaborate on Sweetwater. Where was it, exactly? How far was it from the road system? He was inviting the witness to elaborate. The young man hemmed and then confessed he didn't actually know about Sweetwater. He had been asked to include it in his testimony to make sure someone mentioned it. He was mortified, and so was the chairman. The local congressman, who opposed protection, pounced. He said the environmentalists don't know what they are talking about. The chairman should pay attention to the local opponents, who really know the area.

So don't lie. Be prepared. Tell a good story, but don't even stretch the truth.

Be sure not to gossip or disparage anyone, especially your adversaries. You'd be amazed how it gets back to them. One of my mentors will never live down the day, early in his career, when he belittled a senior senator while chatting with a friend in a booth at a Capitol Hill bar. A little later a man got up from the adjacent booth and introduced himself as the senator's chief of staff. "Don't bother to come to our office in the future," he said.

If others do it, don't join in. Be respectful; it may even help you earn more respect yourself.

I Am Shocked—
Shocked—to Find That Politics
Is Going on in Here!

Lobbying is about the politics of an issue, not simply the merits of the case. Politics may be something that many activists find distasteful, so much so that earnest activists obsess over the merits of their case and ignore the political realities of the situation.

As previously mentioned, a successful lobby visit is like a conversation where both parties speak, where both parties learn and react to what they've heard. Building a successful relationship means that the member's staff is happy to meet, chat on the phone, or email because he finds your information helpful. The good news is that not only is your communication with the office staff absolutely necessary, but it also helps the member of Congress get to know you, respect you, and even come to appreciate your viewpoint. In the best relationships, he comes to trust you enough to provide information to you that he may not want to be widely known. If the member trusts your information, you are in a firm position to make your case based on the politics.

Politics? What About Facts?

Simply laying out the facts "proving" your side won't get a lawmaker to decide to vote in your favor on an issue; facts are important but not decisive. Each side in a political process does a pretty good job mustering facts to support their argument. But an elected official is not like a wise judge who listens to each side's strongest arguments and then renders an objective verdict. Rather, you need to make the political case that your side of the issue can be popular with constituents or other stakeholders that matter to the member. That's not distasteful. That's the reality of how one does good things in our system.

One of my mentors, Ernie Dickerman, who represented The Wilderness Society on the Hill, taught me a lot one day when I heard him tell activists that members of Congress were nice enough people. All they want to do is be well-liked, especially in their district, and be re-elected. If you can show how your wilderness proposal will be popular, then they will likely be for it.

Or as Sierra Club lobbyist John Zierold once said, "The first order of business for a legislator is to get re-elected. My job is to associate our cause with his."

Certainly, there are plenty of experts on the Hill and plenty of courageous votes cast. But not every vote is courageous. Members don't last long defying their constituents.

But not every issue is equally important to the politics of a constituency. Sometimes a member has already won the support of a constituency based on other issues, and can afford to be on an opposite side to support your issue. Other times a member may be disappointing your side on an issue and looking for an opportunity to show he can be favorable elsewhere.

Occasionally a member will simply take a courageous position because she likes you and she likes your people. That doesn't happen all the time, but, if you are likable and trustworthy, you are more likely to win the close ones. In the best lobby efforts, the member of Congress will tell you who and what is important to her. If you can find a way to fit your goals around what she thinks is important and work to ally with the constituents she feels are important, there is a very good chance that she will find that your cause is reasonable and something she can get behind.

Bring Me the Broomstick of the Wicked Witch of the West

Let's say your campaign to protect the proposed Ouijaboard Wilderness is off the ground. You have gathered local support, received a favorable editorial in the local paper, several area businesses publicly like you, and you have established a good relationship with the conservative member of Congress who represents this area. He has shown interest and has said he is impressed with your proposal. But he has not said he will introduce a bill to protect the place you wish to protect. And wilderness areas require Congress to enact a law.

When I reach this point—good relationship, no commitment—I am usually candid with the member or the staff. I ask, what could we do to persuade you to introduce and move a bill to protect this special place? We can ask this type of question after we've developed a good relationship and good communications with the decision makers. There is no reason to guess about this. We need to hear from our prospective champion.

Maybe the member isn't sure what he wants. But often he has a specific request. For example, he might ask: "Have you spoken with Tom Smith? He has a grazing allotment in your wilderness proposal. Does he support it? If he doesn't, I'm not sure I can introduce this."

So he's telling you two things. First, rancher Smith is important. Broad public support is great, but it is not sufficient. Certain people, certain interests, are particularly important to him in this instance. Second, he is probably saying that, unless Smith is an absolutely unreasonable person, you will need his support, or at least his acquiescence. Until you get it, you are probably not going to get this place protected.

So when the wizard says you don't get home to Kansas without bringing him the broomstick, you'd better find a way past those flying monkeys and get the stick. Otherwise, your campaign is going to have to go a different route.

For unknown reasons, some campaign leaders are very shy about communication with the decision maker, at least in the beginning. Perhaps their politics are different and they don't feel comfortable speaking with people who don't share their views. But it's absolutely necessary; without it your strategy is based on guesswork. "Will the member respond to this? Or to that? What did she mean when she said something cryptic last week at her press conference?" And unfortunately, sometimes guesswork leads to some pretty paranoid thinking.

Even the most unreasonable of them are not like North Korea. You don't have to guess what their actions mean and based on those guesses, make threats in return. You can make an effort to get to know whether the member ever agrees with you or not. You can find out directly how they view situations and who they believe are important. Perhaps, over time, you can even find some areas where you can collaborate, even if you can't see eye to eye on most things. Members can change, and so can we.

Don't Be Angry; Be Disappointed but Resolute

Let's suppose that you've done everything right. You've gained support, you've lobbied well, and you have built a reasonable relationship with the member and his staff. You even visited rancher Smith and he said that if you modified your wilderness boundary a little bit to accommodate his stock tanks, he would not oppose your proposal. But when you go back to your member of Congress, he says he just can't do it—at least he just can't do it now.

How do you respond? You may feel anger. And your supporters back home may be very angry. It's a predictable response, but it's not the right response.

I once worked with a local leader from the Pacific Northwest. I'll call her Dora. She was trying to gain protection for a place that involved more than simply local politics. Larger interest groups, including regional and national timber associations, opposed her. As she gathered support, she learned that she needed the support of the most senior representative in the delegation. He was from a conservative district and was often an advocate for the timber industry. As the end of the congressional session approached, time was running out for her bill.

She had done a good job over the previous two years of getting to know the staffer; she was also well liked and respected in every office she needed to visit. But this was a hard decision for the senior member, and the staff had asked her to come by. She was hopeful that this could be the breakthrough and asked that I accompany her.

The aide spoke kindly and quietly, saying he knew she had put a lot into this and they knew she really cared. "Dora, I'm awfully sorry to tell you but my boss can't support you at this time." We waited for her reaction to being given the news after repeated trips from the West Coast.

She paused at first, took a breath, and then she said simply, "I have a three-year-old son at home. And I do this for him. It pains me to leave him behind when I fly every few weeks to come here. And I have to ask my sister to care for him. It's not easy for her. She has two children of her own. And I miss my son so much. But next year, I'm going to ask my sister again. And I'm going to tell my son that I have to come back."

The staffer was a Hill lifer and widely known for being curmudgeonly. But he was biting his lip. And he reached out and said, "I'm sorry, Dora. I understand. I'm sure we can figure something out next year."

Had Dora been angry, the gruff senior staffer could have also reacted in anger. And if she just left without saying anything, he might have shrugged and thought, *Well, I did the best I could. Not my problem.* But because she reacted the way she did, she evoked deep sympathy. The staffer did figure it out: He worked hard the next year to fix the political problems that were blocking her proposal. It passed with minor changes. That's some good lobbying.

The Importance of Being You

I tell that story not only (I hope) so you won't get angry during an office visit, but to show the power a local volunteer leader has relative to a professional who represents an interest group.

I often hear from local activists that they feel they're in over their head. That they are overmatched by wealthy interest groups who can wrangle backroom deals and steer big campaign contributions. Even for those of us who can't steer big contributions, the professional can develop a lot of relationships and pick up a reservoir of experience on the law and procedure that can be valuable to the member of Congress. He has more information about what is going on with other committees, interest groups, or the other side of the Hill. Those are skills and powers that a local activist may not possess.

However, the professional is just that. He's paid; he's not doing this out of the goodness of his heart. He's not a constituent. He doesn't have the personal story of a Dora. She did this for her son, and that made the gruff old aide care about it and want to help her. That's the power of the local advocate.

So many beginners want to make sure they master every fact. And it is very helpful for the member if a local advocate becomes known as a trusted source of information. But you can always say, "I don't know the answer to that, but I can find out and get back to you." And that works

on several levels. You have found out what is important to the member. You can take time to make sure you have the information and that it is correct. And you are guaranteed a return visit or phone call.

The real power of the local activist as lobbyist flows from the personal bonds you make. If the member and staff get to know you, like you, trust you, and like the people around you, that member will want to help you. You may not get everything you are looking for. But they will find a way to give you all they can. And that gets the cat fed.

Resources

Legislation and Congress

Asbell, Bernard. *The Senate Nobody Knows.* Baltimore: The Johns Hopkins University Press, 1981. (Interesting in that it discusses passing the Clean Air Act legislation.) http://www.amazon.com/Senate-Nobody -Professor-Bernard-Asbell/dp/0801826209.

Redman, Eric. *The Dance of Legislation: An Insider's Account of the Workings of the United States Senate.* Seattle: University of Washington Press, 2001. (Predates the partisanship and stasis of recent congresses.) http://www.amazon.com/ The-Dance-Legislation-Insiders-Workings/ dp/0295980230.

Lobbying

Levine, Bertram J. *The Art of Lobbying: Building Trust and Selling Policy.* Thousand Oaks, Calif.: CQ Press, 2008. http://www.neebo.com/neebo/ art-of-lobbying-0872894622-9780872894624.

Libby, Patricia J. *The Lobbying Strategy Handbook: 10 Steps to Advancing Any Cause Effectively.* Thousand Oaks, Calif.: SAGE Publications, Inc., 2011. https://www.goodreads.com/book/ show/11322986-the-lobbying-strategy- handbook.

Negotiation

Ury, W., R. Fisher, and B. Patton. *Getting to Yes: Negotiating Agreement Without Giving In.* 2d ed. London: Penguin Books, 1991. http://www.amazon.com/ Getting-Yes-Negotiating-Agreement-Without/ dp/0140157352.

Wheeler, Michael. *The Art of Negotiation: How to Improvise Agreement in a Chaotic World.* New York: Simon & Schuster, 2013. (On how good negotiation can lead to improvisation and ideas that neither party considered prior to negotiation; may be good but I haven't read this book yet.) http:// www.amazon.com/Art-Negotiation-Improvise- Agreement-Chaotic/dp/1476757917/ref=tmm_ pap_swatch_0?_encoding=UTF8&sr=&qid=.

Wilderness Legislation and History

Roth, Dennis. *The Wilderness Movement and the National Forests.* Second ed. College Station, Texas: Intaglio Press, 1995. http://www.amazon.com/ The-Wilderness-Movement-National- Forests/dp/0944091059.

Winter sports athletes, corporate partners, and industry trade groups gathered in Washington, DC in 2013 to meet with members of Congress and urge them to support a strong climate policy. *Photo Courtesy of Protect Our Winters*

What We Learned About Lobbying

We at Protect Our Winters may not be lobbyists, but we do find ourselves in Washington, DC, quite often advocating for climate issues on behalf of the snow sports community. So given that we're not Beltway insiders or trained lobbyists, it can be hard to know whether or not we're truly effective on Capitol Hill. Like many in the nonprofit world, we're learning through common sense and plenty of practice.

Problem is, you have only one shot to be effective during those short conversations with politicians and influencers. That's why the segment at the Tools Conference by Tim Mahoney—that accelerated the learning curve—gave us some real insight from a lobbying vet about the best way to be direct and purpose-driven on Capitol Hill.

Protect Our Winters recently spent time in Washington, DC, supporting the EPA's proposed carbon standards rule, which will reduce carbon emissions from industrial power plants—the source of most of our carbon problem. Whenever I found myself in a conversation with a congressman, I kept thinking about the mantra Tim had said during his presentation: "Be respectful and keep things on track." That alone has been immensely helpful.

In fact, through constructive and candid conversations we've been able to build relationships with some pretty tough senators, many of whom told us they too were skiers and appreciated our work. That's a good start.

– Chris Steinkamp

157

Sunset on the wild California coast. King Range, California.
Bob Wick/Bureau of Land Management

California North Coast Wilderness

Ryan Henson

From 2001 to 2006, the California Wilderness Coalition and local volunteers tried to convince Congress to protect 275,000 acres (more than 429 square miles) of threatened federal public land on California's North Coast, despite a hostile political environment in Washington.

For decades, activists had fought to protect places in the area like the King Range National Conservation Area (part of California's famed "Lost Coast," so named because of its wild and undeveloped nature) from logging and other threats. Furthermore, we knew that if we could get Congress to protect the King Range and other special places as "wilderness" (the highest form of protection that exists for government land under federal law), these areas would be off-limits to development in perpetuity.

The first step involved in getting Congress to act was to win the support of North Coast Representative Mike Thompson, a moderate Democrat representing Napa and other nearby counties at the time. When we met with his staff in 2001, we asked them to work with us to protect fifteen proposed wilderness areas. We summarized the ecological and social importance of each area, and explained how they were threatened. We also presented the staff with 500 form letters and a petition with a thousand names in support of our proposals. The staffers said they would present the information to Representative Thompson and then get back to us.

They also offered us some advice: One heartfelt, personalized letter was worth dozens of form letters, and petitions were of very little value. They also pointed out that many environmentalists in the past who had sought Rep. Thompson's help were sloppy with the facts, unwilling to build support beyond the activist community and to meet with opponents and potential opponents, and always seemed to forget to say "thank you" before demanding more. If we wanted Rep. Thompson's help, we had better behave more wisely than that.

Two months later Rep. Thompson himself agreed to meet with us. We prepared for every conceivable question he might ask and recruited some local elected officials and business owners to join us since we knew it was more effective to have them be our messengers. At the end of our presentation, while Rep. Thompson seemed sympathetic, he was also noncommittal. He explained that he would consider being our champion only if we could build a very strong base of community support in his district, support that went far beyond "preaching to the choir," and resolve all of the reasonable concerns of affected stakeholders. He stressed that that was just some of what it would take to get a bill through a difficult Congress that was fairly hostile to wilderness.

To meet these challenges, we began an aggressive support-building effort in the community, focusing on recruiting a diverse assortment of supporters, ranging from clergy and business owners to tribes, hunters, ranchers, elected officials, and even loggers. We also met with every potentially affected stakeholder and possible opponent we could identify. We listened carefully and respectfully to their concerns and sometimes modified our wilderness proposals as a result. Even when we were unable to compromise, just listening to them and establishing a relationship blunted their opposition. As one conservative rancher said after we had coffee with him, "I thought you people would have horns on your head, but you actually seem pretty reasonable." Many of these stakeholders eventually became supporters. When we met again with Rep. Thompson and updated him on our efforts, he announced he would convene a town hall meeting to get public input on our proposals.

Wilderness supporters dominated the town hall meeting, and we were careful to have as many nontraditional allies as possible speak instead of environmentalists. We were also so well prepared that none of our opponents was able to offer any substantive arguments against our proposals. We had an elected official give Rep. Thompson more than 300 letters of support for our cause, no two of which were alike. After the meeting, he paid us the following compliment: "More pro-wilderness people were wearing cowboy hats than the anti-wilderness people." We were extremely proud of that.

Satisfied with our efforts to lay the groundwork for legislation, in 2002 Rep. Thompson introduced his bill, the Northern California Coastal Wild Heritage Wilderness Act (US Senator Barbara Boxer of California introduced a companion bill in the Senate). Many political difficulties and controversies arose both in Washington and at the local level as we advanced the measure through a Republican-controlled House of Representatives.

Our primary hurdle was to get the bill through the House Natural Resources Committee, chaired by Richard Pombo, a Republican and confirmed opponent of wilderness who had ominously changed the name of the committee

by removing the word "Natural" from its title. Chairman Pombo held our bill at bay for years as we continued to build support back home and use facts and credible spokespeople to overcome opposition to the legislation. For example, when opponents argued that wilderness protection would hamper firefighting, we recruited firefighters to dispute those claims. When people argued that we would somehow affect private property rights, we found private landowners who were willing to speak the truth. Even as we continued to build support, we were ready to counter any misinformation at a moment's notice.

The only wilderness bills Chairman Pombo eventually allowed through the Resources Committee were Republican-sponsored or at least bipartisan bills with influential Senate sponsors. Our bill was the one exception. Senator Boxer, later joined by her California colleague Senator Dianne Feinstein, were Democrats, but they were certainly influential and their work with Rep. Thompson resulted in our bill becoming the only Democrat-sponsored wilderness bill to make it through the Resources Committee and to pass both houses during Chairman Pombo's four-year tenure. This was due in no small part to our staff and volunteers demonstrating the competence, in-depth knowledge, strong work ethic, responsiveness, honesty, and political savvy that it took to win and maintain the confidence of our political champions.

The Northern California Coastal Wild Heritage Wilderness Act was signed into law on October 17, 2006. At the victory party, Rep. Thompson told us that he so enjoyed the experience that he would be willing to introduce more conservation bills in the future if we could run our campaigns in an equally effective fashion—a commitment he has kept. Today, when you visit a place like the King Range Wilderness, remember that a small band of determined citizens, including many local volunteers of very modest means with no previous political experience, won protection for the area by working as a coordinated team with their champions in Congress.

The mountains plunge straight into the ocean. King Range, California. *Melissa Farlow/National Geographic Creative*

Denis Hayes was fired as director of the federal Solar Energy Research Institute by President Reagan because he was too enthusiastic. A grant promised from the Ford Foundation was jointly vetoed by Robert McNamara and McGeorge Bundy because he was too radical. Then he took Earth Day to 160 nations and built the greenest office building in the world.

Denis Hayes

2003 KEYNOTE SPEAKER

Epiphany

I grew up in Camas, then a very small paper mill town on the Washington state bank of the Columbia River. My father ran the number 10 paper machine.

My family background was not uncommon back in those days. My father's father died when dad was twelve years old. Dad was the oldest man in the family, so he did what was expected. He quit school in the sixth grade and went to work, and he worked the rest of his life. Similarly, my mother didn't finish high school. She was a beautician.

Camas was surrounded by some of the most scenic land in the world. The Columbia River Gorge was an easy bicycle ride away. On a clear day, you could see Mount Hood, Mount St. Helens, and Mount Adams. Nearby forests were rich with wildlife and old-growth trees.

But Camas was far from a hotbed of environmentalism. The mill—the largest specialty paper mill in the world—chewed up every forest it could. My friends and I regularly fished on the Columbia River. Every now and then, we would come across a gigantic, stinky, scum-filled pool with thousands of dead fish. Until I moved away to college, I woke up every single morning with a sore throat from the sulfur dioxide and the hydrogen sulfide that laced the air. People were aware of the air pollution, of course. Camas was largely defined in the region by its smell. The sulfur compounds were mixing with rain to produce acids that ate away the paint jobs on automobiles. The mill owner, Crown Zellerbach, installed a shower at the mill's big parking lot. When workers drove their cars out at the end of the shift, they could spray off all the accumulated crap. Our cars kept their shiny finishes, but our lungs suffered.

The paper company made no attempt whatsoever to control any air or water pollution, and gave no thought to the sustainability of its logging operations. The mill workers took a manly pride in braving the noise (everyone was deaf by fifty) and the acrid odors ("the smell of prosperity"). My youth was spent astride these two worlds: the rich, healthy, lustrous splendor of the natural environment and the toxic, stinking industrial behemoth that provided virtually all the jobs in town and controlled the politics.

I did very well academically in high school. But no one in my family had been to college. I was far too parochial to think about college at all strategically, and I didn't have a guidance counselor to lay out the options. I'd been working thirty hours a week from seventh grade on and had a little bit of money saved, but my parents were in no position to supplement it. When my parish priest offered me a full scholarship—a free ride—to a small Catholic college, I didn't hesitate.

But I found it alien and awful and, frankly, just weird. I lasted less than a week.

I hitchhiked back to Camas. My options at that point were to attend Clark College, the local community college, or go to work in the mill. I went to Clark and worked nights at a Dairy Queen; that gave me a lot of time to read. And for the first time in my life I began to get an education that was more than the regurgitation of facts.

I was moved by *Silent Spring*, which was published that year, and read Rachel Carson's beautiful marine books, too.

As I learned more about the real world, the myths I'd grown up not questioning were shredded. But I hadn't acquired a coherent worldview to replace them. Not uncommon for an eighteen-year-old, I became deeply alienated and depressed. I was not a joy to hang out with. I was still living at my parents' house, but I had become a complete mystery to them. My father, who subscribed to the Joe McCarthy school of conservatism—the last presidential candidate for whom he cast a vote was George Wallace—worried aloud that I was becoming a commie.

In truth, I wasn't becoming an anything. During those years, I digested everything from Ayn Rand to Herbert Marcuse, from Henry David Thoreau to Frantz Fanon. I read some Freud and a lot by acolytes of B. F. Skinner. I absorbed it all, but none of it gave me the foundation I was looking for.

I was convinced that pretty much everything was going to hell, quickly, and I felt utterly helpless to do anything about it. Camas was quite some distance from any corridors of power.

So at the age of nineteen, I threw some clothes into a backpack and set out to find something that would give meaning to my life.

I was gone for three years.

I spent one summer being driven to my job at an elite Tokyo club in a chauffeured Rolls-Royce, followed by nine months of living on eighty cents a day. I once attempted to exchange black market currency with a gentleman in Ghana who turned out to be the American ambassador. A group of fundamentalist Christian Korean housewives, encountering this long-haired, long-bearded, ragged guy with Western features, became convinced that I was the Second Coming; I escaped out a back door and disappeared. My diet on the road was rice, peanut butter, and vitamin pills. I lost forty-five pounds and was once so sick I slept for three days straight.

PG. 162 Wandering deep into the Sossusvlei Namib Desert. *Jim Martinello*
ABOVE The effluent treatment canal comes right out of the Crown Zellerbach
Paper Mill, ca. 1973. Camas, Washington. *Alamy*

I needed, every now and then, to replenish my cash. I was a disc jockey and a swimming coach. I taught conversational English to bank executives, was a male model for a wide variety of Yamaha products, and rented surfboards in Hawai'i.

But most of the time I was devoted to a quest for answers to the big questions. I spent a lot of time in Japan, studying traditional Japanese values, radical new politics, Buddhism, and judo. I took the Trans-Siberian Railway across the Soviet Union at a time when that just wasn't done by young Americans, spending rubles obtained in Afghanistan at one-tenth the official exchange rate. I made good friends in Poland, Czechoslovakia, and Hungary who showed me the bleakest, most depressing realities of Communism up close and personal. I hitchhiked around places like Syria, Iraq, and the Sudan, where it would be suicidal to hitch-hike today. I visited Algeria to see what had happened to Frantz Fanon's "new man," baptized in the cleansing fires of revolution. I roamed around India, nearly drowning in the richness of its confusing stew of cultures that I couldn't absorb.

And, in the end, all this led to an epiphany.

It occurred in what is now the nation of Namibia. I was hitchhiking from Windhoek toward Cape Town. On a whim, I diverted about fifty miles out to the coastal town of Lüderitz. After wandering around a bit, I decided to head back to the main north-south highway. My driver turned north; I was going south. So I walked out into the desert a ways and unrolled my sleeping bag.

I was exhausted and hungry. I'd been extremely hot all day, and the cold desert night was closing in. I'd had occasional brief relationships along the way, but I had mostly been alone with my thoughts for a very long time. These were almost biblical conditions for having a vision, or at least its secular equivalent.

For some reason, I began thinking about an ecology institute I'd attended after my junior year in high school. Sponsored by the National Science Foundation, we mostly studied dragonflies. I'd never heard of ecology until I was approached about attending the institute—but it was in Ohio, a long way from Camas, and that was enough. That summer I'd read much of Eugene Odum's classic text, but it hadn't affected my life in any particular way. Ecology then was as devoid of political content as botany or molecular biology—it was just a branch of biology.

But that night a few years later, things came together in a different way in my mind.

I realized that people, of course, are animals. For most of the history of *Homo sapiens*, we were governed by the same principles of ecology as elk and tigers and dragonflies. The currency of life is solar energy—captured by plants through photosynthesis, stored in carbon-hydrogen bonds, and released through oxidative phosphorylation. That is literally the source of all work, all organization, all counter-entropy, in the world. And the formula for biological success was to use that energy just as efficiently as possible.

Humans had begun breaking a lot of little laws when we learned to unleash sunlight that had been bottled up millions of years earlier in coal, petroleum, and natural gas, and efficient energy use had ceased to be of interest. But now the big laws, nature's laws, were catching up to us. What, I wondered, would the world look like if industrial civilization had been designed in concert with fundamental principles of ecology?

There was no vocabulary to address such questions. I'd never heard of human ecology, and no one had yet uttered such terms as urban ecology, industrial ecology, ecological economics, or biomimicry. But without the aid of a relevant vocabulary, those were concepts I spent the night trying to get my arms around. They seemed to offer much more insight into health, sustainability, war, competition, the value of diversity, and even the pursuit of happiness than anything I'd read from Marx, Adam Smith, Montesquieu, Freud, or Jefferson.

That random evening in the middle of the Namib Desert turned out to be the great dividing line in my life. When I rolled out my sleeping bag that evening, I was still a confused, rudderless hitchhiker trying to fall asleep in the middle of nowhere. When I arose the next morning, I had begun to construct a road map for how I would live the rest of my life.

A fawn pauses in a meadow on the edge of the Columbia River Gorge, Oregon. *Corey Arnold*

CHAPTER 09

Working with Businesses

John Sterling

Most of what I know about working with businesses I learned by watching nonprofits make mistakes in their efforts to engage companies in conservation efforts. One day, while serving as director of environmental programs at Patagonia, Inc., I received a phone call from the head of one of the conservation groups we funded. His organization was working to protect old-growth forests in Canada by getting companies to promise not to use any wood products made from Canadian old-growth. Our conversation went something like this:

Q   Hi, John. I wanted to let you know that we are going to run a full-page ad in the *New York Times* that identifies companies that have pledged not to use products that contain Canadian old-growth. The ad will also call out companies that choose not to make that pledge. Does Patagonia want to be on the good list?

A   Well, of course we do, but I need to make sure we can live up to that promise. (For a company with offices and retail stores in the United States, Japan, and Europe, it's harder than you might think to guarantee that not a single sheet of paper containing old-growth pulp might make it into a supply cabinet.)

Q   OK, but let me know ASAP, because we go to print in one week.

A   That's not much time. What other companies are you contacting?

At this point, he rattled off a list of more than twenty companies, most of which would likely make a "no old-growth pledge" if given enough time to work with their supply chains to ensure they could keep the promise.

Fortunately for me, Patagonia had already removed all old-growth from our supply chain, so we were able to put our name on the "good list." The ad went to press, and I later learned that many of the other companies scrambled to promise to go old-growth-free because they did not want to appear in the *Times* ad as a company that wouldn't make that pledge. These companies felt bullied by the organization, but managed to get their names on the right list.

After the ad ran, a trade association for the Canadian wood products industry launched a boycott of the companies that promised not to use old-growth products. Each of the companies on the good list now had to deal with angry Canadians claiming that their pledge was killing jobs in Canada. When these companies asked the conservation

PG.168   John Sterling, executive director of The Conservation Alliance, discusses the nuances of working with businesses at the 2015 Tools Conference. Fallen Leaf Lake, California. *Amy Kumler*   PG.169   An ancient juniper holds court in the Oregon Badlands Wilderness, which was protected by the Oregon Badlands Wilderness Act passed in 2008 thanks in part to a successful partnership between the Oregon Natural Desert Association and local business leaders. *Greg Burke* group for a plan to respond to the boycott, the group basically said, "You're on your own." In the end, the conservationist got what he wanted: a high-profile ad with lots of corporate logos promising not to use old-growth products. But, he also left a trail of frustration among my colleagues at those other companies, none of whom would trust a conservationist again for many years.

This is a cautionary tale about working with businesses. Companies can be powerful partners in conservation, but you need to bring the same respect to your relationship with them that you would to any other ally.

Why Work with Businesses?

Businesses determine nearly everything about our lives: the food we eat, the news we receive, the music we hear. Given the enormous role businesses play in all of our lives, it's astonishing how few companies support environmental work. Businesses contribute only 4.6 percent of all financial support to nonprofit groups, less than one-third that of foundations (which contribute 13 percent). And even fewer businesses get directly involved in any form of advocacy, even though their advocacy can have an outsized influence on decision makers.

Part of the problem is that most environmental groups fail to *ask* businesses for either financial or advocacy support. Groups are accustomed to writing foundation grant proposals, major donor letters, and year-end appeals to individuals, but few groups have developed a consistent program for seeking financial and advocacy support from businesses. They should, and here's why:

Businesses Have Credibility on Economic Issues

Since the global economic catastrophe of 2008, decision makers view every issue through the lens of the economy. Conservation groups can present solid arguments for the economic benefits of protecting wildlands and rivers, but business leaders are the most effective messengers of those arguments. At the nadir of the Great Recession in 2009, the US Senate was debating a bill that eventually protected three million acres of federal land and a thousand river miles. Two senators spoke from the floor about how important outdoor recreation is to businesses in their states, and how passing this legislation was an investment in our economic future.

Businesses Have Visibility

Largely through their efforts to sell their products (via tools such as ads, catalogs, websites), businesses are familiar to the communities they serve. A successful business builds a loyal customer base that believes in that business's products, and would be inclined to pay attention to a cause that company supports. When I was at Patagonia, customers regularly contacted our Environmental Programs department to ask our advice on specific issues.

Businesses Employ People

Behind the desks are people who are likely to support environmental efforts. Working with a business gives a nonprofit access to a new group of potential supporters.

(Some) Businesses Have Money

Some businesses are a potential source of financial support.

The Nature of Business

Businesses are fundamentally different from environmental groups. One of the benefits of working for an environmental organization is that you and your colleagues go to work each day with the purpose of "saving the planet" or at least some small part of it. The purpose of a business is to sell a product or service, and to make money. Even the most progressive, socially conscious business must tend to the bottom line. It's important to remember this when entering into a relationship with a business. With few exceptions, businesses need to know "What's in it for me?" when dedicating resources to something that does not generate revenue for the business.

Increasingly, however, businesses are aware that supporting good works pays off both in public relations and in customer and employee loyalty. So, in general, businesses and their leaders want to do the right thing, but it's easier for them to do so if there is a direct or indirect value. In my current position as executive director of The Conservation Alliance, I lead a coalition of nearly 200 businesses that pool annual membership dues to fund conservation work in North America. Every time we talk to a company about joining The Conservation Alliance, we discuss how that brand can leverage their membership to build a deeper and stronger relationship with their customers.

What Your Group Can Get from Businesses

Every business is different, and some are likely to offer more support than others. Below are some types of support you should consider requesting from businesses.

Spokespeople

Business leaders can make great spokespeople for your issues. Decision makers are used to hearing from advocacy groups about how desperately a certain place needs to be protected. But when a business leader makes the same plea, it often carries more weight. I regularly lead groups of business leaders to Washington, DC, to talk to members of Congress about protecting wilderness and wild rivers. The first time I organized one of these trips, we met with a member of Congress who listened to our group of business representatives, and said, "I've never heard anyone say that conservation is good for business." He then went on to co-sponsor the wilderness bill we were advocating.

Access to Decision Makers

Business leaders often have strong relationships with elected officials. Building a connection to businesses can give you greater access to these decision makers, and greater credibility when you meet with them. Lean on your business supporters to get access to decision makers,

and include them in your meetings with elected officials. Everyone in politics wants to help a job creator.

Board Members and Volunteers

Environmental groups can learn a lot from business leaders about running an organization. From a business, you can get help with marketing, finance, and sales as well as board members.

Cash

Whether through a formal program or on an informal basis, many businesses give money directly to environmental groups. Some have funding programs that operate according to specific guidelines. Always know those guidelines before asking for anything from such a business, and follow the guidelines when making a request. Companies that do not have funding programs may also be willing to contribute, but will likely require more of your time and more persuasion.

Product Donations

Every company sells a product, whether it's a shirt, a guided trip through the Grand Canyon, or auditing services. In many cases, products are the easiest form of support a company can offer, and most companies are willing to do so. Product donations also serve as free marketing for the business. Using company products as membership incentives or auction items is good grassroots marketing for any brand.

Non-Product, In-Kind Support

Companies can offer an array of non-cash services that include donating meeting space, allowing employees to participate in environmental group activities during work hours, or donating graphic design services. In-kind donations are often a great way to introduce a business to your organization's work, and often lead to increased support on other levels.

Fees for Services

Some environmental groups can offer services to businesses, and be compensated for this. One example is for a group to offer a "team-building" opportunity to a business through which the company pays the group to take its employees on a guided trip to the area that the group seeks to protect. The employees spend a weekend together in the outdoors, and end up working more effectively together when they return to the office. In the process, those company employees learn about the group, and are more likely to become individual supporters.

Marketing and Branding Expertise

Most profitable companies are skilled at communicating with the public. They call it *marketing* for products, and *branding* for the company as a whole. Environmental groups can learn marketing and branding from companies, and adapt business communication skills to environmental work.

What You Can Offer Businesses

Believe it or not, your small non-profit can be of great benefit to businesses. Here are some examples of why.

Market Advantages

Increasingly, many businesses compete in saturated markets and are looking for ways to differentiate themselves from their competition. Supporting environmental work adds value to a company's products as more and more customers are scrutinizing a company's ethics when deciding which brand to buy.

Building Company Culture

Most businesses are interested in building a distinct culture that reflects the company's values and helps attract and retain good employees. A commitment to conservation and the environment can be a key pillar for a company's culture, and partnerships with conservation organizations can help build that foundation.

Employee Loyalty

Companies are constantly looking for ways to boost employee morale. By actively supporting environmental groups, a company gives its employees a feeling that they are part of something bigger than the company's products. I have given countless presentations about The Conservation Alliance to employees at our member companies. At nearly every talk I give, I hear from employees that they feel better about their employer because of the company's participation in the Alliance.

Opportunity to Be Part of Something They Can't Do Themselves

Most businesses focus solely on their products and don't have enough time to engage deeply in conservation. Environmental groups give companies an easy way to participate in protection efforts without having to initiate or organize them.

A Chance to Simply Do the Right Thing

Though supporting conservation provides market advantages, some companies sincerely want to do the right thing with the purest intentions. Environmental groups give them that opportunity.

Getting Started

For most groups, simply starting a relationship with a business is the greatest challenge. Overcoming that challenge requires that a group answer two questions: (1) What companies should you approach? and (2) What element of your work should you ask the company to support?

What Companies Should I Approach?

Determining which businesses to approach is largely common sense, but highly variable. Groups should consider working with companies:

- at which the group has a personal contact
- that have a vested interest in the group's efforts
- that have expressed interest in the group's issue
- that may be able to influence key decision makers
- whose products have a connection to the group's issue
- that have a history of involvement in community and/or environmental issues.

It makes sense to start with sympathetic companies, but don't rule out the others. Give companies an opportunity to participate in your work at whatever level is comfortable for them. From companies that meet any or all of the above criteria, groups might expect a greater degree of participation than from less engaged businesses. For starters, ask the "second tier" businesses to sign a statement in support of your work, then keep them informed. Over time, work to grow their participation until they become one of your key business partners.

What Element of My Group's Work Should I Ask Them to Support?

In most cases, companies want to be involved in specific campaigns, and in particular, campaigns that are easily defined and have a reasonable chance of success in one to three years. Consistent with their entrepreneurial nature, companies need to know what to expect as a return on investment in a group's work. At The Conservation Alliance, we keep track of every acre of land and mile of river our grantees protect. At the end of the year, we give our member companies a tally of what we accomplished that year: their Return On Investment (ROI). The best campaigns for businesses are those that, if successful, allow the company to point to a river or a piece of habitat and say, "Our support helped protect that place."

Not all business/environmental group relationships are project specific. In some cases, companies may want to partner with a group solely to benefit from association with the organization. This is most common in "co-branding" efforts when a company engages in a partnership with a group to gain access to that group's constituency for marketing purposes. Many grassroots environmental groups are too small and their constituency too local to participate in this kind of partnership. But, co-branding represents one situation in which an environmental group might try to start a relationship based on the organization's positive profile in a community rather than a specific campaign.

Above all, start your business outreach with a coherent strategy. Think about what you want from business relationships, and what resources you're willing to spend to secure those relationships. How much staff time and budget are you willing to commit to a business partnership? Nurture the relationships by treating businesses

the way you would any trusted partner. Meet with the owner, get to know the employees, and keep the businesses engaged. And if your work succeeds, include the businesses in the celebration.

Tips for Securing and Maintaining a Successful Relationship with a Business

Once a group identifies likely business partners and determines which component of the group's work might interest the companies, the following tips may help to bring those relationships to fruition.

Think Relationship

Most businesses like to engage in long-term relationships, and their commitment will grow as the relationship evolves. As with any relationship, don't overwhelm the business right away. Give them time to ease into your work. It may take two to three years for the relationship to flourish. Persist but don't annoy.

Start Small, Then Build

At first, don't ask for much from the business. Request a meeting, learn more about the company, and tell them about your work. Then ask for something small: a product donation, or the opportunity to give a slide presentation to employees. Gradually work up to larger requests. People and businesses crave consistency. If they've said yes to you once, it's difficult to say no farther down the road.

Get Employees Involved

It's a lot easier for a business leader to say no to you than it is to say no to one of his or her work colleagues. Most employers want to build a company culture that keeps their team motivated. Culture is usually based on shared values, and care for the environment can be one of those values. If your work appeals to employees, and you give them meaningful and fun ways to be involved in your efforts, the boss will likely appreciate your efforts. If you can get company employees' buy-in to your issues, then they become internal lobbyists on your behalf. Make a slide presentation, plan a work day, host an event that engages employees. Once you have the staff members hooked, keep in touch with them via email or social media. If you successfully integrate employees in a way that builds company morale, company management will appreciate your efforts and be more likely to continue to support those efforts, and your organization. Also, many companies match employee contributions to nonprofit groups. Learn all you can about these employer-matching programs, and remind employees of this easy way to support your organization.

Make Sure the Business Has a Good Initial Experience

Give a lot of thought to the first thing you ask a business to do on your behalf. Make sure they know about any possible downsides to supporting your work. If you want them to support a piece of wilderness legislation, let them know that the local ATV club might disagree with their position. If the effort goes smoothly, make sure they get the credit they deserve. Thank them, and if possible, have others thank them.

Talk to the Right Person

Many companies have an environmental or community relations person. Some merely have an employee who gravitates to environmental advocacy. Regardless, find the right person, and initiate your conversation with him or her.

Learn All You Can About the Business

Before meeting with a business representative, become familiar with the company. Study its website and catalogs; anything you can find. Know the company's history and heritage, look for common ground, and be aware of potential conflicts with your work. Remember, it's a relationship.

Don't Leave a Business "Out to Dry"

If a company sticks its neck out on your behalf, support them. This sounds obvious, but some environmental groups take what they can get from companies, then abandon them. The best environmental group/business relationships are those in which both parties stand to benefit, and each treats the other with respect.

Think Like a Marketer

Without compromising the integrity of your advocacy efforts, think about how the business can benefit in the market by working with your group. Assume every business leader wants to know how the company benefits from the partnership. Similarly, be clear and focused when presenting your work to a company. What one message do you want the company to understand about your work? You'll have the opportunity to tell them more over time, but stay focused at first. Rather than talking about your organization's history, and all your programs, tell them how their involvement will help accomplish one specific thing.

Consider Your Competition

Unlike many foundations, which have specific areas of interest, businesses receive requests from a wide range of causes: homeless shelters, local arts programs, youth programs, charity golf tournaments. When presenting your program to a business, be aware that you need to be not only the most compelling environmental cause, but the most compelling cause period.

Tell Them Why It Matters to *Them*

Why does your effort to protect a wild area or stretch of river matter to the company? Some connections are obvious: your group is working to protect a fly-fishing stream, and you are asking a fishing gear manufacturer for support. Others are not so clear. Few companies have a direct product connection to climate change, but the issue affects everyone. Regardless, make whatever connection you can to the company's self-interest, no matter how tenuous. I've lately noticed many clean water organizations working with micro-brewers, making the case that good beer requires good water.

Leverage Business Support

In certain cases, peer pressure works well. It may be effective for you to seek support from several companies in the same industry. First target the leaders, the companies with which others want to be associated. Then go to the others with the pitch that "X, Y, and Z companies are supporting us, and we plan to publicly acknowledge that support. Would you like to join them?" Few companies want to be left out of a winning proposition. In these situations, however, be careful not to appear manipulative.

Don't Be Surprised When a Company's Priorities Change

Personnel changes, sales fluctuations, and ownership transitions can all abruptly alter your relationship with a company. One day your primary advocate at a company leaves, or their donations budget gets slashed because sales have dropped. Don't be surprised or deterred—and don't whine. Find out whom to contact next, and ask politely how to proceed.

Always Thank Them Publicly

Companies love the kudos they receive from environmental groups. It's like free advertising, but it's much more meaningful and credible. If possible, acknowledge the support of a business when a company representative (the higher ranking, the better) is surrounded by your members or other supporters: at an annual fundraising event, retreat, or other special event.

Support the Companies that Support You!

If a company supports your work, buy their products (if indeed you need the products they make). Don't assume that an environmentally conscious business will always be around. In many cases, these companies put themselves at risk by taking public stands on controversial issues. One of the best ways to support these businesses is to buy their products. There are too few environmentally conscious companies out there, and each environmental group's work will be easier if these companies thrive and other companies adopt their practices.

Conclusion

Environmental groups and businesses both stand to gain from working together. But in many cases, and for both parties, these relationships travel unmapped roads with unfamiliar companions. Done right, though, environmental groups can build strong allies in companies whose voices carry weight in public debates increasingly—and unfortunately—dominated by corporate interests. It takes time and savvy to build these relationships. In the process, environmental groups may not only gain key supporters, but also slowly and incrementally transform the nature of business.

Resources

Barcott, Bruce. "As a Matter of Fact, Money Does Grow on Trees." *Outside Magazine.* March 1, 2005. http://www.outsideonline.com/outdoor-adventure/As-a-Matter-of-Fact-Money-Does-Grow-on-Trees.html.

Headwaters Economics. (This organization has conducted countless studies showing that public lands are far more valuable as protected areas than as one-time assets for resource extraction.) http://headwaterseconomics.org/.

Outdoor Industry Association. "Outdoor Recreation Economy." (The Outdoor Industry Association published a study that attempts to quantify the economic contribution that outdoor recreation makes to the overall economy. This data can be helpful in making the case that conservation is good for business. And these talking points are great coming out of the mouths of business leaders.) http://outdoorindustry.org/advocacy/recreation/economy.html.

Schwartz, Tony, and Christine Porathmay. "Why You Hate Work." *New York Times Sunday Review.* May 30, 2014. http://www.nytimes.com/2014/06/01/opinion/sunday/why-you-hate-work.html.

Alaska Coalition

The Arctic Refuge has consistently faced attempts to turn "America's Last Great Wilderness" into an industrial oil field. Back in 2005, the coalition faced a daunting challenge. Leaders in both houses of the Republican-controlled Congress were attempting to tuck an Arctic Refuge drilling provision into the federal budget bill. Rather than try to sway all 535 members of Congress about the folly of this proposal, the Alaska Coalition's strategy targeted a handful of moderate House Republicans. They organized a rally in front of the Capitol with 1,500 Arctic advocates wearing blue "Save the Arctic Refuge" shirts. The attendees were from the districts of the targeted members of Congress and represented a good cross-section of influential voters in these districts. Following the rally, each constituent attended meetings with their representatives.

Their lobbying was a turning point in the campaign. The day after the campaign successfully beat back the drilling effort, NBC News reported:

"For a quarter-century, environmentalists have succeeded in blocking efforts to drill for oil in what they consider a pristine, cherished patch of tundra .... But with sky-high fuel prices and a wider Republican majority in Congress, their long fight to keep oil companies out of the refuge looked to be in trouble. Then they got some help from an unexpected place: House Republicans.

"Last week, the Senate voted 51-48 to endorse a requirement for the Interior Department to begin lease sales .... The House seemed on the same path.

"Environmentalists already had launched an intense lobbying campaign both in the congressional districts of moderate Republicans and on Capitol Hill. Although the House had passed [Arctic Refuge drilling legislation] five times, the environmentalists believed their best chance to block it this time was not in the Senate, but in the House where GOP moderates were viewed as ready to buck their leaders.

"Rep. Dave Reichert (R-WA) was among two dozen GOP moderates who on Thursday displayed pictures of scores of his constituents who had come to Washington to urge him not to approve [Arctic Refuge] drilling. 'You have to listen to the people you represent,' he said."

– Brian O'Donnell

Caribou crossing a river near their calving grounds in the Arctic National Wildlife Refuge, Alaska. *Karsten Heuer*

180

Oregon Badlands

Brent Fenty

The fight to protect the Oregon Badlands, a 30,000-acre area east of Bend, Oregon, was a classic environmental battle pitting wilderness advocates against off-road vehicle enthusiasts. After years of debate, the fight had come to a draw despite the obvious merits of the area—juniper trees nearly two thousand years old, geologic formations found nowhere else in the world, and brilliant spring wildflower blooms. Despite these virtues, the Badlands remained unprotected and lacked a congressional champion.

With these facts in mind, the Bend-based Oregon Natural Desert Association (ONDA), which had led protection efforts for a couple of decades, turned the focus of the campaign to Central Oregon's business community. Local businesses had great relationships with Oregon's congressional delegation and credibility in the region during a time when the national economy was slumping. And like Badlands advocates, many of the business leaders had moved to or stayed in Central Oregon because of the natural environment.

Campaign transitions don't come easy. They require admission that a past approach is not a winning strategy. Working with businesses can be particularly challenging for environmental advocates since some activists feel that to engage with businesses, even when there is an agreed-upon goal, is "selling out." This simply doesn't make sense. Most of us work somewhere; a failure to engage with businesses is ignoring a major force in our daily lives. And although some businesses impact the natural environment, many are run by people who cherish the community they live in; they want to keep it a good place to live, or make it an even better place to live. They are often thoughtful and articulate and therefore have much to offer to a campaign.

The campaign conversion for the Badlands started with the convening of a group of business leaders to complete a study about the subject of possible partnership that was conducted by Headwaters Economics. Many of these leaders ultimately became the face of the Badlands protection efforts. The study helped them better understand how Badlands wilderness was valuable to the local economy and allowed them to speak out in ways they had not done previously. As Teague Hatfield, owner of the local shoe store FootZone, said in a letter of support, "People are drawn here for many reasons …. Open space and recreation are a part of that lifestyle for many. If we do not take the opportunities available to us now, we will erode the character that makes this a wonderful place to live, work, and play."

However, this group of leaders could not be successful on their own. They needed support. We reached out to other local business owners knowing that asking them to advocate for wilderness might be challenging. A few things were key to our success. First, we identified businesses based on their standing in the community, rated them based on their likelihood to support wilderness in the Badlands, and started with businesses we knew were already "with us." Our hope was that developing a base of business supporters would make other businesses more likely to take the leap of faith. Second, we developed clear and concise messages about why the Oregon

Badlands should be wilderness, we were up-front about the level of opposition, and we provided simple talking points with possible responses. Third, we made clear that our purpose was not to solicit a donation. The single greatest asset the business owners could offer was their support (of course, donations were not refused!). Lastly, we emphasized how we planned to recognize them in the future via advertising and letters of support. Simply put, no surprises.

What was surprising is the immense support that such an approach generated within the region. Over 200 businesses ultimately signed on in support of the Oregon Badlands Wilderness campaign, including most of Central Oregon's top ten employers. Our presentations moved from the tried and true churches and environmental organizations to chambers of commerce, visitors associations, and city clubs. What was also surprising was the initiative and innovation that businesses brought to their sponsorship. They developed store displays and created craft beers featuring the Badlands and, in one instance, a local café printed "We Support Badlands Wilderness" on their menu when they found out the chief of staff for Oregon's senior senator would be dining there.

This level of effort ultimately won over support from Oregon's entire congressional delegation—Republicans and Democrats alike. As Gary Fish, founder of Oregon craft beer maker Deschutes Brewery, put it, "When it seems that partisanship mars nearly everything that Congress does these days, it was heartening to learn …that our senators … both have the public interest at heart and will work together toward passage of the Oregon Badlands Wilderness Act …. The Badlands is truly a unique and amazing wild treasure, and if our lawmakers can get this bill to the president's desk quickly, our children and theirs will be the real winners."

Most important, business support was garnered without diminishing the proposed size or type of protection for this area. On March 30, 2009, the Oregon Badlands Wilderness was permanently protected for future generations. An amazing area got the protection it deserves, and the relationships we developed established the groundwork for continued conservation efforts throughout the region.

Oregon Badlands Wilderness, Oregon. *Greg Burke*

Dr. Jane Goodall

2008 KEYNOTE SPEAKER

Sowing Seeds of Hope

PG.184 Teaching children how to plant trees at the Jane Goodall Institute Tchimpounga Chimpanzee Rehabilitation Center, Republic of Congo. *Fernando Turmo/Jane Goodall Institute* ABOVE A rare shot of Dr. Jane Goodall at rest. Lake Tanganyika, Tanzania. *Michael Christopher Brown/Magnum Photos*

Since 1986 I have traveled about 300 days a year around the globe and seen firsthand the damage we have caused. I know just how bad it is and, pretty well, how it got that way. And I am not surprised that I meet so many individuals who seem to have little hope for the future, believing that there is nothing that can be done to turn things around, and who have become apathetic, depressed, or angry. Of course, they may be right. It may be true, as some scientists maintain, that it is too late to reverse the progression of shrinking fresh water supplies, pollution, climate change, species extinctions, and population growth. We may well be doomed to slide into total ecosystem collapse and the end of life on Earth.

Yet I truly believe there is a window of time in which we can at least slow down these horrors. And this is what gives me the energy to carry on. For one thing, I continually meet or hear of amazing people doing amazing work in protecting or restoring environments, saving species from the brink of extinction, alleviating poverty, inventing new technologies that will enable us to live in greater harmony with nature and each other. I learn of companies that have realized that the bottom line is not the only thing that matters; they are taking social responsibility and environmental sustainability seriously. In other words, I know what is going on outside the reporting of the mainstream media that operates on the (unfortunately true) belief that "bad news sells."

We need good news, too.

The resilience of nature *is* good news. By 1990 all the trees around the tiny Gombe National Park had been cut down by villagers desperate to grow food or make money from charcoal. Realizing that we could only hope to save the chimpanzees if we could alleviate the desperate poverty of the people, we initiated a holistic program, TACARE, and this was so successful that eventually the people agreed to set aside village land to form a buffer around the park. Fifteen years later the chimpanzees had three times more forest, thanks to the regenerative power of the land.

Perhaps my greatest reason for hope is our youth. When I left Gombe and began traveling around the world trying to raise awareness, I met so many young people who seemed apathetic, depressed, or angry. I asked them what was wrong and they all said more or less the same: "You (older generations) have compromised our future and there is nothing we can do about it." We have indeed compromised their future; every time I see a child and think how we have harmed the planet since I was their age, I feel ashamed of our species. But I refused to accept that there was nothing they could do about it. And so in 1991 I started Jane Goodall's Roots & Shoots program with twelve high school students in Dar es Salaam, Tanzania. Its main message: "Every one of us matters and has a role to play. Every one of us makes an impact on the world around us—every day. And we can choose what sort of impact we can make."

Children are quick to realize that the cumulative effect of millions, even billions, of people making ethical choices as to how they live each day can lead to major change. We encourage people to think about the consequences of what they buy, wear, and eat. Where was it made? Did it involve child slave labor? Cruelty to animals? Harm to the environment? Indeed, organic food, fair trade clothing, and so on may cost a bit more—but then one buys only what one needs, wastes less, values the purchase more. Eventually this will force more and more businesses to adopt ethical practices.

When young people understand the problems, when we listen to their voices and empower them to take action, they are a force to be reckoned with. And now, at the start of 2015, we have Roots & Shoots in 139 countries with members of all ages from preschool through university, and about 100,000 groups. Each of these groups tackles three projects of their choice—one to help people, one to help animals, and one to help the environment. And there is a theme of learning to live in peace and harmony with each other and with Mother Nature and to respect other forms of life and ways of thinking that differ from our own. My vision is for a critical mass of young people who understand that while we need money to live, we should not live for money.

It was during the Climate March in New York in September 2014 that I found another reason for hope. Social media. As I walked, I could see all around, people with their cell phones and iPads and other devices. They were using Facebook and Twitter to urge their friends to come and join in. Those organizing the march had expected perhaps 100,000. In fact there were, in the end, almost 400,000. They just kept coming. And the march was not only in New York—there were 2,646 separate events in 162 countries, attended by more than 100 heads of state. It was the largest global march in history. The same year the March for Elephants and Rhinos took place in more than 120 locations. Hundreds of thousands of people marched—and the numbers swelled as the different events were posted in cities around the world. Without social media, these and other events would have been very different.

For years I have been saying that every individual matters. Now this is truer than ever—social media helps make our voices count. In this new way we can involve thousands—millions—of people. This is how we can stand up to the giant multinationals that are harming our planet to satisfy their lust for immediate profit, never thinking of those who will inherit the world that they are selfishly degrading and destroying.

It is bizarre, is it not, that the most intellectual creature to have walked the planet is destroying its only home? We seem to have lost wisdom. When we make a major decision we tend to ask, "How will this benefit me now? Or the next shareholders meeting? Or my next political campaign?" when we should be asking how the decision will affect future generations. It seems to me that only when head and heart work in harmony can human beings attain their true potential. And that potential is huge. My job is to give people hope—for without hope, we do nothing.

We must not give up. Too much is at stake for our children for future generations.

Dr. Jane Goodall and Roots & Shoots members plant trees at
the Singapore American School, Singapore. *Chris Dickinson*

(10)

Utilizing the Economics of Conservation

Ben Alexander

In the mid-1970s when my family moved to Bozeman, Montana, we found a university town surrounded by productive agricultural lands. These in turn were encircled by public lands and forested mountains that produced timber for area mills. Bozeman had a small cinder-block airport, and Interstate 90 passed by east to west. We found a place that was friendly but a little wary of newcomers, and thought of itself as an agricultural hub and land-grant university town.

After graduating from Bozeman High School, I fled the constraints of a small town for the larger world. My parents stayed, and I returned over the years to visit. As I did, I fell in love again with the landscape of southwest Montana and noticed the influx of people who did not seem to be just visiting as tourists en route to Yellowstone National Park but were actually living here. In the mid-1990s, I decided to make Bozeman my home again.

I had recently completed graduate school and secretly thought that moving back to Montana might be career suicide. I should not have worried. Bozeman at the time was part of a broader demographic and economic shift in the West that saw a natural resource economy transformed into a thriving human resource economy. As I realized the power of place to attract (and retain) talent, I began to understand that the environment and the quality of the environment now are economic, competitive advantages for today's more dynamic and productive businesses, and for a growing number of communities across the West.

Change Is Difficult

In 2006, along with several colleagues, I co-founded Headwaters Economics, a think tank focused on improving community development and land management in the West. We set out to help community leaders and others to better understand the new competitive advantage of the West, and to assist them as they considered public policies and priorities that would allow them to succeed in an expanding economy that rewards skills and quality.

There was one problem. Even though the West of our childhoods no longer exists, by and large as a society we pretend it does. While inevitable, change is threatening; it creates uncertainty—and real winners and losers. One response to change is to stick to what we know. Many former timber towns, for example, struggle to envision a new future. Failing this, they fall back on a hope that the past's abundance and rewards will return.

The landscape and architecture of the West tempt us to misrecognize change as well. We look out on vast expanses of rangeland and assume ranching is the dominant economic activity; or we see retail shops with brick façades on Main Street catering to visitors and assume tourism is the main economic driver.

At the same time, much of the conservation community remains in the past, focusing narrowly on the perils of natural resource industries and seeing businesses of any kind as a threat.

Change in the West

While it can sometimes be confusing as to whether we are in the Old West or the New West, or the "New Old West" to quote one of my favorite Nevada billboards, the economy has moved on.

The West referred to here consists of the eleven western states in the continental United States, a stretch of land from Montana south to New Mexico and out to the West Coast. These states are home to the bulk of our nation's federal public lands, including multiple-use lands supporting commodity extraction and a range of protected areas such as wilderness and national parks.

During the last four decades, the western economy has outperformed the rest of the US economy in key measures of growth: employment (fig.1), population, and personal income. During this time, for example, the region created jobs at twice the rate of the rest of the United States.[1]

The reason is that the West has more successfully diversified its economy to include fast-growing and higher-paying services industry jobs—high-tech, finance, and health care—and attracted talent and entrepreneurs who create tomorrow's companies. This is happening in both large cities and small towns across the region.

In effect, the economy of the West has shifted from a largely natural resource–based economy to a knowledge-based economy (fig.2). This development mirrors changes in the United States economy as a whole, which is no longer a competitive low-cost producer of basic goods. Today, the region and the nation's competitiveness centers on the ability to cultivate and attract innovative companies and an educated workforce that produce a more complex mix of higher-value goods and services.

The magnitude of this economic shift has left more than a few people confused. During the last four decades, nearly all net new jobs in the West—more than 19 million new jobs—were created in services industries. Services include low-wage industries such as hotels and food service as well as high-wage industries such as architecture, engineering, and computer programming. By comparison, almost no net new jobs were created in more traditional industries, such as mining, forestry, and agriculture.[2]

These trends have shifted the industry balance in seismic ways. The most recent data indicate that services now account for 72 percent of all jobs in the West, while the rest of the private sector, including traditional natural resource industries, make up about 14 percent of all jobs in the region. Government employment accounts for the remaining jobs.[3]

Both larger cities and more rural parts of the West are experiencing these shifts. Small communities in the region have historically played second fiddle to larger towns and cities, providing raw materials to be processed and sold elsewhere. This extractive relationship still exists, but in fewer places as more towns and small cities connect to the burgeoning services economy. Today, nearly half of all western counties

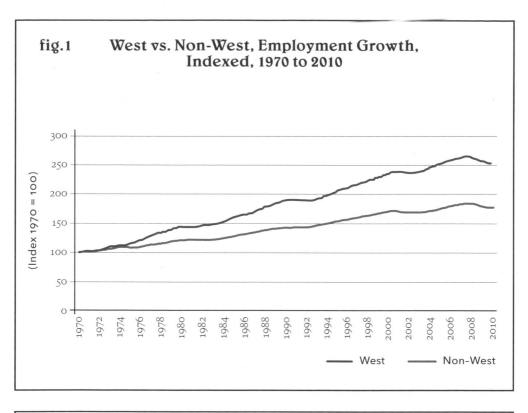

fig.1 West vs. Non-West, Employment Growth, Indexed, 1970 to 2010

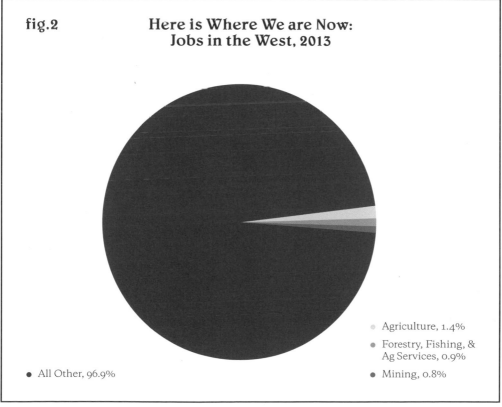

fig.2 Here is Where We are Now: Jobs in the West, 2013

- Agriculture, 1.4%
- Forestry, Fishing, & Ag Services, 0.9%
- All Other, 96.9%
- Mining, 0.8%

GO WEST, ENTREPRENEUR

The American West has spent the past four decades outpacing the rest of the U.S. in several important economic measures. Embracing the new economy, which is shifting toward service industries, not to mention the unparalleled quality of life offered by the region's bounty of protected public lands, make the West the best place for America's most innovative people and companies.

Changing and growing economy

The rise of the West can be attributed in part to the region's success in developing and attracting a diverse services economy.

CHANGE IN EMPLOYMENT IN THE WEST BY INDUSTRY, 2001 TO 2010

Industry	Change
Health care and social assistance	786,810
Real estate and rental and leasing	500,815
Finance and insurance	391,851
Government and government enterprises	372,458
Professional and technical services	359,646
Educational services	241,049
Accommodation and food services	234,298
Arts, entertainment, and recreation	143,751
Other services, except public administration	141,910
Administrative and waste services	105,925
Mining, oil and gas	76,135
Transportation and warehousing	20,234
Forestry, fishing, related activities, and other	16,726
Utilities	7,428
Wholesale trade	-2,107
Wood products manufacturing	-7,890
Retail trade	-14,161
Management of companies and enterprises	-45,889
Farm employment	-51,825
Information	-184,679
Construction	-367,436
Manufacturing	-766,738

-1,000,000 -600,000 -200,000 200,000 600,000 1,000,000

HIGH-WAGE SERVICES, AVERAGE EARNINGS PER JOB, 2010

Not only are services jobs growing, many of them pay well

$97,808	$96,216	$95,565	$84,061	$79,906	$65,500
Management of Companies and Enterprises	Information	Utilities	Professional, Scientific, and Technical Services	Finance and Insurance	Wholesale Trade

Attracting talent through attractive surroundings

As the Western economy shifts from reliance on extracting and processing natural materials businesses are no longer necessarily bound by geography. Economists say entrepreneurs are increasingly choosing to locate in Western states thanks in part to the prevalence and accessibility of public lands, replete with wild rivers, forests, and mountains and outstanding recreational opportunities; in other words —quality of life— which offers a competitive advantage in attracting top talent.

PERCENT CHANGE IN EMPLOYMENT, WESTERN NON-METRO COUNTIES, 1970-2010

Percent of county lands federally protected

More than 30% Protected	345%
More than 20% Protected	297%
Less than 10% Protected	108%
0% Protected	83%

0% 50% 100% 150% 200% 250% 300% 350%

West is best—for your wallet, too

The more protected public lands, the higher per-capita income becomes. On average, western non-metro counties have a per capita income that is **$436 higher** for every 10,000 acres of federal protected lands within their boundaries.

AVERAGE INCREASE IN PER CAPITA INCOME FROM PROTECTED PUBLIC ACREAGE, NON-METRO WEST, 2010

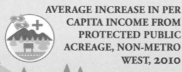 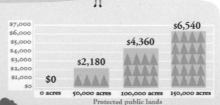

0 acres	$0
50,000 acres	$2,180
100,000 acres	$4,360
150,000 acres	$6,540

Protected public lands

HEADWATERS ECONOMICS

http://headwaterseconomics.org/land/west-is-best-value-of-public-lands/

have an economy in which services account for more than 70 percent of all jobs.[4]

In effect, the economic playing field between smaller towns and larger cities in the West has become more level. For the first time, small to midsized towns are successfully competing for higher-value aspects of the global economy, including knowledge-based industries that pay higher wages. These include information, finance, management, professional, scientific, and technical services, among others. Today, four in ten western counties have an economy in which more than 15 percent of all jobs are in high-wage services industries, with almost as many rural as metropolitan counties succeeding here.[5]

A good example of this is Sandpoint, a small town of less than 7,500 people in northern Idaho. This former timber town has morphed into a quality-of-life community, trading on the appeal of Lake Pend Oreille and the surrounding Selkirk and Cabinet Mountains. It has attracted retirees and appealed to younger people with families who work in knowledge-intensive industries such as aerospace manufacturing, pharmaceuticals, and software development. These individuals and companies rely on the Internet and access to Spokane's airport in Spokane, Washington, to sustain business relationships. They are building their companies in Sandpoint because it's a great place to enjoy the outdoors, raise a family, and live in a friendly community.

Despite these encouraging statistics, portions of the rural West are not doing well economically. These places do not enjoy the benefits of connecting to today's more diverse services economy for a variety of reasons—competitive pressures on remaining traditional industries, limited civic capacity, and lack of amenities (including attractive landscapes and protected public lands, and isolation). As a result, they have more limited opportunities and often rely on struggling traditional industries that are shedding jobs or are locked into a low-cost battle for survival. The economies of these places typically are not growing—the exception can be found in energy boomtowns that ride the swells and troughs of energy markets and new discoveries—even as youth are leaving and show no signs of return.

Location and Quality of Life

With advances in transportation and communications, more people and companies have the opportunity to choose where they will locate, and more of them are choosing places with a high quality of life.

Communities across the West have begun to realize that they can succeed by investing in and marketing their community character and outdoor quality of life. This is critical because, as Enrico Moretti observes in *The New Geography of Jobs,* "In the twentieth century, competition was about accumulating physical capital. Today it is about attracting the best human capital."[6]

For a growing number of companies and individuals, this business climate is closely tied to attractive natural landscapes and outdoor recreation. As "footloose" businesses whose success is relatively independent of location, these companies are more sensitive to the preferences of CEOs, and recruitment and retention factors that allow them to compete for and retain talented employees.

One corporate recruiter recently observed that "Increasingly over the years, amenities have become more a part of the discussion with our clients and more important to candidates' decisions about taking a job. It's not just what the job is any longer, but where the job is that matters."

As this logic becomes more pervasive, businesses are emphasizing the quality of place and investing in organizations that protect this competitive advantage. In Montana, for example, Business for Montana's Outdoors has joined a growing number of companies—across a range of competitive fields that include advertising, high-tech manufacturing, entertainment, architecture, and more—that are not hesitant to speak out about how the outdoors allows them to actively recruit talent. Their motto is "Reserving our outdoor assets for tomorrow's entrepreneurs."

The Value of Public Lands

In this economy, the West has a clear competitive advantage in its scenic natural lands, many of which are publicly owned. The West has more federal public lands and protected public lands (such as national parks and monuments) than any other region of the country. These lands offer

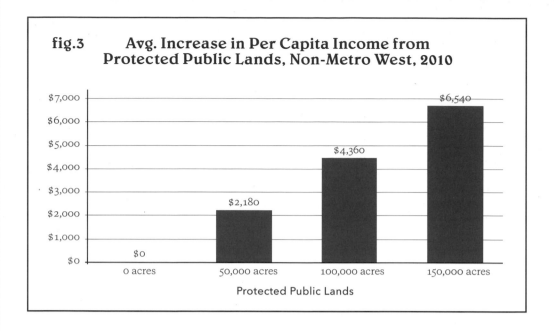

fig.3   Avg. Increase in Per Capita Income from Protected Public Lands, Non-Metro West, 2010

Protected Public Lands

hiking, fishing, hunting, skiing, boating, and other recreation, and provide a scenic backdrop to the region's communities. They are accessible and enjoyed by the West's residents at higher rates than in the rest of the country. Public lands stimulate tourism and outdoor recreation. More importantly, these lands are one reason why people and companies across a broad range of industries are coming to the region and diversifying the economy.

A growing body of research has analyzed the economic role of federal public lands, including the economic role of protected federal public lands, and established a connection between protected land and robust economies. Recent research by Headwaters Economics found above-average employment and income benefits in communities and counties with nearby protected federal public lands (fig.3).

During the last forty years, rural western counties with more than 30 percent of the county's land base in federal protected status created jobs four times faster than rural western counties without federal protected lands. In 2010, rural western counties had a per capita income that was $436 higher for every 10,000 acres of protected federal lands within their boundaries—or more than 10 percent of average per capita income in rural counties across the West.[7]

In 2011 these findings led more than 100 US economists and related academics—including three Nobel Laureates—to sign a letter urging President Obama to "create jobs and support businesses by investing in our public lands infrastructure and establishing new protected areas such as parks, wilderness, and monuments."

Small business owners understand this logic as well. A recent Small Business Majority poll conducted in Arizona, Colorado, Nevada, and New Mexico found that "Small business owners believe protecting public lands would positively impact small business opportunities, local job growth, state economies and more: 65 percent of owners believe designating new national parks and monuments would enhance local jobs and the economy ... and 52 percent agree it would help their state attract and retain new business and entrepreneurs."[8]

Conservation Takeaways

The environment and environmental quality is now an economic competitive advantage for today's more dynamic and productive businesses, and for a growing number of communities across the West. As a result, conservation advocates can play an important role supporting economic well-being, and also can benefit from the power of working with new allies, including business and civic leaders, in their efforts to protect the environment.

Suggested guideposts for making progress in this territory:

Be Relevant

Conservation cannot succeed without broader and more influential support. Americans consistently tell us they care about other issues as much as or more than the environment. In addition, as the environment has become an increasingly partisan issue, the constituency for conservation has narrowed, and leadership has become less effective. Bridging to more mainstream issues and building constructive ties with new allies are important to safeguarding a healthy environment.

A good example of linking conservation values to broader values can be found in efforts to increase federal funding for the Land and Water Conservation Fund (LWCF), which protects and enhances natural resources and outdoor recreation opportunities. LWCF partners emphasize how these investments preserve many aspects of America's history and culture, support a growing recreation economy and sportsmen's access, provide close-to-home recreation for the nation's urban populations, and protect working forests and ranches while resolving land use conflicts and saving the US treasury tax dollars.

Do Not Oversell

Protecting the environment by itself may or may not yield economic benefits. Put another way, while protected land and water resources often appeal to workers, businesses, and retirees, conservation efforts should embrace a broader strategy of encouraging community and economic development through investments in education, transportation, and communications. If the environmental quality argument alone is oversold or taken out of context, it is less likely to be believed and may fall flat altogether—harming the credibility and effectiveness of future conservation work.

Know What You Are Talking About

Take the time to learn the issues and research findings before integrating them into a campaign. There are organizations and publicly available data that can assist with developing research to show how natural amenities and a healthy environment contribute to various economic advantages—for a start, see the list of resources at the end of this chapter.

Tell a Story

Information by itself rarely changes the world. Economists may be the last ones to grasp this point. Conservationists, who typically excel at marshaling data in logical ways to buttress an argument, should not make the same mistake. Whenever possible, link solid research to compelling personal, business, or community stories to show how real people benefit from environmental protection.

For example, knowing that most people move to central Oregon because of the spectacular landscape is less compelling than hearing from the founder of Ruffwear, a thriving local company, about why he brought the company to Bend and uses the quality of life there as a marketing and recruiting tool.

Let Partners Speak

It can be difficult for conservation advocates to be credible on economic development matters. Let others who are more respected voices on the economy be messengers. These can be business owners, corporate recruiters, chamber of commerce members, retired workers, etc. They can tell their story and reach a broader audience with a message about the alignment between environmental protection and economic competitiveness.

Culture Matters

When most people talk about economic efficiency and maximizing profit as reasons why they cannot afford to protect the environment, they are really talking about broader values. Few of us are truly rational economic actors. Ranchers, for example, generally do not ranch because it is the best way for them to make the most money—more likely it is because ranching is what they know and love. (Ranchers have been known to joke that they will stay in "business" until the money runs out.) Environmentalists tend to argue that protecting the land is important in itself or, as we argue here, good for the economy. But an appeal to economic self-interest should also consider broader values, such as love of place or the outdoors, or the well-being of children. These values are commonly held and persuasive across the political spectrum.

Know Where You Are

Not all places are alike, or have the same economic opportunities. Despite the broad trends discussed in this chapter that create new competitive advantages for many towns and cities in the West, some places are not doing well. For these parts of the West—whose economies are in decline and where newer forms of economic activity seem unlikely—a conservation approach may avoid economics altogether. Alternatively, it may focus on retooling existing industries (for example, in agriculture or forestry) around better practices and new markets, or even addressing longstanding environmental damage through restoration, which has immediate economic benefits.

Final Words

Conservationists can be savvier about the growing synergy between environmental and business health, and creative about how to deploy this information. It is time to broaden the focus beyond the perils of natural resource industries to work toward solutions with rapidly expanding businesses whose financial bottom line increasingly is aligned with environmental quality.

Outdoors manufacturing and retail businesses have been particularly receptive to partnering with conservation groups to advance mutually beneficial outcomes. The Outdoor Industry of America, for example, publishes an annual report estimating the economic magnitude of their industry nationally and for each state, and uses these findings to advocate for public policies that protect their business interests, including land and water protection.

This is an important step. However, the larger opportunity lies in grasping that the success today of the US economy as a whole relies on quality. This includes environmental quality, which has become a competitive advantage in attracting talent and fostering innovation for many of the nation's fastest-growing companies across a range of economic sectors. Now more than ever, protecting the environment is part of a winning economic strategy.

As I write this, I am looking through office windows at mountains that stretch, largely roadless, to Yellowstone National Park. The trees that drape these mountains now have more value left standing than cut and turned into lumber. The businesses in Bozeman took a long time to realize this. It may have taken the high-profile purchase of a local software company by a Silicon Valley giant to bring the point home. But we get it now. And we are talking to our neighbors and elected officials about how to protect and restore the environment that sustains our community.

FOOTNOTES

1   US Department of Commerce. 2012. Bureau of Economic Analysis, Regional Economic Information System, Washington, D.C. Tables CA25 and CA25N.

2   Ibid.

3   US Department of Commerce. 2012. Bureau of Economic Analysis, Regional Economic Information System, Washington, D.C. Tables CA25 and CA25N.

4   Ibid.

5   Ibid

6   Moretti, Enrico. The New Geography of Jobs. Boston: Houghton Mifflin Harcourt, 2012. Pp. 10, 66.

7   See http://headwaterseconomics.org/land/west-is-best-value-of-public-lands.

8   Small Business Majority. 2012. Polling results available at: http://headwaterseconomics.org/land/west-is-best-value-of-public-lands.

Resources

Economic Profile System. Free software that produces detailed socioeconomic reports of communities, counties, states, and regions, including custom aggregations and comparisons. http://headwaterseconomics.org/tools/eps-hdt.

Economists' Letter to President. Letter from more than 100 economists urging the President to protect important public lands. http://headwaterseconomics.org/land/economists-president-public-lands.

National Monument Economics. Reviews the economic importance of major national monuments in the West to local communities. http://headwaterseconomics.org/interactive/national-monuments.

National Park Economics. Reviews the economic impact of visitation and expenditures for every national park service unit in the country. http://headwaterseconomics.org/interactive/national-park-service-units.

Protected Federal Lands in Non-Metro West Increase Per Capital Income. Research on the amount of per capita income explained by protected federal lands for every non-metro county in the West. http://headwaterseconomics.org/land/protected-public-lands-increase-per-capita-income.

The Economic Impacts of Restoration in Central Idaho. A straightforward way to calculate the economic impacts of natural resource restoration activities to nearby communities. http://headwaterseconomics.org/land/reports/idaho-restoration-impacts.

The Value of Protected Public Lands. A summary of resources on the economic value of protected federal lands. http://headwaterseconomics.org/land/reports/protected-lands-value.

West is Best: Protected Lands Promote Jobs and Higher Incomes. Research on how public lands in the West create a competitive economic advantage. http://headwaterseconomics.org/land/west-is-best-value-of-public-lands.

West-Wide Economic Atlas. Interactive map of economic and land use trends for every county and state in the West. http://headwaterseconomics.org/interactive/west-wide-atlas.

Castle Valley

Fifty million years ago, a massive salt dome collapsed far beneath the landscape east of what is now Moab, Utah. The surface dropped hundreds of feet. Today, 300 people live at the bottom surrounded by the high edges of spectacular Wingate Sandstone cliffs, dark canyons, and the iconic spires of the Castleton Tower climbing area. The Bureau of Land Management (BLM) has identified the landscape surrounding Castle Valley as having wilderness qualities.

The School and Institutional Trust Lands Administration (SITLA), created in 1994, controlled much of the land surrounding the Castle Valley residents' homes.

At the time of statehood in 1896, the map of Utah was divided into townships—each consisting of thirty-six sections. Originally, three of these sections were called trust lands and granted to the state by Congress. Trust lands were to generate revenue for that area's public schools, hospitals, teaching colleges, and universities. Since its inception, the fund managed by SITLA has grown from $50 million to $2 billion through oil, gas, and mineral leases, rent, and royalties, and real estate development and sales. Because these lands are held in trust, they are managed more like private lands, without the environmental oversight required when developing public lands.

Due to various land trades, Castle Valley ended up with more than its share of trust lands, subjecting over half of its area to possible oil, gas, and real estate development.

A "For Sale" sign went up in 1999. That sign came down twice.

Details of the first time are sketchy—we only know that vandals removed it one night from Castle Valley and mysteriously re-installed it beside Turret Arch in Arches National Park. The point was made: Developers will sell anything, even national parks.

The sign came down for good a few months later when the Castle Rock Collaboration, a small group of valley residents who organized to protect their homes from unwanted SITLA development, announced they'd bought the parcel after receiving a check from an anonymous donor. Support continued to grow from the Grand Canyon Trust, Utah Open Lands, and The Nature Conservancy—which discovered two threatened plant species, Jones cycladenia and the Schultz stickleaf, on three of the SITLA parcels.

Valley residents David Erley and Laura Kamala had led the charge. With support from the outdoor equipment companies Black Diamond, Patagonia, Petzl, and the local climbing community, they worked tirelessly with the Access Fund to keep the area adjacent to the Castleton Tower climbing area open to climbers and hikers. Erley and Utah Open Lands—the land trust that managed the entire process and would oversee the conservation easements attached to these parcels—went to great effort to design and build a campground to better accommodate the growing number of climbers coming to test themselves on these iconic routes.

Protecting the land at the base of Castle Rock was only part of the challenge. Across the road a 4,000-acre block of SITLA land surrounded the town on the east and southeast. In an effort that would take more than a decade, Laura Kamala engaged SITLA in a conversation that would result in last year's bipartisan legislation involving a trade of the land between SITLA and BLM.

Looking back, the Castle Valley success was based on three factors:

1   Involvement of local residents who weren't going anywhere and who had the most at stake
2   Engagement of strange bedfellows, including the climbing community, industry, and The Nature Conservancy
3   Extreme patience. Start to finish, it took fifteen years.

– Brooke Williams

Castle Rock rises from the fog. Castle Valley, Utah. *Tom Till*

Organ Mountains, Chihuahuan Desert, New Mexico. *Tim Fitzharris/ Minden Pictures/National Geographic Creative*

Organ Mountains-Desert Peaks National Monument

Nathan Small

Piercing a Southwest sky, the Organ Mountains rise above Las Cruces, New Mexico. Morning sun spills over their 9,000-foot peaks, lighting the Doña Ana, Robledo, Las Uvas, and Potrillo Mountains. On May 21, 2014, President Barack Obama protected this land with the creation of the 496,330-acre Organ Mountains-Desert Peaks National Monument. Diverse local support, economic opportunity, collaboration, and endless elbow grease are campaign guideposts that mark the way to more monuments and better communities.

It was good policy and smart politics when the Obama administration created this national monument. Opinion polls consistently showed more than 60 percent support, and local governments passed multiple resolutions endorsing conservation. Business, religious, community, and sportsmen's organizations joined sovereign Native American nations, local elected governments, and US Senators Martin Heinrich, Tom Udall, and Jeff Bingaman (retired) to protect

our mountains. Two practices generated and sustained support: relentless focus on comprehensive, not piecemeal, conservation, and identifying individual and cultural reasons to take ownership of conservation efforts.

In 2008, Rep. Steve Pearce (R-NM) introduced "conservation" legislation that released wilderness study areas, permanently preventing them from being designated wilderness. Advocates seized on the subterfuge. Five days after the introduction, a press conference featuring sportsmen, business leaders, elected officials, and other conservation supporters denounced Rep. Pearce's legislation and refocused on comprehensive conservation.

Advocates supported the national monument for many reasons. One shared reason was expanding economic opportunity. Driven by a 2006 Headwaters Economics study, which showed that wilderness designation coincided with higher per capita income and higher income growth in peer counties, we reached out to businesses and associations to create the Wilderness Economics Conference. The event brought together local and national leaders to discuss the economic benefits of protected lands. Some attendees, like David Crider from Southwest Expeditions, http://www.swexpeditions.com, are now building outdoor-focused businesses connected to the new national monument.

An independent 2013 study sponsored by the Las Cruces Green Chamber of Commerce predicted national monument benefits totaling $7.4 million generated annually and eighty-eight jobs created.

Wayne and Kiki Suggs, owners of Las Cruces–based Classic New Mexico Homes, included monument photos in their sales book. These pictures attracted business. A doctor came from the Eastern Seaboard, entranced by the majestic mountains and blue skies. Another buyer called the Organ Mountains the "Tetons of the Southwest."

Victor Gallegos owns Nopalitos Restaurant and Nopalitos Galería, both in Las Cruces, http://www.nopalitosrestaurants.com. He hosted history talks, *placticas*, about Billy the Kid at his gallery, where patrons discovered that Billy and his gang left their initials on Outlaw Rock—just a few miles away in the monument. Victor's connections to cultural heritage and economic opportunity made support of the monument the right personal and professional choice for him.

The mayor of Mesilla, Nora Barraza, made many trips to Washington, DC, to advocate for the national monument. Tourism revenues drive Mesilla's budget. Every year, the town's residents re-enact the 1848 signing of the Treaty of Guadalupe Hidalgo (which ended the Mexican-American War and resulted in the US gaining land that includes present-day Arizona, California, New Mexico, and parts of Colorado, Nevada, and Utah), whose markers are still visible in the monument. Mayor Barraza uses ceremony, education, and celebrations to showcase Mesilla's national monument connection and attract more tourists.

We invited and welcomed new supporters and leveraged strong leadership, and eventually overshadowed the dwindling opposition. National monument designation has already driven economic success, with two conferences and a new climbing festival recently choosing Las Cruces because of its proximity to the monument. Now, sovereign Native American nations, sportsmen, and many others are working together for monument management planning. Together, we are exploring new ways to share the treasures of the Organ Mountains-Desert Peaks, and by so doing, expanding our own economic opportunities.

Andy Knight on Tooth or Consequences 5.10a, High Horns,
Organ Mountains, New Mexico. *Andrew Burr*

Terry Tempest Williams is a citizen writer who is passionate about wilderness, words, and birds. She is involved with the Environmental Humanities Graduate Program at the University of Utah, where students are exploring activism through the lens of storytelling as they focus on oil shale and tar sand development in America's Red Rock Wilderness. Her book, The Hour of Land: A Personal Topography of America's National Parks, *will be published in 2016.*

Terry Tempest Williams

2002 KEYNOTE SPEAKER

Ghost Deer

Ghost deer—this is what the locals call white deer living inside the Seneca Army Depot in upstate New York. My friend, a resident of the Finger Lakes region, and I were driving on our way from Geneva to Ithaca. She told me we might be lucky enough to witness them. How many of you have seen the white deer? My eyes scanned the gray, leafless winter-changing-to-spring landscape, eager to see such a rarity. And sure enough, one ghost deer, a female, was browsing with three brown white-tailed deer. She stood behind the tall chain-link fence like an apparition.

We pulled off the road. Through my binoculars, I watched the pure white deer, her large brown eyes, the way she stood out in the dark woods like a beacon of light. Normally, my naturalist mind would begin a rapid line of questioning: why, where, when, how. But this time, my lust for facts disappeared under the spell cast by this strange, unexpected presence and the irony of such purity feeding on the edge of a military reservation where the groundwater is contaminated with volatile organic compounds, where Percy missiles were once housed, and where unexploded ordinance still waits for the surprised foot, paw, hoof, or wing.

To see the deer is to bear witness to the restorative power of beauty—rare, unexpected beauty in the midst of terror.

The white deer at the Seneca Army Depot stand out. They are vulnerable. I know there's a biological explanation to the pigmentation of these deer that is different from albinism. They are mutations. And I'm sure there are endless studies about to their rise in population from one sighting in 1941 to approximately one hundred individuals on the reservation today in 2002. But for now, may these ghost deer stand as a source of inspiration at a time when I am searching for symbols, metaphors, images.

Perhaps the power of the white deer is that they appear inside the military complex as a question. Their very presence within the fenced army depot is both a mystery and a path toward inquiry. And they are full of grace and gentleness, true to the nature of deer.

My friends who live between Cayuga and Seneca Lakes tell me that the white deer population is now protected, that one of the highest uses of the now-closed Seneca Army Depot is to be a wildlife sanctuary, a sanctuary alongside a state prison. A few miles from the army depot is the town of Seneca Falls, the birthplace of American feminism, where on July 19 and 20, 1848, the Declaration of Sentiments was written.

Patterned after the Declaration of Independence, it reads, "We hold these truths to be self-evident, that all men and women are created equal, that they are endowed by their creator with certain inalienable rights, that among these are life, liberty, and the pursuit of happiness. That to secure these rights, governments are instituted, deriving their just powers from the consent of the governed. Whenever any form of government becomes destructive of these ends, it is the right of those who suffer from it to refuse allegiance to it. The history of mankind," it continues, "is a history of repeated injuries and usurpations on the part of man toward woman, having in direct object the establishment of an absolute tyranny over her. To prove this, let facts be submitted to a candid world." And then the list of facts are in fact submitted.

210

These are brave words—words from brave Americans that I believe were written from the heart, especially the heart of democracy. The women went on to say, "And entering upon the great work before us, we anticipate no small amount of misconception, misrepresentation, and ridicule."

And this they found. This evidence found, they stood out, they were vulnerable. But they also found a path to a more enlightened and egalitarian society where justice was not only addressed, but enacted. They dared to speak truth to power. They were fearless in the questions they chose to ask and the requests they chose to make.

I kept thinking as I read their words that we would never be that bold and brave to write what they wrote. But we need to become that brave. The white deer and the suffragers from the Burned-Over District remind me of what is possible within my own home ground of America's Redrock Wilderness.

We are in a time of great transformation. Around the world, we seem to be holding these two opposing worldviews. On one hand, a world of fundamentalism with strong allegiances and boundaries, where a fear of change fuels violence. On the other hand, a world of global awareness and compassion, where the embrace of all life is the embrace of peace. One bows to the absolutes, the certainty of righteousness; the other bows and sits with the questions. One builds armies, the other builds communities. Both worldviews dwell inside each one of us. How might we bring our two hands together in prayer?

For my own peace of mind, I will visit the white deer often in my imagination, hoping for a break in the fence so that they will one day walk through in the name of freedom. And I will think of the women in Seneca Falls who dared to commit their names to paper, one after the other, in the name of justice for all.

Postscript: More than a decade later, citizens from Seneca Lake continue to uphold the noble tradition of resistance and insistence in the name of social justice. They have organized around an anti-fracking campaign in order to preserve the water quality of the Finger Lakes region. "We Are Seneca Lake" supports ongoing civil disobedience to thwart fossil-fuel development in New York state. Hundreds of residents have been arrested and served time in jail to ensure that "the open space of democracy" remains exactly that.

On December 17, 2014, Governor Andrew Cuomo heard the cries of his constituents and banned fracking in the state of New York.

On January 16, 2015, the Grandmothers' and Mothers' Blockade blocked the local entrance of Texas-based energy company Crestwood Midstream in subfreezing temperatures to protest its intention to store fracking materials in nearby gas tanks. The women with their children shut down the facility from all traffic coming and going for nearly six hours.

The ghost deer are watching.

(11)

Visualizing Data

Tanya Birch &
Karin Tuxen-Bettman

In 2005, residents of the Santa Cruz Mountains, in Northern California, received a letter in the mail. It was a notice from a local water company of their intentions to selectively log, in perpetuity, more than 1,000 acres of redwood and conifer forests in the heart of the community. The letter also included a sketchy black-and-white map that purported to show the boundaries of the logging area (fig.1).

From this map, can you tell where the proposed logging zone is? The community residents couldn't either. It was nearly impossible to distinguish the logging boundary from the roads and topographic contour lines, even for residents familiar with the area. Perhaps that was the point.

One resident of the area, Rebecca Moore, who was also a computer scientist at Google, decided to re-create the map using Google Earth, a new tool that had been introduced two months earlier. She obtained digital parcel data of the proposed 1,000-acre logging area from the county planning department, and added other information such as rivers, photos, and even a 3D model of a helicopter carrying logs over the canyon. She was able to build a new map that made it easy to visualize the logging proposal plan (fig.2). She presented this during a community meeting, which spurred the local residents to form a new community group, Neighbors Against Irresponsible Logging (NAIL).

In their fight to stop the logging plan, NAIL used Google Earth to show where the logging would happen, but more importantly, to prove that the proposal was illegal. Two years later, the California Department of Forestry ruled the logging plan ineligible. Rebecca's pioneering work helped NAIL achieve a victory for environmental advocacy, and also showed that Google Earth can increase public awareness of community issues and therefore facilitate real social change.

Following this success, Rebecca, the computer scientist who created the NAIL map, proposed that Google establish an official program called Google Earth Outreach. The program was created to help nonprofits and other public benefit groups use Google Earth and other mapping tools to help visualize, analyze, and raise awareness for environmental and humanitarian projects all over the world.

Since the program's inception, Google Earth Outreach has part-nered with many organizations around the world. The program trains nonprofits on how to use mapping tools to enhance their work. It helps promote the good work these groups are doing, from stopping illegal logging for palm oil to preserving indigenous culture by putting points of interest like sacred sites and hunting regions on the map.

Appalachian Voices used Google mapping tools to visualize the devastation caused by mountaintop removal in West Virginia—something that can only be seen from above. The Surui Tribe in the Brazilian Amazon used Google mapping tools to build a map of places and events of cultural and natural significance, and the United States Holocaust Memorial Museum employed them to map the genocide in Darfur, Sudan.

The Power of Seeing

Spatial visualization is a key component to any environmental campaign. You are trying to save a place and nothing shows it better than a map, a video, or pictures. We've seen the power of this kind of presentation to make a visual argument when others have failed, and drum up support for projects that work to save the three-dimensional world, our common home.

Telling Stories with Google Earth

If you're one of the one billion people who have downloaded Google Earth, you're familiar with the 3D model it creates of our world. You may have even created your own point, line, or polygon annotations on top of Google Earth. Many nonprofits we've worked with wanted to use the rich storytelling capabilities of a 3D globe, but lacked the technical resources to program Google Earth to tell stories like the ones at google.com/cop15. (Check out CoalRiverWind.org's tour at http://www.youtube.com/watch?v=vIwO9Z3llRo. It is a great example of using Google Earth to visualize the economic potential of a wind farm as an alternative to blowing up the mountaintop to get at the coal underneath.) So the Google team created Google Tour Builder to make storytelling using Google Maps and Google Earth easier.

Google Tour Builder is an online storytelling tool that flies viewers from one location to the next within a map view, while displaying information and stories about that location on a panel next to the map. Nonprofit organizations and other groups have used it to tell stories about any issue where location is especially important.

Furthermore, Tour Builder makes map creation and storytelling much simpler so more organizations can reach more people through social media or other online communications strategies.

Visualizing Change with Timelapse

The Landsat program, managed by the US Geological Survey, has been acquiring images of the earth's surface since 1972. These Landsat satellite images provide critical scientific information about our changing planet.

Timelapse (http://earthengine.google.org/timelapse) is a visualization tool that takes millions of Landsat satellite images and combines them to create annual composites for every year since 1984. The result is a panable and zoomable animated map through time (fig.3). You can view or search for any location on the planet and explore a global time-lapse constructed from Landsat satellite imagery. Each frame of the Timelapse map is constructed from a year of Landsat satellite data, constituting an annual 1.7-terapixel snapshot of the Earth at thirty-meter resolution. The whole thing is powered by Google Earth Engine, Google's geospatial analysis platform.

This tool is extremely helpful for environmental activists to communicate the change that's happened in the landscape over the past few decades. Watch as forests are cut down, and as glaciers recede. Learn as lakes and rivers dry up and as urban landscapes develop. Visualize as mines transform grasslands, and as tar sands develop.

fig.1   Water Company Map

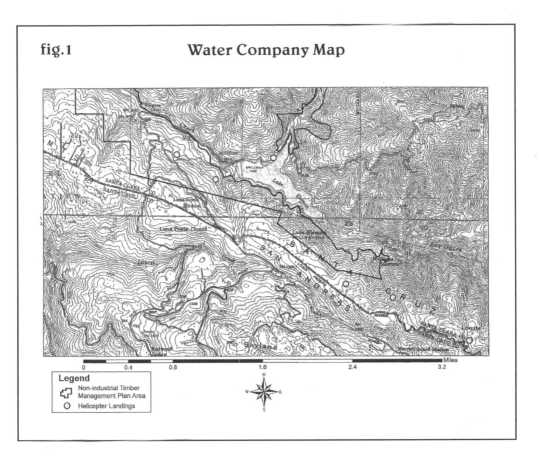

fig.2   Google Earth Flyover

fig.3   Timelapse, Powered by Google Earth Engine

Start exploring now at https://earthengine.google.org/timelapse. You can share the maps on your website, blog, or social media.

A Movie Is Worth a Million Words: YouTube

YouTube is the second largest search engine in the world, so it's a great way to tell your story and engage citizens in your cause. We've all seen the power of good communications strategy with examples like *The Story of Stuff*. This twenty-minute video on YouTube is a fact-filled, fast-paced look at the underside of our production and consumption patterns. (Watch the video at http://storyofstuff.org/movies/story-of-stuff/.)

Since it was uploaded to YouTube in 2007, the video has gotten over 30 million views. How did The Stuff Project get such traction?

1. They spent time researching the issue, and condensing all that information into an understandable format.
2. They focused on a campaign, or an ask. The video presented a *Challenge,* allowed the viewer to be the *Hero,* and told him or her clearly how to *Take Action.*
3. They brought it to the greater online community by embedding the video on hundreds of blogs and websites on the day of launch and beyond.

Get started by creating your own YouTube channel at youtube.com, which you can customize with a banner. You can also put pop-up annotations and other embedded links in your YouTube videos. You can even enable a donation module to raise funds. Subscribe to the YouTube Help channel for video tips, tricks, and how-to's.

More Tools That Can Help Your Campaign

Maps and videos can have a profound impact on your project, but there are even more tools that can help you to reach and engage supporters, improve your operations, and help to raise awareness for your cause. The first step is to visit google.com/nonprofits. Here you will find all sorts of great information, and you can sign up to be an official Google Nonprofit. Once approved, you can enroll to get free advertising in Google search results with Google Ad Grants (more on that below), request free access to the Google Apps suite, and more.

Let's now focus on how you might use some of these tools!

Create a Campaign Plan Collaboratively: Google Docs

Nothing is better than getting help from your team on a campaign plan, or any document where a lot of editing needs to take place. Google Docs is a collaborative document editor that allows you and your team to simultaneously edit a document, such as a campaign plan.

Finish your draft, then click the "Share" button to share it with your teammates. All of you can edit content, add images and graphs, and even leave comments for others to address. You can also choose to give teammates view access, or full edit access. All revisions are saved, so you can always revert back to a previous version if you want to reference earlier changes.

All of your team members can be connected and collaborate on calendars, documents, spreadsheets, and more. All you need is a Gmail or a Google Apps for Nonprofits account email.

Managing Your People Lists: Google Sheets

Organizations like yours need to manage "people lists," including members, volunteers, and donors. For example, Samasource connects women, youth, and refugees living in poverty to work over the Internet. They used Google Sheets to keep a collaborative, live list of all their partners, so everyone shares the most current information. Just like Google Docs, Sheets are collaborative and all the revision history is saved. You can use Google Sheets in several ways:

- MANAGE A LIST OF YOUR MEMBERS, VOLUNTEERS, AND DONORS. Keep it private, or share it with just your core team, such as your volunteer coordinator. If the contact

PG.217   A copy of the original map (Fig.1) distributed by a local water company to the residents of the Santa Cruz Mountains, California, as compared to the Google Earth Flyover map (Fig.2) that resident Rebecca Moore built in response to the confusion the original map created. *Images Courtesy of a resident of the Santa Cruz Mountains and Google*   LEFT   Stills from the Google timelapse showing the increase in development, and subsequent decrease in the water table, around Las Vegas, Nevada, and Lake Mead. The years shown here are 1987, 2002, and 2012. *Images Courtesy of Google* information is in the spreadsheet, you can easily import it to a private Google My Map so that you can know where they are concentrated. This might help you focus your outreach efforts in areas where they will be most effective.

- ACCEPT SIGN-UPS DURING EVENTS. If you create a Google Form, you can have a laptop at the farmers' market table, at the back of the room during your City Council Meeting, or even embedded on your website, and people can enter their contact information right on your form. You'll save time by not having to enter all that information by hand, and you can easily keep all the information in a Google Sheet. Samasource also used Google Forms to collect data from staff and aggregate that data into a Google Sheet without having to manually transfer data.

Visit http://www.google.com/nonprofits/community/samasource.html to learn about other tools Samasource used to help them save tens of thousands of dollars and get their new nonprofit off the ground quickly.

Visualize Your Data
Interactively: Fusion Tables

If you manage any data in spreadsheets, you probably need to map or graph that data from time to time. Fusion Tables helps you create quick and easy data visualizations, such as maps, pie charts, or timelines. For example:

- View data with addresses in a table format, as cards, or plotted on a map.
- With a spreadsheet of donor addresses and amount donated and when, you can see what kinds of fundraising events are most successful. You can display your data as interactive line charts, bar charts, or pie charts.
- With a spreadsheet of volunteer addresses, you can email only those volunteers who live near a specific location, e.g. a beach where you are organizing a cleanup, or a farmers' market where you are hosting a table.

Whether it's a quick map or a pie chart, "Fusion Tables" is really powerful—you just need a spreadsheet of data and Google does the heavy lifting for you to create these great visualizations.

Broadcast Your Message:
Google Advertising

Google for Nonprofits also offers Google Ad Grants to eligible nonprofit organizations. Google Ad Grants empowers nonprofit organizations with free AdWords advertising to promote their missions and initiatives on Google search pages. By advertising alongside search results, you can reach and engage more of your supporters and attract new donors. Small organizations with little to no marketing budget or prior online marketing experience have utilized this free service to promote their mission nationwide and drive monetary donations. One such organization is AmpleHarvest.org. Their mission is to connect millions of Americans with excess food in their garden to local food pantries to feed the needy and prevent food from going to waste. AmpleHarvest.org's Google Ad Grants have enabled them to drive over one million clicks in five years and over 60,000 conversions in just a few months. They have received more than 7,000 food pantry registrations since launching their AdWords campaigns in 2009, as well as a significant amount of press coverage and support.

Resources

You can learn more about the NAIL story at http://www.google.com/earth/outreach/stories/nail.html.

Even more stories can be seen at www.google.com/earth/outreach/stories.

You can find more on Tour Builder, here. https://tourbuilder.withgoogle.com/.

For more on fusion tables, go to google.com/fusiontables, click "Create a Fusion Table," and then import your spreadsheet of data.

To apply for a Google Ad Grant visit http://static.googleusercontent.com/media/www.google.com/en//grants/pdf/us-marketing-playbook.pdf.

Dr. Jane Goodall with chimpanzee Freud at Gombe
Stream National Park, Tanzania. *Michael Neugebauer*

The Jane Goodall Institute

Lilian Pintea & Shawn Sweeney

Our closest living relatives, chimpanzees, are threatened by habitat loss and degradation, illegal bushmeat hunting, disease, and illegal pet trade. The Jane Goodall Institute's (JGI) thirty-year mission focus is to protect 85 percent of chimpanzees and their habitats in Africa. This is an ambitious challenge and can be achieved only through engaging a diversity of stakeholders—from government-managed national parks to community village reserves and privately owned forest patches—to jointly manage chimpanzee populations. The institute leverages lessons learned from its site-specific projects, to scale up and address the threats to chimpanzees within larger ranges.

These include the use of innovative geospatial technologies, from the use of very high-resolution DigitalGlobe satellite imagery to community data collected using the Open Data Kit (ODK) mobile app and Android smartphones and tablets. However, until recently the only way to communicate and share this rich geographic content with a nontechnical audience was through static maps. Thanks to breakthroughs in web-mapping technologies and storytelling tools such as Google Earth Tour Builder, conservation data from local to global scales can now be easily visualized and shared with everyone.

JGI's first Google Earth Tour Builder tour brought together a variety of mapping data and complemented it with text, photos, and videos to tell the story of Dr. Jane Goodall, chimpanzee research and conservation in Gombe, Tanzania, and how the institute is learning from Gombe to scale up and protect chimpanzees in Africa. For example, the Chimpanzee Conservation page of the tour shows village forest reserves established by land use planning efforts facilitated by the institute. It shows communities patrolling these reserves using data collected by village forest monitors using Android smartphones or tablets and the ODK app. It also shows that these efforts are paying off, and in some villages the forests are coming back through natural regeneration as detected by the DigitalGlobe satellite imagery from 2005 and 2013 (imagery displayed in the upper left corner of the tour). Most importantly, the users of the tour can navigate and explore content in 3D to better understand our work in Gombe and how this fits into the larger JGI mission to protect chimpanzees within their large range in Africa.

While JGI's conservation efforts in Africa address immediate threats to chimpanzees, long-term conservation requires a generation of young people who understand the importance of protecting habitats and species. And so, JGI has endeavored to engage young people in meaningful experiences (which they define based on genuine needs in their own communities) for the benefit of people, animals, and the environment. Jane Goodall's Roots & Shoots, the youth-led community action and learning program of the Jane Goodall Institute, uses Dr. Goodall's story to inspire and engage them in their service efforts. The tour illustrates Jane's life from the time she was a young girl through her incredible pioneering discoveries, to JGI's work today. Educators can use the tour in their classes to provide valuable lessons about Dr. Goodall's historical contributions and about chimpanzee behavior and ecology. Experiencing Jane's story in an interactive way through the tour can help young people feel inspired by her impact in the world and excited to "be like Dr. Jane." Jane's story also gives young people a springboard to think about what kind of impact they want to make in their own communities and, with JGI there to help, get them started as tomorrow's change makers today.

LEFT   Regeneration of miombo woodland in the Kigalye village forest reserve, Tanzania, as detected by 2005 and 2014 high-resolution satellite imagery. *Images Courtesy of Lilian Pintea/ Jane Goodall Institute; Map Data: Google, Digitalglobe*   ABOVE   A Village Forest Monitor from Kigalye Village, Tanzania, using an Android tablet and Open Data Kit (ODK) free mobile app to record and report a tree illegally cut in the village forest reserve. *Photo Courtesy of Lilian Pintea/Jane Goodall Institute*

225

Shoko Tsuru is one of the key figures in the campaign to remove the Arase Dam on the Kuma River. Recognized for her long-term efforts on environmental issues caused by the dam, she received the grand prize at Japan's Nature Conservation Society awards in 2015. She is the president of the Kumamoto chapter of the Nature Conservation Educator.

球磨川の荒瀬ダム撤去運動の主要人物の一人。長期にわたるダムの環境問題に取り組んだことが評価されて、2015年日本自然保護大賞を受賞。自然観察指導員熊本県連絡会会長。

Shoko Tsuru

2012 KEYNOTE SPEAKER,
JAPAN TOOLS CONFERENCE

Japan's First Dam Removal: The Arase Dam

O n March 19, 2015, for the first time in sixty years, the Kuma River began flowing forcefully again, two and a half years since the start of the Arase Dam removal. This was a day to commemorate the fulfillment of the residents' wish: "Give the Kuma River back to us." Getting to this point had involved many days of suffering and struggle that the watershed residents endured as a result of the construction of the dam.

The local people used the Kuma River for many purposes, as was the case with many rivers in Japan until very recently. Fish such as Japanese trout and eels (along with a wide variety of other organisms) were food sources as well as the source of regular jobs. The river also provided for everyday water use and a transportation option. People built houses right beside the river and reaped its benefits, handling the periodic flooding with their knowledge of how to keep the damage to a minimum. The people who lived on the river were well aware of their blessings, and were touched with admiration and awe. Children were raised being told in the local dialect, "Don't empty your bladder facing the river." When the Japanese trout-fishing season started, they asked the gods for support for another year, requesting permission to enter the river. They made a sacred offering of sake, and with the first drink they made a toast "to the gods living upstream," and with the second drink, made a toast to "the gods in charge here."

The river was also a recreation area. Since my earliest memories, I had played in the Kuma River. When I wasn't in school, I was in the river. Children would catch and sell trout and eels to help pay for their school supplies and supplement household budgets. It was the same for the tidal wetlands of the estuary. If you walked on them, you couldn't help but step on crabs or flounder, and Japanese littleneck clams and common clams were piled up like gravel. If you scraped the tidal wetlands, you could fill a bucket with Japanese tiger prawns in less than an

PG.226 As the sediment returns to the mudflats of the Kuma River, more people enjoy catching Japanese mud shrimp. Kumamoto, Japan. *Photo Courtesy of Shoko Tsuru* ABOVE Halfway through the removal of the Arase Dam, Kumamoto, Japan. *Photo Courtesy of Shoko Tsuru*

hour. Various kinds of fish gathered in the eelgrass at the edge of the tidal wetlands to rest or lay eggs, and the water was so clear that from the surface to several meters below at the root of the eelgrass you could clearly see each individual egg.

However, a dam was built on the river to make up for power shortages after the war. This structure suddenly appeared and drastically changed the life of the people and the river. There was a dramatic decrease in the number of both trout and eels, which had previously been so numerous that the depths of the river looked black at times. The regular jobs that depended on the river almost totally disappeared.

What was most difficult to endure was the increased flood damage. This was a region already challenged by yearly floods, yet these were expected and there was not much damage. It was possible to predict the rising waters by the way the rain was falling and how fast the river's water volume was increasing. Precautions could be taken. Residents could lift tatami mats and household items as the rains fell, then sweep out the scratchy sand that remained after the water receded, replacing the paper screens on sliding doors and putting the tatami mats back down. They looked at it as a major cleaning once a year.

The floodwaters after the dam was constructed were completely different from what they had faced before. Water levels rose so suddenly that there was no time to raise up the tatami mats, and it was all people could do to escape with their lives. Once people returned to their homes, they found their streets and the inside of their houses blanketed in foul-smelling mud that was difficult to remove without heavy machinery. Household furnishings were carried away by the water, or covered in mud and unusable. There was no choice but to rebuild or move. As the effects of the flooding accumulated over time, the population decreased, and the village became desolate.

While this was going on, a construction plan was proposed for a new, large-scale dam on the Kawabe River, the largest tributary of the Kuma. The site to be submerged was Itsuki Village, but opposition emerged among its residents. The opposition movement that occurred at Hitoyoshi City, which is midstream, expanded in and around the prefecture from Sakamoto-machi to Yatsushiro City downstream. It included not just people who experienced flood damage and farm families who were supposed to be beneficiaries of the dam, but also watershed residents, fishermen, as well as many environmental organizations, scholars, attorneys, and assembly members inside and outside the prefecture. Popular sentiment grew, and starting with Sagara Village, which was the planned spot for the dam, it came to the point that local chief executives opposed the dam in Hitoyoshi City and Yatsushiro City.

At this time, the Arase Dam was up for water rights renewal. Naturally, the Kawabe Dam opposition movement joined with the Arase Dam removal movement. Especially compelling were both the desire to take back the old Kuma River and the Sakamoto Village residents' wish to remove the dam, since they had repeatedly suffered extensive damage due to construction of the Arase Dam. Petitions were repeatedly sent to the Kumamoto Prefecture from the village assembly, which said, "We have endured fifty years of this. It's time to give the Kuma River back to us." Pushed not only by the rise in public anti-dam sentiment, but also by electricity deregulation and an increase in maintenance and control expenses, in December 2003 the governor of Kumamoto Prefecture decided to remove the Arase Dam. The plans for the Kawabe Dam also hit an impasse.

The gates of the Arase opened completely in April 2010, and dam removal started in September 2012. If progress is smooth, the plan is to be finished in March 2018. The right riverbank side of the dam has been removed, and almost all of the old current has been restored.

From the time that the gates were fully opened, the river and tidal wetlands have gradually changed. Places that had become a stagnant, muddy lake have returned to the flow of a snaking river. The layers of the terrible-smelling mud that had accumulated at the bottom of the lake have changed to a pebbled riverside. The riverboats have returned, along with people fishing for Japanese trout. In the side streams that recovered quickly, schools of those trout have returned—along with playing children.

Sand is once again being supplied to the tidal wetlands at the mouth of the river, and this has fueled the regeneration of an expanding area of eelgrass—which had completely disappeared after construction of the dam. The volume of catches of fish, eel, and crab are also starting to recover.

Nature's recovery is faster than we imagined it would be.

However, while we can see the effects of removing the Arase Dam, the effects of the Setoishi Dam ten kilometers upstream are also becoming evident. Regeneration of the Kuma River is still a difficult task, and we are working toward the removal of the Setoishi Dam as well.

In Japan, where construction of useless dams is forced upon us, the Kuma River, site of the removal of a major dam and cancellation of another, is becoming a happy river. The day is very near when we will see many children playing and schools of fish moving freely in the Kuma River once again.

ABOUT THE ARASE DAM

This was a dam built specifically for power generation in 1954 at Hagi Arase in Sakamoto-machi, Yatsushiro City (formerly Sakamoto Village), located approximately twenty kilometers from the mouth of the Kuma River in the southern Kumamoto Prefecture. Twenty-five meters high, the dam's length was 210 meters, and the electric power generation volume was 18,200 kW. The business operator was Kumamoto Prefecture. A decision was made in 2003 to remove it, with the removal project beginning in 2012. The cost of removal is approximately 8.8 billion yen ($73,000,000 at 2015 exchange rates). The removal work duration is six years.

Three days after the dam removal, the Kuma River's natural flow returns for the first time in sixty years. Kumamoto, Japan. *Photo Courtesy of Shoko Tsuru*

Dave Foreman was the first keynote speaker at our first Tools Conference in 1994, shortly after the FBI spent $3 million and used a full-time undercover agent in an attempt to frame him for "eco-terrorism." A federal judge later dismissed the charges. Foreman was selected by the National Audubon Society in 1998 as one of the "100 Champions of Conservation" over the past 100 years.

Dave Foreman

2004 KEYNOTE SPEAKER

The Dancing Planet

We must tie our battles together under a grand overreaching vision of peaceful co-existence between human civilization and the whole wild diversity of native North American fauna and flora, a different vision than the world of malls and sleazy suburban development, clear cuts and parking lots that our opponents are offering. People of the entire continent need a new vision.

So I always go back to Aldo Leopold's story. More than a hundred years ago, he graduated from the Yale School of Forestry with a master's degree. He caught the train for the territory of Arizona to go to work for the newly created US Forest Service. His first job in the Apache National Forest in eastern Arizona was to cruise timber. At that time, the White Mountains, the Mogollon Rim, the Blue River country was a huge, wild place without roads. There was no way the Forest Service could log the forest. But they wanted to know how many trees were there so they could plan logging thirty or forty years in the future. Leopold's job was to go into the forest on horseback for two weeks at a time with a crew of men and calculate the standing board volume.

One day in 1909 on one of these trips, Aldo Leopold and his men stopped for lunch on a rimrock overlooking a rushing stream below them, and as they ate their lunch they saw a large animal ford the stream. They thought it was a doe because she had long legs. But when they saw a bunch of wolf pups run out of the willows on the other side of the stream they realized it was an old mama wolf.

PG.232 A gray wolf at the Lockwood Animal Rescue Center, California. *Tim Davis* ABOVE An endangered Mexican gray wolf with her pup in a captive breeding program at the Sedgewick County Zoo, Wichita, Kansas. *Joel Sartore*

In those days before World War I, any wolf you saw was a wolf you shot. Leopold and his men ran to their horses and pulled their 30/30s out of their scabbards and blasted away. Those of you who hunt know it's hard to aim downhill. But Leopold and his men shot enough lead down the hill that day, and old mama wolf went down. And one of the pups dragged her shattered legs back into the willows to die a slow death. Leopold and his men mounted up and rode down the hill to skin the wolves and pack the pelts back to Springerville to sell.

But something happened that day. Leopold wrote about it decades later in *A Sand County Almanac*:

"We reached the old wolf in time to watch a fierce green fire dying in her eyes. I realized then, and I've known ever since, there was something new to me in those eyes. Something known only to the wolf and to the mountain. I was young then and full of trigger itch. Fewer wolves meant more deer. I believed no wolves would mean a hunters' paradise. But after watching the green fire die, I realized that neither wolf nor mountain agreed with such a view."

So more than one hundred years later, here we are. We need that green fire in the land. We need it in our own eyes. We've got to communicate that to the people of America. Leopold also wrote: "A deep chesty bawl echoes from rimrock to rimrock and rolls down the mountainside and fades into the far blackness of the night. It's a cry of wild defiant sorrow and contempt for every adversity on earth."

A couple of years ago in the Boundary Waters of Minnesota, I awoke in the middle of the night and the storm had stopped. There was a noise out there; it wasn't loons, it wasn't wind, it was a pack of wolves. Leopold was right. The howl of wolves is the cry of wild defiance, sorrow, and contempt for adversity. But it's something else too. The sound of joy. It's the music of this whole, glorious, fecund, buzzing, blossoming dance of life that we all love. It tells us why we're in this. Why we're fighting. Why we're standing up for forests and wolves and parrots. Why we're defending rangelands and rivers. Because of the joy in life. Because of the love we have for the evolutionary dance.

In Yeats's poem about the center not holding and the blood-dimmed tide being loose, he says the best are without all conviction, and the worst are full of passionate intensity. I think all of us today know that the worst are full of passion and intensity. And we know that they will win if the best—us—are without conviction.

We need nuts and bolts. We need the technical skills, but we've got to remember why we're in it. Why we have conviction. Because of love for this beautiful dancing lovely Earth and all its species.

Authors' Bios

CHAPTERS

Ben Alexander

Ben Alexander is co-founder of Headwaters Economics, an independent nonprofit research group whose mission is to improve community development and land management decisions in the West. He has worked with land management agencies, elected officials, rural development specialists, and landowners in the West for the last fifteen years. Ben has published in the areas of agricultural and energy economics, the value of public lands, and community development.

Owen Bailey

Owen Bailey is the executive director of the Environmental Defense Center (EDC) in Santa Barbara California. He joined EDC after almost ten years at the Sierra Club, where he began working with their California coastal campaign, Great Coastal Places. Over this time he had the opportunity to work with Sierra Club chapters and other organizations and individuals throughout the state, helping to engage community for coastal protection. With the Sierra Club, Owen developed and implemented community organizing strategies for several significant conservation victories including the defeat of BHP Billiton's proposed offshore Liquefied Natural Gas terminal and the preservation of Monterey's Del Monte Forest.

Tanya Birch & Karin Tuxen-Bettman

Tanya Birch focuses on mapping data collected from the field using Android mobile devices. She also created the grants program, providing mapping software to thousands of nonprofits for free. With an academic background in geography and environmental studies at the University of California at Santa Barbara, she has been at Google for ten years. Prior to Google, she researched human elephant conflict in Sri Lanka with the Sri Lanka Wildlife Conservation Society.

Karin Tuxen-Bettman has been with Google Earth Outreach since 2008 helping nonprofits use Google's mapping tools for their work. She focuses much of her work on helping them collect ground-level street view imagery of the amazing places in which they work. Her most recent project involves the measurement and mapping of air quality information for climate change and human health. Her background is in GIS and remote sensing, and she earned her graduate degree in environmental science from UC Berkeley in 2007.

Melinda Booth

Melinda Booth received a BS in Environmental Biology from UC Davis and an MS from the University of Montana in Environmental Studies. With a passion for conservation and a desire to do more, Melinda began fundraising as a means to an end and has since specialized in development for environmental nonprofits. Currently the film festival director for SYRCL's Wild & Scenic Film Festival, Melinda has been organizing large events since 1999. When not working, Melinda enjoys extreme tubing, hiking with her husband and dog, yurt improvement projects, and dreaming of the house she will build one day soon.

Diane Brown

Diane Brown went from tadpole and mosquito habitat research behind her house in Painesville, Ohio, at age six to helping grassroots activists in over 200 communities raise a million dollars in a one-day walk-a-thon. As a thirty-year consultant with The Non-Profit Assistance Group in Sebastopol, California, Diane has worked with hundreds of organizations and community activist hell-raisers. She has relished being a presenter at every Patagonia Tools for Grassroots Activists conference, grasping tightly to her bubble gun and herding benevolent bank robbers in the mighty cause of making fundraising fun for the enviro-masses.

Yvon Chouinard

Yvon Chouinard is a noted alpinist and the founder and co-owner of Patagonia, Inc. He's also the co-founder, with Craig Mathews, of 1% for the Planet, an alliance of businesses that contribute at least 1 percent of their annual revenues to environmental causes. An avid surfer and fly fisherman as well as climber, he lives in Ventura, California, and Moose, Wyoming, with his wife, Malinda.

Kristen Grimm

As founder and president of Spitfire Strategies, a leading communication and campaign strategy

PG.236-237 In 2014, over 400,000 people took to the streets in the largest march on climate change to date. New York City, New York. *Emma Cassidy/Survival Media Agency* PG.238-239 The Bering Sea at sunset. *Corey Arnold*

241

firm, Kristen Grimm has helped thousands of non-profits and foundations develop strategies to create lasting social change. Recent accomplishments include crafting a winning campaign effort to restore the ecosystems in the Gulf of Mexico for the Walton Family, coordinating state efforts to ensure children have quality health care coverage for the David and Lucile Packard Foundation, message guidance to support grantees working to improve education throughout the United States for the Bill and Melinda Gates Foundation, and creation of a food oasis program in Georgia for the Arthur M. Blank Foundation. Kristen has authored numerous publications including the communication strategy-planning tools Smart Chart 3.0 and Planning to Win, which helps organizations craft winning campaign strategies.

Beth Kanter

Beth Kanter is a well-established international leader in nonprofits' use of networks, social media, data, and learning. Her first book, *The Networked Nonprofit,* introduced the sector to a new way of thinking and operating in a connected world. Her second book, *Measuring the Networked Nonprofit*, is a practical guide for using measurement and learning to achieve social impact. She is the author of Beth's Blog: How Nonprofits Can Leverage Networks and Data, considered the go-to source for how nonprofits can use networks, data, learning, and social media for social change. Beth has thirty-five years of experience working in the nonprofit sector in technology, training, and capacity, and has facilitated trainings for nonprofits on every continent in the world (except Antarctica). Named one of the most influential women in technology by *Fast Company* and one of *BusinessWeek*'s "Voices of Innovation for Social Media," Beth was Visiting Scholar at the David and Lucile Packard Foundation 2009-2013 and has worked with the Knight Foundation, Robert Wood Johnson Foundation, and others

Jim Little

Jim Little came to Patagonia marketing in 1998 from the world of weekly newspapers, where he spent a decade planning and producing issues and covering everything from wildfires to general plan updates. A regular at the Tools Conference, he's reviewed hundreds of publications produced by environmental groups for their editorial content. Jim works on brand, environmental, and sportswear projects for Patagonia, where he's also served on our environmental grants council and sits on our employee environmental internship committee.

Tim Mahoney

Over a forty-year career, Tim Mahoney has represented several environmental organizations and four Alaska Native corporations. He has advocated for wilderness bills encompassing tens of millions of acres, conservation easements, and purchases for more than one hundred thousand acres in parks and refuges. He has worked on public lands laws signed by the last six presidents.

Brian O'Donnell

Brian O'Donnell is the executive director of the Conservation Lands Foundation. Throughout his career he has designed and led campaigns to protect several million acres of land in the form of new Wilderness Areas, National Monuments, and National Conservation Areas across the United States. He lives in Durango, Colorado.

Vincent Stanley

Vincent Stanley has worked at Patagonia off and on since its beginning in 1973. He is the co-author with Yvon Chouinard of *The Responsible Company.* Stanley is also a poet whose work has appeared in *Best American Poetry.*

John Sterling

John Sterling is executive director of The Conservation Alliance, a group of 185 outdoor industry companies that support conservation efforts. Prior to his current role, he was director of Environmental Programs at Patagonia, Inc., where he helped implement the company's wide range of services to grassroots environmental organizations.

Strick Walker

Strick Walker is currently the chief marketing officer at Spindrift Beverage Co. He has spent more than fifteen years at the intersection of consumer engagement and environmental responsibility. Prior to Spindrift, he was the director of global marketing at Patagonia. He also spent three years as chief marketing & development officer at 1% For The Planet. Strick lives in Concord, Massachusetts, with his wife, Leanna, and their kids, Ruby and Fred.

Bill Boland

Bill Boland, global creative director, joined Patagonia's marketing department more than twenty years ago as a graphic designer. He leads both the digital and brand creative teams, directing design for print advertising, catalogs, and the Patagonia website. Partnering with Patagonia's environmental department, Bill led creative development of The Footprint Chronicles in 2004, and worked on the Vote the Environment campaigns in 2012, 2013, and 2014. He lives in Ventura with his wife and three children.

Bob Ekey

A former award-winning journalist, Bob Ekey has served a leadership role in many environmental campaigns for the past twenty-three years, including campaigns to protect Yellowstone National Park from gold mining, protecting vast forested roadless areas in the Northern Rockies, and working to gain wilderness protection for places like the Rocky Mountain Front. He currently is senior director of The Wilderness Society's national energy campaign, working to guide energy development away from wild places and addressing climate change issues. He lives in Bozeman, Montana, with his wife and two children, and he is torn between being an advocate for today's pressing issues and being in the mountains skiing and fly fishing.

Brent Fenty

Brent Fenty is the executive director of the Oregon Natural Desert Association (ONDA). During his time with ONDA, Brent has worked on successful efforts to protect Steens Mountain, the Badlands, and Spring Basin as Oregon's only desert wilderness areas, and he led a citizen's wilderness inventory of millions of acres of unprotected wilderness. Other experiences include working on deforestation policy at the United Nations, hiking the Pacific Crest Trail, volunteering for the Peace Corps in West Africa, and leading water quality and fisheries research projects in Alaska. When he doesn't have his nose in a book, he enjoys whitewater rafting, fishing, hiking, biking, and spending time with his wife, daughter, and dog in wild country.

Karen Gardner

Karen Gardner has spent a decade in the nonprofit field, primarily in the areas of environmental education and fundraising. She currently lives in Santa Rosa, California, and serves as board treasurer for the Salmonid Restoration Federation, as well as development director for Food For Thought, a nonprofit food bank. Karen has a BA from Humboldt State University in political science, and a MPA in nonprofit agency management from Sonoma State University.

Ryan Henson

Ryan Henson was born into a family of loggers and farm laborers in Mendocino County, California. After serving in the Navy, he became the first member of his family to graduate from college in 1993. Ryan began working for the California Wilderness Coalition in 1994. His greatest achievements thus far are defending dozens of threatened wild areas from development, directing the first-ever effort to map all of California's wilderness-eligible lands from 1998–2001, the passage of the Northern California Coastal Wild Heritage Wilderness Act in 2006, and the passage of the Omnibus Public Land Management Act of 2009. He currently resides in Shasta County, California.

Mary Anne Hitt

Mary Anne Hitt is director of the Sierra Club's Beyond Coal Campaign, which is working to eliminate coal pollution, stop climate disruption, and repower the nation with clean energy. She previously served as executive director of Appalachian Voices (where she was one of the creators of the award-winning campaign to end mountaintop removal, iLoveMountains.org), the Ecology Center, and the Southern Appalachian Biodiversity Project. She received a BA from the University of Tennessee and a MS from the University of Montana. She grew up in the Smoky Mountains of East Tennessee and now lives in West Virginia with her family.

Lilian Pintea

Dr. Lilian Pintea is vice president of conservation science at the Jane Goodall Institute (JGI). He has more than twenty years of experience using satellite imagery and Geographic Information

Systems. Dr. Pintea is considered a pioneer in the application of cutting-edge geospatial, mobile, and cloud-based mapping technologies to support conservation in practice. This includes community mapping, innovative use of spatial analysis and tools to develop and implement conservation and participatory village land use plans, and the use of mobile devices to empower local communities to monitor their forests and be better stewards of their natural resources and custodians of chimpanzees.

Nathan Small

Nathan Small is serving his second term as Las Cruces City Councilor for District 4. He continues to focus on existing neighborhoods, expanding economic opportunity, and city sustainability. Nathan has worked for the New Mexico Wilderness Alliance since 2004, currently as conservation coordinator. Nathan is a third-generation New Mexican. After working on a commercial fishing vessel in Alaska and graduating from college, he returned home. A lifelong outdoorsman and sportsman, Nathan enjoys the outdoor and recreation opportunities near Las Cruces. He is married to Xochitl Torres Small.

Katharine Wroth

Katharine Wroth has spent ten years working at Grist—an independent nonprofit media organization that shapes the country's environmental conversations—as a writer, editor, grant writer, special projects manager, and currently senior editor. She co-edited Grist's first book, *Wake Up and Smell the Planet*. She is unlikely to ever produce 100,000 tweets, but she enjoys chronicling and participating in Grist's social-media adventures. Grist has been featured by media including *The Washington Post,* NBC's *The Today Show,* and *Time*, and has won many prestigious awards for its pioneering media work.

EDITORS

Nora Gallagher

Nora Gallagher is the environmental editor for Patagonia. Since the mid-1980s, she has developed, assigned and edited Patagonia's environmental campaign essays and all other environmental communications. She is part of a team that is continuing to develop Patagonia's environmental goals and strategy. She is also the author of a best-selling memoir, *Things Seen and Unseen*, and a New York Times Editor's Choice novel, *Changing Light*. She edited the award-winning *Patagonia: Notes from the Field*. She lives in Santa Barbara, California.

Lisa Myers

Lisa Myers is Patagonia's environmental grants manager. She has worked for Patagonia since 2001, where she has been involved in organizing and implementing the Tools for Grassroots Activists Conference that hosts seventy-five environmental activists every two years at South Lake Tahoe. She lives in Oak View, California.

The Santa Barbara chapter of Surfrider, Santa Barbara Channelkeeper, the Environmental Defense Center, and Patagonia hold a paddle-out to raise awareness for four bills moving through the California legislature to prevent future spills like the 2015 Refugio oil spill. Goleta, California. *Tim Davis*

Index

patagonia®

tools for grassroots activists

Best Practices for Success in the Environmental Movement

FIRST EDITION
Editors: Nora Gallagher,
Lisa Myers, and John Dutton
Art Director: Scott Massey
Photo Editor: Eugénie Frerichs
Project Manager: Jennifer Patrick
Production: Rafael Dunn
and Jordan Damron

Printed in Canada by Prolific
on 100% recycled paper

ISBN 978-1-938340-44-4
E-Book ISBN 978-1-938340-45-1
Library of Congress Control Number
2015958531

One percent of the sales from this
book go to the preservation and
restoration of the natural environment.

Dale Gribble walks the line in front of the Hunter Power Plant, Castle Dale, Utah. *Andrew Burr*

Travis Rummel stands on a beautifully preserved old-growth cedar stump at the bottom of Lake Aldwell. With the Elwha Dam removed, the river has carved its course through the drained reservoir, the wetlands at the river's mouth are rebuilding, and life is returning to the river corridor. Washington. *Ben Knight*   ABOVE   Hetch Hetchy's infamous O'Shaughnessy Dam with new signage. Yosemite National Park, California. *David J. Cross*

In 2013, members of the Klabona Keepers and their supporters peacefully occupied two drill pads for two weeks in the Tl'Abona territory (Sacred Headwaters). These actions, in addition to years of blockades and downstream support, paved the way toward permanent protection of this area. British Columbia. *Tamo Campos*